# ENGLISH ON THE BONIN
# (OGASAWARA) ISLANDS

# ENGLISH ON THE BONIN (OGASAWARA) ISLANDS

DANIEL LONG

*Tokyo Metropolitan University*

Publication of the
American Dialect Society

·

Number 91

·

*Published by Duke University Press
for the American Dialect Society*

*Supplement to* American Speech, *Volume 81*

PUBLICATION OF THE AMERICAN DIALECT SOCIETY

*Editor*: ROBERT BAYLEY, *University of California, Davis*
*Managing Editor*: CHARLES E. CARSON, *Duke University*


Number 91
Copyright © 2007
American Dialect Society
ISBN: 978-0-8223-6671-3


Library of Congress Cataloging-in-Publication Data

Long, Daniel, 1963–
    English on the Bonin (Ogasawara) Islands / Daniel Long
        p. cm. — (Publication of the American Dialect Society ; no. 91)
    Includes bibliographical references.
    ISBN-13: 978-0-8223-6671-3 (cloth : alk. paper)
    1. English language—Variation—Japan—Bonin Islands.  2. Bonin
Islands (Japan)—Languages.  3. Pidgin English—Japan—Bonin Islands.
4. Creole dialects, English—Japan—Bonin Islands.  5. Bonin Islands
(Japan)—Sociolinguistics.  6. North Pacific Region—Languages.
I. Title
PE3502.J3L66 2007
427.952'8–dc22                                    2006032806


British Library Cataloguing-in-Publication Data available

*For my Momma and Pappa*
*who gave me roots to take me back to Tennessee*
*and fins to bring me back to the Bonins*

# CONTENTS

# ACKNOWLEDGMENTS

The following sections have appeared previously, although they have been extensively reorganized for this book:

Portions of chapter 3 (Long 1999)
Portions of chapter 5 (Long and Trudgill 2004)
Sections 6.4, 7.1, 8.5 (Long 2000)
Section 11.6 (Long 2004)
Portions of section 1.5 and chapter 11 (Long 2001b)

Data and analyses in this book were originally presented at the following academic meetings: Osaka Shōin Women's College (Dec. 19, 1997), Kokugo Mondai Kyōgikai (May 23, 1998), Austronesian Circle of Hawaii (Sept. 17, 1998), New Ways of Analyzing Variation in English (NWAVE) 27 (Oct. 1, 1998), Kōnan University (Oct. 24, 1998), American Dialect Society (Jan. 7, 1999), NWAVE 29 (Oct. 7, 2000), and Asian Studies Conference Japan (July 21, 2003).

I would like to thank Robert Eldridge and Erich Berendt for giving me the opportunity to speak at the Asiatic Society of Japan on February 17, 2003. As far as I know, this was the second talk at the Asiatic Society to deal with the Bonin Islands. The first was presented on March 15, 1876, by Russell Robertson, recently returned from the islands. His paper was subsequently published as "The Bonin Islands" in the *Transactions of the Asiatic Society of Japan* 4: 111–43.

This research has received the kind support of the Island Cultures Research Centre at Macquarie University, Sydney, where I am currently a research fellow. The contrasts I was able to draw in this book with the Norfolk Island situation would not have been possible without the support of this institution, in particular its director, Philip Hayward. Further support was provided by a Special

Research Grant from Osaka Shōin Women's College, and by the following Grants-in-Aid for Scientific Research from the Japanese Ministry of Education and the Japan Society for the Promotion of Science: #10710259 (1998, 1999), #11480052, (1999, 2000), #12039233 (2000), #13019205 (2001), #13410139 (2002, 2003), #14390043 (2002, 2003, 2004), and #16652033 (2004, 2005).

I wish to thank the many people who helped me by making comments and suggestions or by providing me with data: Janet Fuller, Franz Muller-Gotama, Peter Mühlhäusler, Dennis Preston, Mikael Parkvall, Edgar Schneider, Michael Wescoat, Robert Eldridge, Junko Konishi, Paul Cunningham, Richard Burg (for giving me the Van Buskirk and King manuscripts), and Sebastian Dobson (for the Quin, Taylor, Sakanishi, and Sewall sources). Alterations and additions to the analysis of the shipwrecked sailors' word list were offered by Ross Clark, Joel Bradshaw, Kenneth Rehg, and others. On the island, I received the help of Shin Abe, Makoto Inaba, Yuka Kato, Marcel Knapp, Kinuko Shimada, Fusazō Shimada, Hajime Suzuki, Manami Yamaguchi, Takaya Yasui, and above all Fuyuo Nobushima. I am also grateful to Tetsuya Sogabe of Nippon Broadcasting System, who encouraged me on an early survey. Beret Strong kindly lent me materials from her great-aunt, Mary Shepardson. Ron Butters and Robert Bayley shepherded this manuscript to publication with the warmth and patience that only true mentors exhibit. My friends Peter and Jean Trudgill accompanied me to the island on the roughest seas I have experienced, and Peter's analysis appears as chapter 5 of this book. My deepest gratitude goes to Yasuko Akama, Regina Barcinas, Jeffrey Gilley, Stanley and Noriko Gilley, Ed Gunderson, Minoru Ikeda, Able Savory, Irene Savory Lambert, Gail Savory Cruz, Minnie Savory, Ethel Savory Pack, Elsie Savory and John Wick, Jonathan and Etsuko Savory, Hendrick (Nicky) Savory, Mary June Washington Miyagawa, Margie Yahagi, Edith Washington, John and Jeannie Washington, Rance Washington, and the other Bonin Islanders who lent their cooperation and assistance with this research.

# ABBREVIATIONS

| | |
|---|---|
| COP | copula |
| FP | (phrase-)final particle |
| GEN | genitive particle |
| LOC | locative particle |
| NOM | nominative particle |
| QUOT | quotative particle |
| TOP | topical particle |
| Q | question (interrogative) particle |
| CAUS | causative verb ending |
| COND | conditional |
| PASS | passive verb ending |
| PRES | present-tense verb ending |
| PAST | past-tense verb ending |
| PL | plural suffix |
| NML | nominalizer |
| CONJ | conjunction |

# PART I
# BEFORE THE ARRIVAL
# OF JAPANESE

# 1. THE LINGUISTIC HISTORY
# OF THE BONIN ISLANDS

İT IS A LITTLE KNOWN LINGUISTIC FACT that among a group of Western Pacific islands English is maintained as a community language of the indigenous population. These are the Bonin Islands. Today, these islands (also called the Ogasawara Islands) are part of Japan and their population, Japanese citizens, but the English language has survived there, as both a tool of communication and a marker of their unique identity. This book attempts to provide an outline of the English of the Bonin Islands in its various forms and incarnations from 1830 to the present.

I begin in chapter 1 with a sketch of the islands' history. Throughout their history, English has existed on the islands as a language system unto itself and as a contributing portion of other language systems. I outline these language varieties in chapter 2. Chapter 3 examines historical and social factors behind the evolution of the pidginized English that served as the local lingua franca among early-nineteenth-century settlers and proposes that a creoloid developed from this unstable pidgin into the FIRST LANGUAGE of island-born speakers.

Chapters 4 and 5 examine varieties of English used on the Bonins in the late nineteenth century subsequent to the arrival of the Japanese language on the islands. In the former, I examine the historical state and social role of the creoloid English that evolved during this period and came to be used diglossically with Japanese as bilingualism progressed. The latter chapter presents a linguistic analysis of late-nineteenth-century Bonin English in the form of a case study. Chapters 6 and 7 parallel these chapters, with the former providing an examination of the sociohistorical issues behind Bonin varieties of English in the early twentieth century, as Japanese began to usurp the role of English in one domain after another, and the latter coordinating the available information concerning linguistic features of the English of this period. Chapters 8–10 deal with the U.S. Navy Era. I begin this section with an overview of the historical and social background of the era. Chapter 9 provides a description of the English of speakers raised during this period. Chapter 10 analyzes the processes by which the English of the twentieth-century Bonins became intertwined with Japanese to form a MIXED LANGUAGE. Chapter 11 looks at English and other island language varieties following the reversion. Finally, chapter 12 puts the Bonins in context by comparing and contrasting them with other island language communities.

## 1.1. LANGUAGE CONTACT TERMINOLOGY

Before starting our examination of the Bonin Islands, let us clarify the meanings of several terms used in the study of language contact: PIDGIN, PIDGINIZED, CREOLE, CREOLOID, and ABRUPT CREOLIZATION.

1.1.1. PIDGINIZATION AND PIDGIN. A pidgin is a language system that evolves when speakers of two, three, or more languages come into contact with each other and cannot understand one another's language. Typically, the language of the people with "power" (through economics, technology, warfare, sheer numbers, etc.) is learned imperfectly by the other groups. These groups acquire lexical morphemes from the powerful LEXIFIER (or SUPERSTRATE) LANGUAGE, but their understanding of grammatical morphemes and syntax (the way words are joined together to make meaningful sentences) is influenced by their various native languages (the SUBSTRATE LANGUAGES). Their misinterpretations (reinterpretations) of the grammar of the target language result in the grammatical simplification and restructuring of the language. In the early stages of pidginization, differences are seen among speakers of different native languages. For example, in Hawaii a Tagalog speaker (thinking in verb-initial syntax) might say *Work hard des people* 'These people work hard', while a Korean or Japanese speaker may tend to put the verb at the end of a sentence as their native languages dictate, as in *Name me no like* 'I don't like the name" (Carr 1972; Bickerton and Odo 1976; Bickerton 1981). As pidgins develop, they become more homogeneous with less drastic variation among users; a process that Thomason (2001, 169) terms "crystallization." Thus, pidgins come to have definable grammatical rules. As Sebba (1997, 15) says, "They have vocabulary and grammatical structures, however basic, which are accepted by their speakers. It is not the case that 'anything goes.'"

Some scholars (e.g., Sebba 1997) use the term "stable pidgin" for pidgins that have achieved some degree of homogeneity, while other scholars (e.g., Winford 2003) avoid this redundant terminology. Some researchers use terms like "prepidgin" or "jargon" to distinguish early unstable contact varieties. Holm (2000, 5) writes: "Although individuals can simplify and reduce their language on an ad-hoc basis (for example New Yorkers buying sunglasses in Lisbon), this results not in a pidgin but a jargon with no fixed norms." However, these distinctions are not always clear, and Holm (2000, 69) and other contact linguists speak of "prepidgin continua."

Hymes's (1971, 84) archetypal definition is still current (as evidenced by its inclusion in Winford 2003, 270): "Pidginization is that complex process of sociolinguistic change comprising reduction in inner form, with convergence, in the context of restriction of use. A pidgin is the result of such a process that has achieved autonomy as a norm." In this book I speak of the development of a simplified variety of English through its long-term use by a community of largely nonnative speakers as "pidginization" following Hymes's usage.

There is no evidence that the Bonin contact variety of English reached the level of stable pidgin before it began to be nativized. However, it IS clear that the Bonins community fulfilled one of the central criteria for the development of a simple jargon into a stable pidgin: TERTIARY HYBRIDIZATION (Holm 1988, 5; Sebba 1997, 103). This means, in short, that the pidginized English was used not just by nonnatives and native English speakers to communicate but as a third-party means of communication between two different nonnative language groups as a form of communication. (This is discussed at length in section 3.2.)

I refer to that contact variety throughout this book as "Bonin Pidgin English." I am not claiming that there was a stable pidgin and in this sense the label may be misleading; "Bonin Early Pidgin

English" or "Bonin Unstable Pidgin English" might have served equally well, but the fact is that there is little information on which to base specific labeling anyway.

One thing contact linguists DO agree upon is that pidgins have no native speakers. A user of a pidgin is by definition a native speaker of some other language. A nativized pidgin is a CREOLE.

When speakers use a pidgin to communicate, there may be many complex relationships that the speaker can conceive of (in her mind, in her native language) but cannot verbalize in the pidgin due to its grammatically limited nature. Pidgins are good at expressing ideas like 'I'm tired and hungry' or 'Shut up and work! I'll hit you!' but when the pidgin user conceives of a complex thought like 'Hey, do you think he would threaten to hit me even if I were to tell him I was too hungry to lift these anymore?' she may just have to continue working in silence.

1.1.2. CREOLE, CREOLOID, AND ABRUPT CREOLIZATION. This gap between what a person can think and what she can say does not exist for children who have acquired a pidgin as their native (and often only) language. They expand the grammar of the pidgin and recycle its parts, changing simple words into complex grammatical features, so that, for example, *s'pose* becomes the grammatical feature to make conditional sentences (where the superstrate language English would have used *if*). This developing complexity (not as the result of borrowing from some other language but within the heads of the children) is termed "noncontact induced expansion," (Trudgill 2002, 69–70). Creolization is expansion through the nativization of a pidgin, and the creole language that the children create is a full-fledged language in which there are grammatical structures to express the cognitive relationships that their minds come up with.

In the past, much attention was focused on children nativizing a stable pidgin (a process that has come to be known as "gradual creolization"), but recently another scenario has received much attention. Sebba (1997, 134) writes: "just as we know that children are likely to be born into a settled community where a stable or expanded pidgin is spoken, we can also be sure that children will not WAIT to be born UNTIL a rudimentary pidgin has become a stable one. Thus, there is a possibility, at least in theory, that children may be born under circumstances where the only lingua franca used by adults is a pidgin in an early stage of development—no more than a jargon." Thomason and Kaufman (1988) have termed this process "abrupt creolization."

In abrupt creolization, the pidgin becomes grammatically more complex within the span of a single generation. The expansion process "'repairs' the results of the reduction process which occurred during pidginisation" (Trudgill 2002, 70). An abrupt creolization scenario might go like this. A group of settlers on a previously uninhabited island speak different first languages, so they use pidginized English to communicate with one another. Because the children born into the community seldom hear (standard) English or any of the other native languages of their parents' generation, they acquire the pidginized nonnative English as their native language.

In some speech communities there are many nonnative speakers using an unstable early pidgin English to communicate with one another, but there are also some native English speakers (very few in the case of the Bonins and Pitcairn Island, which I will discuss later) who wield a great deal of influence within the community. The resulting contact language resembles a creole in having admixture (words and features from other languages) and simplification as the result of imperfect learning by large numbers of nonnative adult speakers, but it differs from a creole in that the changes are relatively undramatic and it has not undergone dramatic restructuring of its grammar through the processes of reduction and subsequent expansion. This type of contact language has been termed a creoloid.

The term "creoloid" itself was used by John Platt in 1975 to refer to basilectal Singapore English, which has many features of a creole, due to the influence of the first languages of its users, but does not show the dramatic grammatical restructuring typical of true creoles. The term has subsequently become more widely known as a label for languages like Reunion Creole, which Corne (1982) says has remained structurally closer to French than, say, Mauritian French Creole, because the former remained in contact with French while the latter's lack of subsequent contact with the superstrate language allowed it to develop on its own (Trudgill 1983). Recently Holm (2004) devoted an entire book to the phenomenon, which he (after considering words like "semi-creoles") chooses to term "partially restructured languages" (Holm 2004, xiii).

Sebba (1997, 162) discusses Afrikaans as a creoloid, "meaning that it has creole-like features but is not a full creole," specifically pointing out that "although it shows less radical simplification than other creoles, [it] has nevertheless reduced the Dutch system of tense marking so that it falls in line with the other [creole] languages studied in this chapter" (166).

Trudgill separates the processes that Sebba refers to as "simplification" into "simplification" and "reduction." His discussion of creoloids is worth quoting here at some length:

There are many varieties of language in the world which look like post-creoles but which actually are not. Such varieties demonstrate relatively undramatic admixture and simplification relative to some source language, BUT ARE KNOWN TO HAVE NO PIDGIN HISTORY BEHIND THEM. Such languages, as I have suggested elsewhere (Trudgill 1983, 102), can be called creoloids, and the process which leads to their formation creoloidisation.

The process of creoloidisation thus consists of admixture and simplification. Unlike creoles, however, creoloids have not experienced a history of reduction followed or 'repaired' by expansion. Creoloids were never reduced in the first place. The difference between a creoloid and a partially decreolised creole is thus a historical one; it is not apparent from synchronic inspection. Creoloidisation is, of course, the result of the influence of imperfect learning by relatively large numbers of non-native adult speakers. However, creoloids are varieties which have never been reduced because THEY HAVE MAINTAINED A CONTINUAL NATIVE-SPEAKER TRADITION. A good example of a creoloid is Afrikaans, which is clearly a creoloid relative to Dutch. [Trudgill 2002, 71; emphasis mine]

In this same discussion, Trudgill makes an important and convincing argument for a distinction between languages like Singapore English, which are not natively spoken (he distinguishes these as "non-native creoloids"), and those like Afrikaans, which are the native tongue of an entire community (and which he chooses to term simply "creoloids").

My final comments regard the portions of Trudgill's text which I emphasized. He says that the speech communities in which creoloids develop "are known to have no pidgin history behind them" and "have maintained a continual native-speaker tradition." I argue in this book that the English-based contact language that developed in the mid-nineteenth-century Bonins (and later formed one of the two components of the twentieth-century Mixed Language on the islands) was a creoloid. But I argue that it did have a pidgin (at least an unstable pidgin, or "early pidgin") history behind it and that it maintains a thin, but continuous, native-speaker tradition.

I will attempt, in this book, to show that the evidence for the nineteenth-century Bonins (while sparse and often circumstantial) is consistent with the development of an unstable pidgin English, followed by a creoloid that developed through abrupt creoloidization.

## 1.2. HISTORICAL OVERVIEW

The Bonin Islands appear to have lain completely uninhabited until Pacific Islander women and European and American men of widely varying linguistic backgrounds began to settle there in the early 1800s (see sections 2.1 and 2.2). Evidence from a variety of sources indicates that a Pidgin English (with a substratum formed from the other settlers' native languages) developed as the community's common tongue. Later the children born and raised in this language environment are thought to have acquired this as their native language (i.e., creoloidization occurred).

In the 1860s and 1870s, Japan laid claim to the islands and they experienced a huge influx of Japanese settlers. The Japanese established the first-ever schools on the islands, initiating bilingual (English and Japanese) education. Increasingly intense bilingualism initiated the processes of SYNTACTIC CONVERGENCE, leading to the development of a second contact language (a Mixed Language) comprised of a Japanese substratum and a lexicon supplied by the earlier English-based creoloid.

After World War II, the linguistic situation on the islands took another sharp turn when the U.S. Navy took control, allowing only those islanders of "Western" ancestry to live on the islands and subsequently establishing a school conducted in English. This period of American occupation and absolute isolation from Japanese ended abruptly in 1968 when the islands were returned to Japanese rule and the displaced Japanese islanders (living then in mainland Japan for a quarter century) were allowed to return home. The Ogasawara Mixed Language and Ogasawara Creoloid English have long coexisted with Japanese and English acrolects, but increasing mobility and improved communication technology seem to be accelerating decreoloidization and (dare I say) "de-mixed-language-ization."

In the 170-year linguistic history of the Bonin Islands, the dominant language has shifted from English (from 1830) to Japanese (1876), back to English (1946), and back again to Japanese (1968). Next, I will attempt to reconstruct this complex history, especially those events which relate to language.

The linguistic history of the islands may be divided into four rather distinct periods: Period 1, 1830–75, spans from the arrival of the first known human residents (on these previously uninhabited islands) to the incursion of Japanese settlers. Period 2, 1875–1945, is the period of Japanification and ends with the forced evacuation of all civilian islanders to mainland Japan at the climax of World War II. This period can be subdivided on the basis of some changes in the linguistic situation. During the early part of this period, Westerners acquired Japanese but English remained their first and dominant language. From roughly the first two decades of the twentieth century, many of the Westerners began to acquire Japanese as their first and dominant language, marking the second subperiod. The third linguistic subperiod began about 1937 as the Japanese government began to clamp down on the usage of English in both public and private situations. Period 3, 1946–68, saw a return to an English-dominant society after the U.S. Navy occupation forces (who had taken control of the islands) allowed only those islanders of "Western" lineage to return, and established an English-language school for their children. Two linguistic subperiods may be distinguished here as well: the years from the Western islanders' return in 1946 until the early 1950s when they lived alone on the islands, and the period when Navy personnel and their families lived on the islands permanently and formal English-medium education was conducted. Period 4, 1968–present, has seen a return to Japanese language dominance since the reversion of the islands to Japanese administration and the repatriation of the ethnic-Japanese islanders displaced for a quarter century. (For more detailed historical information, see Head and Daws 1968. Also see Long 1998a for a listing of works about the islands available in English.)

## 1.3. SIGNIFICANCE IN LINGUISTIC RESEARCH

The study of language on the Bonins is important to various areas of linguistics. This book will concentrate on the English of the islands, but in the interest of general linguistic knowledge, I will outline some of the reasons why the islands are important to the study of Japanese linguistics here.

1. The islands were one of the first areas in which Japanese was taught to nonnative speakers (in the late 1800s).
2. There are interesting linguistic characteristics in the Japanese acquired as a second language by the Westerners.
3. The mixing of Japanese dialects has led to the formation of a new local dialect (a koiné).

Over the years also, there have been a few scattered references to the language situation on the island, but these have viewed the language use on the island as simply the usage of both English and Japanese, overlooking what I maintain to be the most important fact: that is, the development of two additional and unique language systems that formed as a result of the language contact there. There were in fact two language-oriented papers almost two decades ago. Tsuda (1988) looked at the mixing of English and Japanese lexical items in conversations between a male in his 30s and his mother in her 50s. She concluded English was employed by the son (1) when discussing topics dealing with U.S. student life, (2) when discussing oneself during the Navy era, (3) in American place-names, and (4) for numbers. The mother used English when discussing topics related to (1) food, clothing, and shelter, (2) public facilities, and (3) the weather. Sekiguchi (1988) analyzed the results of a word questionnaire performed by children on Hahajima and came to the conclusion that some of the children were familiar with some English fish names such as *hammerhead (shark)*. There was also a paper published in the Japanese Phonetics Society Journal (Arima 1985), but it was written by a nonlinguist whose analysis of islanders' English pronunciation is rudimentary.

A few early scattered Japanese references to language on the islands simply mention that the Japanese spoken there is similar to that of Hachijōjima because many of the Japanese settlers (and all of the early ones) were from there (Hirayama 1941). But these characterizations miss the opportunity to discuss possible koiné-ization among the Japanese dialects. Similarly, they ignore non-Japanese aspects of the island such as dialectal or creoloid traits of the Westerners' English, as well as missing any possible language transfer phenomena in the Japanese spoken by the Westerners. Of course, terms like koinéization (discussed in section 2.8) were not in use at the time these papers were written. But Japanese dialectologists of the time were well aware that dialects mixed together and were already studying this phenomenon in Hokkaido and other places. Japanese linguists were also aware that foreigners acquired Japanese in interesting ways, and an entire monthly academic journal (called simply *Nihongo* and published by Nihongo kyōiku shinkōkai from April 1941 to January 1945) existed to study this topic in the colonies of Korea, Manchuria, Taiwan, Micronesia, and so on. Thus, it is not unreasonable to wonder why scholars at the time overlooked the plethora of linguistics research topics on Ogasawara.

Several scholars of Japanese sociolinguistics have commented in recent years on the seemingly inevitable decline of the English language on the Ogasawara Islands (DeChicchis 1993; Maher 1997; Neustupný 1997), and their fears seem warranted as the younger generation of Westerners (born since the 1968 reversion to Japan) are largely monolingual in Japanese. Of critical importance linguistically is not only the disappearance of English in general, but the decline of that unique variety of Bonin English which developed and has been spoken on the islands.

The language varieties of the Bonin Islands are significant within linguistic research for a number of other reasons. First, they are important within the context of Pacific contact languages because of the early date of the original settlement (1830). The period of the widest development and usage of pidgins in the Pacific came well after this. Second, the relative degree of isolation of the islanders here is significant because it means that the contact language here may have had a unique genesis, unlike almost all other Pacific contact languages, which are thought to have developed from a single source and influenced each other during their development due to the language contact and high degree of mobility of speakers. Pitcairnese occupies a unique place within Pacific contact languages because of these two factors (Clark 1979), and it is quite possible that a Bonins contact language would be unique for the same reasons.

The Bonin Islands occupy an important place in the study of English varieties in the Pacific, and indeed of English globally, for the following reasons.

1. They were settled by people from many diverse language backgrounds.
2. The number of native English speakers was small and these people were in the minority on the island. Moreover, they came from different dialects of English (Southeast England, New England United States; see section 2.3).
3. This language contact is thought to have led to the development of a contact variety (an unstable pidginized variety, later creoloid) of English, and even though there are no records of this, some linguistic features of island speech today are thought to originate in these nineteenth-century contact varieties of English.
4. This Bonin Pidgin/Creoloid developed (largely) independently of other Pacific Englishes (most of which are interrelated).
5. In spite of this Bonin Pidgin/Creoloid English, a "mainstream" variety of English seems to have survived alongside this contact variety. (I use "mainstream" in this book to contrast with contact varieties. In other words, "mainstream varieties" are those which have a continuous history of native transmission—whether they standard or nonstandard dialects.)

Although there has been no previous linguistic work on the
Bonins, they are occasionally mentioned in the literature on Pacific
language contact, albeit mostly as a place where more research is
needed. I will briefly look at some of these references here in order
to see what it is that interests linguists in them and to see what
sort of previous knowledge or preconceptions linguists have of the
islands.

Mühlhäusler and Trew (1996, 380–81) write:

They [the Bonin Islands] were settled in the early 19th century by a highly
mixed group of sailors and Polynesian and Micronesian women whose language was a modified but probably not creolized English.... The linguistic
history of Bonin in the 19th century was probably comparable to that of
Pitcairn and it is unfortunate that no samples of Bonin English could be
located. This topic may well be one that could be undertaken with profit
by a Japanese scholar.

Mühlhäusler (1998, 39) also writes of the situation on the
nineteenth-century Bonin Islands, "Given the almost total illiteracy
and the population mix, it seems likely that Pidginization and Creolization must have occurred."

Ehrhart-Kneher (1996, 523) writes, "A comparison of these two
languages [Palmerston English and Pitcairn] with Ngatikese men's
speech and the as yet to be documented Bonin English (both mentioned in this volume) should prove to be of considerable theoretical interest, as should a comparison with new Englishes on isolated
islands elsewhere, such as that spoken on Tristan da Cunha."

Writing about language contact in the Pacific, Mühlhäusler
and Baker (1996, 498) have noted:

In the few locations where English-derived varieties of language developed, these variants came into renewed vigorous contact with outside languages, particularly English, leading to their disappearance, as in the case
of Bonin.

The final part of this statement is, at present, inaccurate (or at
least incomplete). It is true that the Bonins are still home to a community of people who speak English and who ground their identity
largely in that fact, but it is also undeniable that their numbers

who positively espouse this identity are decreasing. Moreover, the English-speaking islanders today control a postcreole continuum (or more accurately a postcreoloid continuum) of varieties that show the influence not only of the original Bonin English, but of Japanese and the U.S. English brought in by the Navy forces who occupied the island from 1946 to 1968. The only chance which linguists have of studying the nineteenth-century contact language thought to have developed on these islands hinges on our ability to identify and separate these subsequent influences from those features of the original language system.

## 1.4. GEOGRAPHY AND PLACE-NAMES

Since the location of the Bonin Islands has played a great role in forming their history, let us examine the geographical position here along with a discussion of place-names.

The Bonin Islands (usually referred to in Japanese as the Ogasawara Islands, 小笠原諸島) are located between the Marianas and Japan (figure 1.1). They occupy a unique position in Japan's history in that the original settlers of the island were not Japanese, but of many various ethnic and linguistic backgrounds. Nonetheless, the study of their linguistic situation has been virtually ignored except by the comments seen in the previous section. The population is extremely small (in 2001, the population of Ogasawara Village numbered 2,366), and the number of English speakers on the island throughout its history has usually been one to two hundred (see figure 1.2).

As an administrative entity, the Village of Ogasawara (part of Tokyo Prefecture) extends from Okino Torishima (沖ノ鳥島, Parece Vela) in the west to Minami Torishima (南鳥島, Marcus Island) in the east. Its core is formed by the Ogasawara Archipelago and the Volcano Islands (Iwojima [硫黄島], Minami Iwojima [南硫黄島], and Kita Iwojima [北硫黄島]), which lie along a north-south line between the Northern Marianas and Japan. The Ogasawara Archipelago itself in turn consists of three chains of islands: the Chichijima Chain (父島列島) in the center, the Mukojima Chain

FIGURE 1.1

## The Location of the Bonin Islands

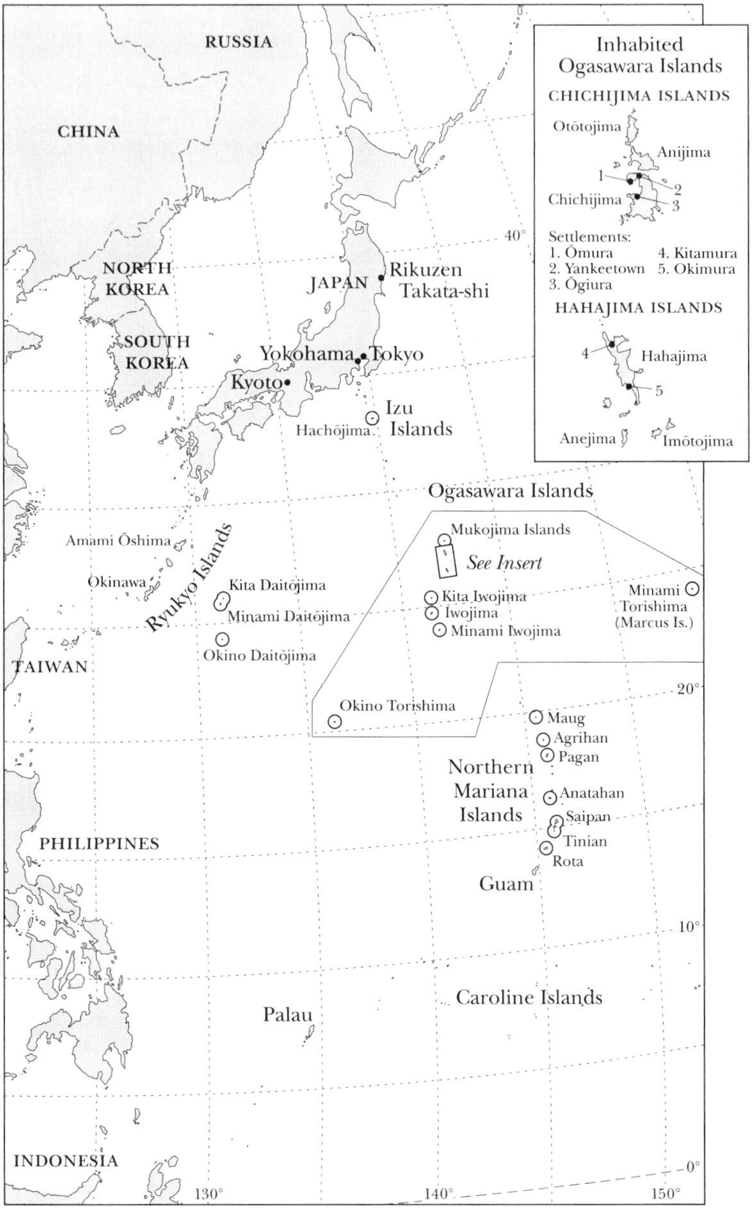

RUSSIA

CHINA

NORTH KOREA

SOUTH KOREA

JAPAN

Rikuzen Takata-shi

Yokohama Tokyo

Kyoto

Hachōjima  Izu Islands

Amami Ōshima

Okinawa

Ryukyu Islands

Kita Daitōjima

Minami Daitōjima

Okino Daitōjima

TAIWAN

Ogasawara Islands

Mukojima Islands

*See Insert*

Kita Iwojima
Iwojima
Minami Iwojima

Minami Torishima (Marcus Is.)

Okino Torishima

Maug
Agrihan
Pagan

Northern Mariana Islands

Anatahan
Saipan
Tinian
Rota

Guam

PHILIPPINES

Caroline Islands

Palau

INDONESIA

40°
20°
10°
0°

130°    140°    150°

### Inhabited Ogasawara Islands

CHICHIJIMA ISLANDS

Otōtojima

Anijima

Chichijima

Settlements:
1. Ōmura          4. Kitamura
2. Yankeetown  5. Okimura
3. Ōgiura

HAHAJIMA ISLANDS

Hahajima

Anejima     Imōtojima

(智島列島) to the north, and the Hahajima Chain (母島列島) to the south. Presently, only two of the Bonin Islands have permanent civilian residents: Hahajima and Chichijima.

Chichijima (with a population of 1,927 in 2001) has dominated Hahajima (pop. 439). This dominance was even more pronounced in the nineteenth century, when the population of Hahajima numbered in the dozens while Chichijima settlers numbered in the hundreds. In the third quarter of the twentieth century, Hahajima reverted to an uninhabited status. Moreover, the distance between the two is less than fifty kilometers and was navigated by canoe. The differences between the two islands were no greater than those within Chichijima, so one may think of the islands as forming a single community. For these reasons, this book uses the terms "the island" in referring to Chichijima and "the islands" in referring to the entire chain, but (except where specifically noted otherwise) this distinction is of little significance for the purposes of this study.

To give readers an idea of the location of the islands in relation to other comparable communities, let us look at the following figures. Chichijima lies at latitude 27°02' north. For comparison, the islands of Okinawa lie between 24° and 27° north. Pitcairn Island (discussed throughout this book for its comparable language contact situation) lies at 25°04' south. Area wise, Chichijima (24 km²) is much larger than Pitcairn (5 km²) but in a different league from Okinawa Island with 1,206 km². For those who prefer to think in more relative terms, one can circle Chichijima by motorboat in about an hour. (See chapter 11 for further comparisons to Pitcairn and other islands.)

There are other islands which lie upon a north-south line similar to that of the Ogasawara Islands. If one imagines a ship headed south-southeast from Tokyo en route to Ogasawara (a relevant exercise since this is the only way to reach the islands today and has been the chief route to them for over a century), leaving in the morning, it would initially encounter the Izu Islands (伊豆諸島). These include Ōshima (大島), Miyakejima (三宅島), and further south, Hachijōjima (八丈島), a name which the reader should remember because it is appears often in the Bonins' linguistic history. Continuing south, the ship must cut across the famous Kuroshio or Black Current, flowing northeasterly at 2–4 knots. During the night, it passes some uninhabited monoliths jutting up from the ocean surface with decidedly non-Japanese names like the Bayonnaise Rocks, Smith Island, and Lot's Wife.

In midmorning of the second day at sea, the ship reaches the largest of the northernmost group of islands in the Ogasawara Archipelago. Mukojima (聟島), literally 'bridegroom island', is still today called by its original English name, Cater Island (*keita* [ケータ] in Japanese). Next in the Mukojima group is Nakōdojima (媒島) 'lit. go-between (matchmaker) island'. The southernmost island in this group is Yomejima (嫁島) 'bride island'.

Just as these islands begin to disappear from sight, the central Chichijima Island Group (父島列島) comes into view. These islands are all named for male family members: Otōtojima (弟島) 'younger brother island', Anijima (兄島) 'elder brother island', and Chichijima (父島) 'father island'.

Fifty kilometers to the south lie the females of the clan: Haha-jima (母島) 'mother island', Anejima 'older sister island' (姉島), and Imōtojima (妹島) 'younger sister island'. Islets and named-rocks include Magojima (孫島) 'grandchild' and Meijima (姪島) 'niece', as well as the nonfamily Minamijima (南島) 'south island', Mukōjima (向島) 'across the way island', and Hirajima (平島) 'flat island'.

Much farther to the south is the Volcano or Iwojima Island (硫黄島列島) chain. Farther south still lie the outlying islands of the Commonwealth of the Northern Mariana Islands, followed by Saipan, Tinian, Rota, and Guam. All of the islands mentioned here lie along similar north-to-south lines where ocean floor disturbances created these islands long ago. It is important to clarify these geographical locations because of the historical and cultural relationships of the region.

## 1.5. PRESETTLEMENT HISTORY

The Bonins may well have been occupied at times by Micronesian peoples from the south. Perhaps Chamorro, the people of today's

Guam and Saipan, once ventured there. Even more likely is that Carolinian mariners reached this far north. These are the world-renowned voyagers who still today travel thousands of kilometers across the open sea relying on ancient navigation techniques, reading star constellations, ocean movement patterns (swells, currents, waves), and looking for biological signs like drifting plants, birds, and so on. Stone tools (adzes) have been discovered on Chichi-jima and Kita Iwojima that are identifiable with these Micronesian cultures (as opposed to Northern Asian cultures like Japan), so it is certain that some of these people navigated their way this far north. What is not certain is whether they were simply traveling or whether they established a permanent community. All we can say for sure is that the islands were uninhabited several hundred years ago when Japanese and Europeans first sighted them.

The first written records of the Bonins date back to when Spanish ships led by Ruy Lopez de Villalobos spotted them in mid-October 1543. (To put events in their historical context, this is the same year that a Portuguese ship landed at Tanegashima south of Kyushu, bringing the first firearms to Japan.) In mid-July 1639, two Dutch ships, the *Graft* (commanded by Abel Tasman) and the *Engel* (commanded by Mathijs Hendriksz Quast), passed the islands (without landing). Chichijima they named Graft Island and Haha-jima Engel Island.

The first people known to have set foot on the islands were Japanese, and they arrived under less than ideal circumstances. In 1670, a ship carrying rice and *mikan* 'citrus fruit' between Wakayama and Edo was caught in a terrible storm. As with other Japanese vessels of the day, it was not designed for the open sea but simply to travel up and down the coast or from island to island. Miraculously, the merchant seamen survived the storm and their damaged vessel drifted until it reached some uninhabited islands that we now know were the Bonins. The men spent 52 days building a makeshift vessel and bravely set back on the open sea hoping to return to Japan. They successfully reached Japan, and the *bakufu* (the feudal government of Japan), curious, devised an elaborate plan—borrowing an oceangoing vessel from the Dutch in Naga-saki—to survey these heretofore unknown South Sea islands. In

1675, the vessel reached the Bonins, and Shimaya Ichizaemon (島谷市左衛門) conducted an accurate survey of them, drawing the first known maps. It was Shimaya who gave these islands their current family-themed names. Thus, as far as modern written historical records are concerned, there is no argument (at least in modern history) that the islands were first landed upon and surveyed by Japanese. But the Japanese expressed little interest in the islands, and they were not colonized.

The term usually used in English to refer to the islands, *Bonin*, actually derives from the Japanese word *bu-nin*, an old reading of the Sino-Japanese kanji characters 無人 meaning 'lit. none + people; uninhabited'. (In modern Japanese, these characters would be read *mu-jin*). The name Ogasawara derives from the name of someone supposed to have been the discoverer of the islands. Related literature in English often mentions a "legend" that these islands were discovered in 1593 by Ogasawara Sadayori (小笠原貞頼), but no serious historians in Japan regard the story as true. This was not a legend, but in fact the result of a hoax perpetrated in 1727 by a samurai named Ogasawara Kunai Sadatō (小笠原宮内貞任) who claimed to have had an ancestor named Sadayori who had ventured to the islands. This masterless (i.e., unemployed) samurai from the landlocked fiefdom now called Nagano petitioned the government for a claim based upon this story. The descriptions of the islands in the documents he filed were fanciful at best, probably based on an spotty reports from Shimaya's exploration. Shimaya's expedition had received a great deal of public attention a half century earlier, but the details of his report were not made public. In actuality Chichijima measures only about five kilometers wide and nine kilometers in length, a fact which Shimaya's accurate maps clearly showed, but Sadatō claimed his ancestor had measured the island at 101 km by 351 km (making it closer to the size of Taiwan). Furthermore, even without the benefit of modern surveying technique, Shimaya's group managed to capture the unique shape of Chichijima, whereas the map Sadatō presented as evidence of his ancestor's find shows a plain circular blob of an island. Sadatō's fantastic descriptions of this island, including shores lined with sea lions (which do not live in tropical waters), do nothing to help his stories' credibility.

In 1735, when the hoax was exposed, Sadatō had all of his property and family estate confiscated by the feudal government and was sentenced to the severest level of banishment (Tanaka 1998). Ironically, a century and a half later, the Meiji government of Japan employed the Ogasawara discovery story in its attempt to support its international territorial claims to the islands. It was at this time that the name of the islands changed in Japan from Bunin to Ogasawara. It is difficult to understand why the nineteenth-century Japanese government felt it necessary to disinter this ancient lie to support their land rights, especially given that it is undisputed that the Japanese castaways and surveyors of the 1670s are the first people known to have landed on the islands.

## 1.6. EARLY SETTLERS

During the early and mid-1830s, a multiethnic band of settlers began to collect on the islands. Of the first-generation settlers on the island, all the women and many of the men were Pacific Islanders. Just among the long-term residents about whom linguistic information can be inferred, one finds over a dozen languages represented.

It is clear from the written records of visitors (examined in section 3.6) that the islanders spoke an "imperfect" English. This is an unremarkable statement since only a small fraction of the total population had English as their native language, and none of the others had formal instruction in English, nor were they literate. The second generation of settlers—those born on the island—acquired a variety of English (one that I contend can be called Bonin Creoloid English) as their native tongue.

## 1.7. ARRIVAL OF JAPANESE

The Japanese eventually learned of the existence of these foreigners living on islands that they had tacitly laid claim to a century and a half earlier, but they ignored them. The islands were not however, totally isolated, and in some years dozens of European and American ships, whalers, sealers, and others pulled into port to purchase fresh water, food, and supplies and sometimes to entertain themselves at the expense of the islanders.

By far the most renowned visitor of this period was one Matthew Calbraith Perry, who visited the islands en route to Japan. While on the islands he met with and purchased land from island leader Nathaniel Savory.

There was an attempt by the Japanese to settle on the Bonins in 1862, but it failed due not to anything that happened on the islands themselves but to the shifting political climate back in Edo.

In 1876, the Japanese settling of the island began in earnest with the arrival of a group of colonizers from Hachijōjima. Before the Japanese colonization began, it is recorded that there were 66 people living on the islands (including three on Hahajima). By the end of 1878, Japanese in-migrants numbered 194 (including one settlement on Hahajima), thus already outnumbering the previous inhabitants. By 1900, the population of Chichijima had climbed to 2,366. The non-Japanese settlers had become an ethnic and linguistic minority on their own island (figure 1.2).

## 1.8. WORLD WAR II

The linguistic situation leading up to World War II will be examined in detail in chapter 4, but there are a few important linguistic and cultural facts which are of import here. Up to the time of the Pacific War, the Westerners had become completely bilingual and their daily "language life" was diglossic. As Japan became a military state, the Westerners and their English language were increasingly the target of suspicion, until finally in 1938 the use of English in public was prohibited on the islands. The Westerner men were conscripted into the Imperial Army, many as translators, and one even served in the emperor's guard. Although there was never a land battle on the Bonin Islands, they were air bombed relentlessly.

The battlegrounds moved from Micronesia through Saipan and closer to Japan. In 1944, with the Pacific War front moving closer to mainland Japan, seven thousand people from the Bonin

FIGURE 1.2

Shifts in Population and Westerners' Percentage of Total Islanders

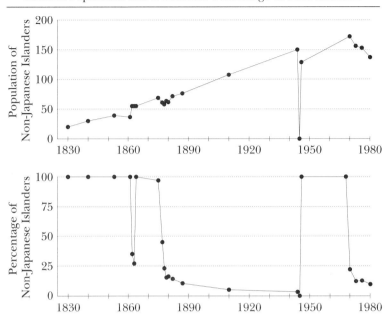

and Volcano (Iwojima) Islands were forcibly moved to the mainland by Japan in the interest of safety. After the Japanese surrender,
Japanese troops were taken off the islands, and for a short period,
the islands reverted to the uninhabited status they had held over a
century prior.

## 1.9. POSTWAR ISOLATION

Following the war, the Westerners approached the U.S. military government in Tokyo and asked that they be allowed to return home.
Although their ethnic Japanese neighbors had accepted their presence as a matter of course on the islands, they experienced suspicion and racial bigotry on the monoethnic Japanese mainland.
(Lizzie Washington, for example, describes such experiences in a
televised documentary [NHK 1987], as does Able Savory in inter-

views with me [Long 2003].) The U.S. military did not allow the ethnic Japanese back on the island, but they had allowed the islanders of Western ancestry (who had been Japanese citizens for several generations) to return to the island in 1946. During the 1950s and 1960s, the Westerners of Ogasawara lived isolated on their island along with a small and rotating deployment of U.S. Navy personnel, their families, and a few select American civilians (schoolteachers, missionaries). During these decades, the Westerners required the permission and the cooperation of the Navy in order to leave the island, and contact with mainland Japan was discouraged.

The ethnic Japanese who had made their homes on the islands for two or three generations were not allowed to reside on the islands, but they were eventually (in May 1965) allowed a small number of limited visits to attend to the graves of their relatives.

This period, sometimes called the Navy Era, brought a return to the usage of English in "high" domains on the islands. A school was established for the island children, and they were educated in English. From tenth grade, they went to Guam and lived with Navy families while attending high school there (taught completely in English).

## 1.10. REVERSION TO JAPAN

In 1968, the United States abruptly announced to the Bonin Islanders that the islands and their inhabitants would be returned to Japan. In a little over a century, the principal language had changed from English to Japanese, then back to English, and now once again back to Japanese. The ethnic-Japanese who peopled the island before the war now began to return. I deal with the post-reversion state of the islands, their people, and their language in chapters 11 and 12.

# 2. LANGUAGE VARIETIES USED ON THE BONINS

THIS CHAPTER WILL briefly outline and delineate the significant language varieties that have been spoken on the Bonin Islands since their inhabitation in 1830. More detailed descriptions of the socio-historical and linguistic processes through which some of them came into existence will be given in subsequent chapters (chapters 3, 4, 6, and 8), as will more detailed descriptions of the linguistic characteristics themselves of these varieties (chapters 5, 7, 9, and 10). The purpose of the chapter at hand is to delineate and label the various language varieties that will be discussed throughout the rest of this book. This is done to aid the reader, because several of these language varieties have similar names, an unavoidable problem since the varieties themselves are so closely related.

The language varieties are outlined below in roughly chronological order; that is, the order in which they were brought to the islands or in which they developed on the islands. Figure 2.1 shows these languages varieties and the approximate dates of their usage on the island. (The relationships among these language varieties, discussed later in section 3.10, is shown graphically in figure 3.1.) The density of the lines is a rough and impressionistic indication of the degree to which a visitor to the islands in that period might have heard that language variety used. This usage indicator is based on several factors, including the following: (1) the number of speakers (native or nonnative) of that particular language variety known to have been on the island at the time (e.g., there was more than one speaker of European languages like German and Portuguese on the islands in the mid 1800s); (2) the frequency with which that language was used based on domain factors (e.g., varieties of "standard" English were used in communicating with the Navy personnel and in school during the Navy Era, but these domains disappeared overnight with the reversion); (3) the frequency with which that language variety was (thought to be) used, taking into account sociopsychological factors (e.g., the usage of Ogasawara

FIGURE 2.1
Language Varieties Found on the Bonin Islands: Approximate Period of Usage and Vitality (Long 2002b, 305)

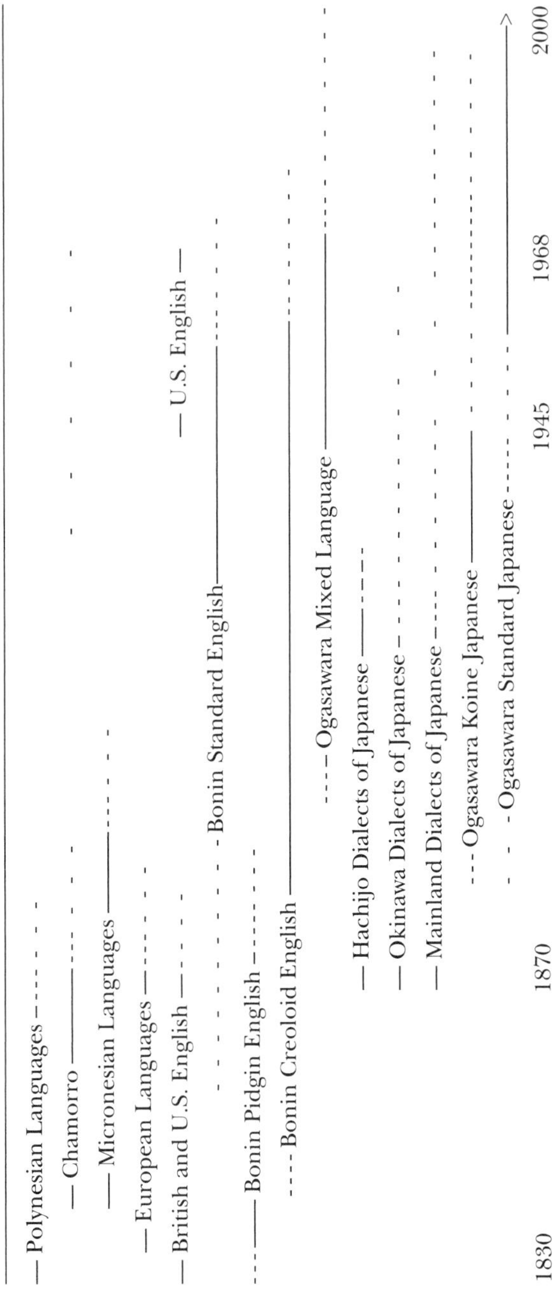

Mixed Language became stigmatized after 1968); and (4) the proficiency of speakers in that language variety (e.g., as the usage of English on the island declined postreversion, speakers report that their English got "rustier").

## 2.1. PACIFIC ISLAND LANGUAGES

Languages from all over the Pacific were spoken on the Bonin Islands throughout the nineteenth and twentieth centuries. Western Malayo-Polynesian languages represented on the island include Chamorro and Malagasy. Oceanic languages (belonging to Eastern Malayo-Polynesian) include the Polynesian languages Hawaiian, Tahitian, North Marquesan, and Rotuman as well as the Micronesian languages Carolinian, Kiribati, Ponapean, and Mokilese. (More detailed data about the individuals who spoke these languages is provided in sections 3.1 and 3.2 along with the historical sources from which such information was gleaned.)

In addition, historical references tell us there were settlers from China and the Philippines, but what languages (or what dialect, in the case of Chinese) they spoke is not known. There was also probably one family from Bougainville Island in Melanesia, although official Japanese records conflict with the "memory culture" (i.e., the information passed down orally) on the island. Some islanders remember being told that this family came from Buka (a small island north of Bougainville), so it is possible that this family spoke Halia-Buka.

## 2.2. EUROPEAN LANGUAGES

Some of the most influential men on the island were native speakers of European languages such as Danish, Italian, French, German, and Portuguese. (English will be dealt with separately.)

Danish is assumed to be the language of Charles Johnson, one of the original settlers of 1830, said to have been from Denmark. He was still on the island in 1838, but there is no record of him after this.

Another of the original settlers was Matteo Mazarro, from Genoa, who thus would have spoken Italian as his native tongue. He was a British citizen and, having been granted governorship of the colony, records show he had quite a degree of influence. He remained on the island from 1830 until he was murdered in 1848. His Chamorro wife Maria delos Santos was subsequently remarried to Nathaniel Savory.

A European islander who did have some degree of social (but apparently little direct linguistic) influence on the island came much later in the person of Louis Leseur. He is said to have been from Brittany in France, and so may have spoken Breton or French or both. He was on the island by at least 1862 and lived on Chichijima until his death in 1885. His wife was a Carolinian woman from Agrihan Island named Pidear, and they had children. He appears to have later married the widow of Marquesan islander John Marquese.

Another late-coming European islander who wielded considerable influence on the island was Frederick Rohlfs, known as "Rose" on the island. He was from Bremen, Germany, but in his case as well, there are no specific examples of his linguistic influence. He lived on Hahajima from 1852 to his death in 1898. His first wife (from 1860–87) was a "Kanaka" woman called Kitty; his second a Japanese woman. ("Kanaka" is a term used in the nineteenth and early twentieth centuries to refer generally to Pacific Islanders.)

Another German islander was William Allen, also said to hail from Bremen. He lived on Chichijima from 1862, married first to a Hawaiian woman called Poconoi, and (from about 1875) subsequently to Maria delos Santos (widowed by Mazarro and then Savory) until his death in 1882.

Within the minute society of the early Bonins, there lived no fewer than four Portuguese speakers. Both Joseph Antonio (a Brazilian Portuguese) and John Roberts (of Lisbon) had resided on the island for four years, and Francis Silva (of the Azores) for one year, when Captain Michael Quin called in 1837. There is no evidence of the subsequent residence of these three or of their leaving descendants, but they formed part of the social fabric of this tiny and isolated community for several years (Quin 1837).

Another person Quin mentions is Joachim Gonzales (commonly called John Bravo), who (in 1837) had been resident at Port Lloyd for five and a half years. He is described as a "mulatto" (Goldschmidt 1927, 4) of the island of Brava in the Cape Verde chain, hence his nickname Bravo. This fact suggests that he may have spoken a creolized variety of Portuguese. Quin (1837) records that three of the total of six children on the island at the time were Gonzales's children. There are several indications (throughout the history of the island) of the subsequent Anglicization of the Gonzales family. Even at this early stage (1837), not only was Joachim himself using the English name John, but he had given English names to his four sons: John, George, Thomas, and Andrew. His descendants made an enormous impact on the island and remain there today.

There is almost no evidence of any direct linguistic influences (loanwords, for example) that these men's native languages had upon the island. Nevertheless, we should not overlook the fact that they spoke English as a second language, just as their Pacific Islander wives did. Almost all children on the island in this formative period of the island's language history were raised in families in which the mother and father did not share a native language. (I will discuss the possible effects of linguistically mixed households in section 3.2.) Moreover, these men were early settlers in the tiny community, and so we must consider the possibility of their influence in terms of Mufwene's (1996) "Founder Principle."

## 2.3. BRITISH AND U.S. ENGLISH

The most prominent native English-speaking settler on the nineteenth-century Bonin Islands was Nathaniel Savory of Massachusetts. He was one of the original islanders and undisputedly the most influential up to his death in 1874. As we shall see later (chapter 5) the influence of this single individual's English appears to have lasted well beyond his death.

There were several other native English speakers on the island besides Savory. Those who remained for long periods and/or who left progeny include William Gilley (England), Thomas Webb (Surrey, England), Aldin B. Chapin (Boston), and Richard J. Millinchamp (England) (Cholmondeley 1915).

In the mid-twentieth century, mainland U.S. varieties of English were spoken on the island by the U.S. Navy personnel who were stationed there. Hawaiian English was quite influential upon young islanders in the mid-twentieth century in the person of George Yokota, a greatly admired and respected teacher of the island children during the 1950s and 1960s. Yokota commands a standard U.S. variety of English which is best described as "standard Hawaiian English." He says that his native tongue is "Hawaiian Pidgin," that is, the creolized vernacular English of those islands (pers. comm., May 4, 2004). (Although I have not done linguistic analysis of his speech, the descriptions in Carr 1972 will give readers a rough idea of what this means.)

## 2.4. PIDGINIZED VARIETIES OF NONNATIVE ENGLISH: BONIN PIDGIN ENGLISH

"Bonin Pidgin English" is the name I use for the nonnative varieties of naturally acquired English used by Pacific Islanders and European residents during the nineteenth century. Little is known about this variety, and indeed its existence (though hardly debatable) is based upon indirect evidence. Perhaps "Bonin Pidginized English" would have been a more accurate label because I do NOT hypothesize that there was a single, homogeneous, and stable variety of Pidgin English on the island, but rather that there was a broad range of imperfectly learned (pidginized) second-language varieties of English. It is, of course, only natural to assume that islanders in this small and closed community influenced each other in the direction of some homogeneity. However, these processes would have been confounded and their importance diminished by two factors. One factor is that before the first-generation settlers had a chance to develop a homogenized pidgin variety second-generation islanders were speaking Bonin Creoloid English as their native language—and second-generation islanders began being born almost as soon as the original settlers arrived. The second factor is that there was a constant influx of additional new nonnative speakers of English throughout the nineteenth century. Considering the tiny number of island settlers overall, one can imagine that just when the established settlers began to achieve some degree of homogeneity among their various nonnative varieties of English, the influx of (say) a dozen new nonnative speakers of English would again increase the degree of interspeaker variation and decrease the pidginized varieties' stability.

## 2.5. BONIN CREOLOID ENGLISH

Bonin Creoloid English is an English-lexified variety that probably developed through the "abrupt creolization" of a locally formed pidgin; it was used on the islands in the nineteenth and early twentieth centuries, but now survives only as residual features in other varieties (Trudgill et al. 2003; Long and Trudgill 2004). The absence of a clear singular-plural distinction and the nonobligatory use of definite and indefinite articles ("zero article" is the norm) are typical features one hears today that are the result of the nineteenth-century language contact on the islands. The same can be said for the usage of [t] and [d] for the *th* sounds.

The Navy brought mainstream U.S. English to the islands and with it decreoloidization. As a result, islanders' English slides along a postcreoloid continuum between the more creoloid traditional varieties used among islanders in informal and ingroup situations and the more mainstream standard English speech they adopt when speaking to English-speaking outsiders.

The historical background of both Bonin Pidgin and Creoloid English will be discussed in chapter 3.

## 2.6. BONIN STANDARD ENGLISH

In this book, I will occasionally use the term "Bonin English" to refer to all the English-related varieties of the islands. This is warranted because of "genetic" relations (i.e., Bonin Pidgin English fed into Bonin Creoloid English) and also stylistic ones, that is, Bonin Creoloid English and Bonin Standard English occupy the two opposite poles along a postcreoloid continuum. (My creation of the term "postcreoloid continuum" here may turn out to have been unnecessary, since, as pointed our earlier in this book, Trudgill [2002, 71] writes, "The difference between a creoloid and a partially decreolised creole is thus a historical one; it is not apparent from synchronic inspection." But I will use the term "postcreoloid" because, if Trudgill is correct about the lack of difference, there seems to be nothing misleading about my coinage and it is consistent with my use of the term "creoloid.")

Bonin Standard English is the language variety that islanders use when talking to outsiders who speak English rather than Japanese. It is important to point out that more standard (or at least mainstream) varieties of English appear to have coexisted with the contact varieties (pidgin and creoloid) throughout the islands' history.

## 2.7. HACHIJŌ DIALECT AND OTHER VARIETIES OF JAPANESE

Hachijōjima, located 290 kilometers from mainland Japan, is the source of the Japanese language varieties brought to late-nineteenth-century Ogasawara. Many of its phonological and lexico-semantic features and a few of its morphosyntactic features are found in the speech of Westerner islanders today. In fact, ironically, if one hears words or phrases from the Hachijō dialect on Ogasawara today, they are more likely to be from the mouths of Westerners than from the postwar generation of Hachijō settler descendants.

The reason for this strange result is as follows. The majority of the early Japanese settlers on the island were from Hachijō. Thus, the spoken Japanese to which the Westerners of this era were exposed was the Hachijō dialect, and the variety of Japanese which they acquired is heavily influenced by this dialect. During the Navy Era, the descendants of the Hachijō islanders were forced to live in various regions of mainland Japan (usually in the Tokyo or Kantō area). Because this exile continued for a quarter century, their children born on the mainland acquired mainland language varieties. During this time, Westerners were living on the Bonin Islands. Younger Westerners' English was influenced by their experiences on Guam and by their contact with Navy personnel. But they lived in isolation from other varieties of Japanese, and their Japanese was not influenced by standard Japanese or other dialects. The Japanese they acquired was that of their parents and other islanders of the prewar generation, heavily influenced by the Hachijō dialect.

This is not to say that they speak the Hachijō dialect as an autonomous language system, but rather that elements of it have been retained in the Koiné Japanese, which is in turn a source language of the Ogasawara Mixed Language (OML) which the Westerners use.

## 2.8. OGASAWARA KOINÉ JAPANESE

Ogasawara Koiné Japanese is heavily influenced by the Hachijōjima dialect (Abe 2002). Since the original Japanese settlers were from Hachijō, this is the result one would expect from the standpoint of Mufwene's (1996) "Founder Principle." Significantly, however, the (koiné) Japanese variety of Ogasawara has a considerable number of words and expressions from many other dialects as well.

Ogasawara Koiné Japanese also incorporates standard and non-standard elements of the Tokyo and surrounding Kantō region dialects, as well as some traits shared with dialects of Kyushu and even Okinawa. There are even similarities with the L2 varieties of Japanese used in Saipan and other former Pacific island colonies, although this is a topic still under study.

There are phonological characteristics of Ogasawara Koiné Japanese. One example is the distinct intonation patterns, particularly a rising intonation on yes-no questions that is not typical of any mainland dialects of Japanese (or of English for that matter).

Other phonological characteristics of Ogasawara Koiné Japanese that would stand out in Tokyo are the occasional vagaries in the short-long vowel distinction, especially in words not used in mainland Japanese, and the lack of a clear distinction between the diphthongs /ai/ and /ae/, which are differentiated in many (but not all) mainland dialects and in the standard.

A fourth example is the lack of clear distinctions in the pitch accents, which (in standard Japanese) distinguish segmentally identical lexical items. For example, in Tokyo Standard Japanese *ame* means 雨 'rain' if pronounced as high-low and means 飴 'candy' if pronounced as low-high. These types of distinctions are vague or nonexistent (depending upon both the word and the speaker) on Ogasawara.

A description of Ogasawara Koiné Japanese is beyond the scope of this book, but it is one of the two elements that make up OML, and as such, aspects of it will be touched upon later in this book. More information is provided in Long and Hashimoto (2005).

## 2.9. OGASAWARA STANDARD JAPANESE

In much the way that Bonin Creoloid English and Bonin Standard English form a continuum, so Ogasawara Standard Japanese and nonstandard Ogasawara Koiné Japanese form a continuum. (Furthermore, there is also a strong Japanese element of OML, which I will discuss later.) In reality, speakers "slide" along this continuum (speaking Japanese that is slightly more or slightly less standard) rather than discretely switching between these varieties.

Visitors often comment that "there is no dialect on the island." Of course they receive these impressions because (1) their contacts during their brief stay are often with mainlanders on the island for six months or a year working as diving guides, bartenders, and so on, or (2) the real islanders with whom they do interact are codeswitching into standard Japanese for their benefit. But when islanders switch into standard Japanese, it is nonetheless Ogasawara Standard Japanese. Although this language variety sounds to the nonlinguist quite similar to the standard Japanese spoken in mainland Tokyo, to linguists who search carefully, there are some notable differences in vocabulary as well as some interesting pragmatic differences in expressions, as well as slight phonological differences.

One difference is lexical. In an otherwise standard Japanese sentence, one hears island words for plants, animals, or foods, such as *yarōdo* 'the indigenous tree *Ochrosia nakaiana*', *sasayo* 'the fish *Kyphosus bigibbus*', and *piimaka* 'raw fish in vinegar dish'. These words have their origins in (respectively) English (from *yellow wood*), the Hachijō dialect, and Hawaiian. (For more information see section 3.7.) These lexical items are quickly picked up by migrants newly arrived from the mainland as well.

There are semantic or discourse features which stand out: *Kono fune de kita?* translates as 'Did you come on this boat?' On the island, *this boat* refers not to a particular vessel but to a particular voyage. There is only one passenger vessel that journeys back and forth to Tokyo (a 25.5-hour voyage at present). The question "Are you going back on this boat?" is asking not which vessel you intend to travel on, but if you intend to return on the only vessel's next voyage to Tokyo.

The ship makes four or five trips a month back and forth to the mainland on varying days of the week. Islanders' lifestyles revolve not around calendar days (Monday, Tuesday, etc.) but around the boat schedule, so that a particular store's regular day off is not "every Wednesday" but "every day-after-the-boat-leaves." Since many tourists come and return on the same "boat," there are more of them for the three or four days when the boat is in dock on the island, and fewer of them during the two or three days that the ship is returning to the mainland. Terms like *binkan* 'lit. between voyages' or *nakabi* 'middle days' refer to this period and are significant for those in the tourist trade. A scuba diving shop may recommend that an island visitor stay for *tsuu booto* 'lit. two boats; the length of two voyages' and wait to dive until the *nakabi*, when the "one-boat" tourists have left the island and the dive boat is less crowded.

The word for the main islands of Japan is not *hondo* as most mainlanders would expect, but *naichi*, a word which was used for the mainland as seen from the colonies before World War II and thus has an outdated, colonial, or even militaristic ring for the uninitiated mainland visitor.

In addition to these lexicosemantic differences, the unique phonological qualities of Ogasawara Koiné Japanese mentioned above often go unchecked when speakers switch their lexicon and syntax to standard Japanese (and understandably so when one considers the generally difficult-to-control nature of phonological characteristics).

## 2.10. OGASAWARA MIXED LANGUAGE

The Ogasawara Mixed Language is a MIXED LANGUAGE in the specific sense of the word as defined and used by Bakker and Mous (1994), that is, a contact language but one that differs significantly from the type of contact languages linguists have traditionally studied—pidgins and creoles in particular—in that there is no major grammatical restructuring present. OML basically consists of an English lexicon on a Japanese grammar, retaining the phonology of both source languages. This language variety is described in chapters 7 and 10 of this book.

## 2.11. ETHNIC GROUPS AND THEIR NAMES

The residents of Ogasawara are commonly grouped into three categories. The descendants of the non-Japanese settlers are called *ōbeikei* (欧米系), which can be rendered literally as '(people of) European and American descent'. These people are also called *zairai tōmin* (在来島民) 'lit. preexisting islanders'. In this book, I translate this term as 'Westerners'.

The descendants of the early Japanese settlers who were resident prior to World War II are called *kyūtōmin* (旧島民) 'old islanders'. (The term *Hachijōkei* [八丈系] is used to refer to the descendants of the Hachijō Island settlers, and since they form the core of the kyūtōmin population, the two terms are often used interchangeably.) The third group of residents are those who migrated to the island after its return to Japanese control in 1968, called *shintōmin* (新島民) 'new islanders'.

In 1877, a "Bermudan Negro" sailor named Robert Morris became the first islander to take Japanese citizenship, and by 1882 all of the settlers had been naturalized. From the beginning of Japanese rule in the 1870s until at least 1930, distinctions are made in the official population records between the kikajin (帰化人 'naturalized people') and the other Japanese islanders. This distinction was abolished not only because it was thought morally wrong to emphasize such a racial distinction, but also because increasing intermarriages were rapidly rendering such distinctions meaningless. Until June 1897 when it was abolished, the Kikajin nyūseki torishimari ni kansuru sho-jōyaku (帰化人入籍取締りに関する諸条約 'Laws concerning the regulation of registered naturalized people') restricted the movement of the kikajin on the Japanese mainland in spite of the fact that they were Japanese citizens (Tsuji 1995, 196). Some ethnic-Japanese on the island today worry that the term *kikajin* sounds ethnically bigoted, but I have never encountered any of the older Westerners who have any strong emotional reactions, negative or otherwise, to the word.

Although I use "Westerner" in this book to describe these people, the term is not without its problems. I have chosen the term after great consideration, deliberation, and consultation with fellow Ogasawara researchers and the islanders themselves. I shall address these problems and look at other terms, both Japanese and English, that have been used at various times to refer to the islanders, both by others and by themselves.

The first problem is that the English term "Westerner" is not commonly used; no one but myself, and perhaps a few people who reference my work, uses the term. On the other hand, the Japanese term *ōbeikei* is commonly used in Japan today. But it is neither embraced nor resented by the people to whom it refers. It is not often heard in their conversations with each other, but they do use it out of convenience when referring to themselves in conversations with ethnic-Japanese listeners. In normal conversation, the Westerners themselves simply use expressions such as "our people" or "we, us" to refer to their own group. When the conversation is in Japanese, similarly vague expressions such as *wareware* (first-person plural pronoun) are used.

A second problem is that in the literature concerning the islands, the term "Westerner" refers to different groups prior to the arrival of the Japanese and afterward. Thus, it is a potential source of confusion. In the pre-Japanese history of the islands, European and American settlers were contrasted with the Pacific Islander settlers. After the arrival of the Japanese, these two groups of previous settlers increasingly intermarried and came to be grouped together as ōbeikei in contrast to the ethnic-Japanese.

A third problem, then, is that the term "Westerner" is misleading when used to refer to twentieth-century islanders. This is because none of these people have completely "European and American" heritage; all are the descendants of marriages between European and American settlers and their Pacific Islander wives. For example, it is often pointed out that many of the islanders today are descendants of the American Nathaniel Savory. Writers tend to overlook the fact that all such islanders also trace their lineage back to his Guamanian wife Maria delos Santos, as well. The people called "Westerners" are today quite conscious and proud of their Pacific Islander roots.

Despite all the problems with the word "Westerner," however, I have chosen to use it throughout this book because it is the term in common use and because various problems could also be cited with the alternatives (e.g., "Bonin Islanders," "Chichijimans," "original settlers").

# 3. ENGLISH BEFORE THE ARRIVAL OF JAPANESE: NATIVE AND CONTACT VARIETIES

THIS CHAPTER CONTENDS that an English-based contact language developed on the Bonin Islands in the nineteenth century and was used as the language of communication among the settlers there. The factors discussed in support of this contention are (1) the diversity in the languages of the first-generation settlers, (2) the abundance of linguistically mixed households, (3) the absence of formal education or literacy, (4) the nature of words reported by Japanese seamen shipwrecked on the island, (5) reports of communication in "English" between islanders and visitors, (6) the off-island experiences of islanders, (7) written references to a contact language, (8) the continued usage of non-English words, and (9) the linguistic outcomes of similar island communities.

As outlined in section 1.3, many scholars of language contact have lamented the virtual absence of data regarding language contact on the Bonins in the nineteenth century. I began research on this topic with the conviction that "virtually" none does not necessarily mean none whatsoever. This chapter aims to reexamine the existing and available materials for linguistically relevant evidence that previous research has overlooked. These, regrettably, are not the sophisticated descriptions of linguistic structure that linguists would prefer, but are nonetheless evidence from the firsthand reports of visitors and from the writings and voices of Bonin Islanders themselves. I have quoted many primary sources, in spite of space limitations, because of their importance to this volume and because most are extremely obscure and difficult to obtain. Taken individually these accounts appear to be merely shreds of information, but taken as a whole and examined in light of linguists' knowledge of how language functions and changes in society, they come together to form a picture of the linguistic situation on the islands in the nineteenth century.

## 3.1. DIVERSITY IN THE LANGUAGES
## OF FIRST-GENERATION SETTLERS

The first known permanent human settlers came to the islands now called the Bonins in 1830. On June 26 of that year, five white men sailing from the Sandwich Islands (Hawaii) brought with them ten Kanaka men and five Kanaka women. English speakers were clearly not in the majority. Of the first five white men to come to the island, only three were native English speakers (Nathaniel Savory and Aldin B. Chapin from the United States, and Richard J. Millinchamp from England); the other two were Genoese and Danish.

It is not known exactly which varieties of Polynesian all the original Kanakas spoke. Since they sailed from Hawaii, it is logical to assume many were Hawaiian. John "Judge" Marquese was from Nuku-hiva, and so it is assumed he spoke Northern Marquesan. Harry Bolla Otaheite was Tahitian, so one can assume he spoke that language. Both arrived in 1830 and lived on the island for many decades (Cholmondeley 1915, v, 92). All three of these languages belong to the Eastern Polynesian branch of the Oceanic language family (which also includes the languages of Micronesia except Chamorro and Palauan). Grimes (1996) reports that Northern Marquesan has about 50% mutual intelligibility with Tahitian, and if we consider only lexical similarities, the estimates range from 45% to 67%. Lexical similarities between these two languages and Hawaiian are also said to be over 70%. These facts indicate that the Pacific Islanders were to some degree able to communicate among themselves without necessarily resorting to a third language such as English.

Following these initial settlers, others arrived in group after small group over the next few decades. Subsequent Pacific Islander settlers spoke various languages of the Austronesian language family. Figure 3.1 shows the genetic distances between the Austronesian languages known to have been spoken on the Bonins, but we derive from these great distances that the Pacific Islander settlers' languages would have been no more mutually intelligible than those of the European settlers.

FIGURE 3.1
## Genetic Relationship among Austronesian Languages Spoken on the Bonins

```
Austronesian
  Malayo-Polynesian
    Central-Eastern Malayo-Polynesian
      Oceanic
        Central-Eastern Oceanic
          Remote Oceanic
            Central Pacific
              East Fijian-Polynesian
                Polynesian
                  Nuclear Polynesian
                    East Polynesian
                      Central Polynesian
                        Marquesic
                          Hawaiian
                          North Marquesan
                        Tahitic
                          Tahitian
              West Fijian-Rotuman
                Rotuman
          Micronesian
            Micronesian Proper
              Ikiribati
                Kiribati
              Ponapeic-Trukic
                Ponapeic
                  Mokilese
                  Ponapean
                Trukic
                  Carolinian
        Western Oceanic
          Meso Melanesian
            New Ireland
              South New Ireland–Northwest Solomonic
                Nehan–North Bougainville
                  Buka
                    Halia
                      Halia
    Western Malayo-Polynesian
      Chamorro
        Chamorro
      Borneo
        Barito
          East Barito
            Malagasy
              Malagasy
```

From the arrival of humans on the island of Chichijima (the main island of the Ogasawara Archipelago), the native languages of the islanders were numerous and genetically varied. Just among the long-term settlers about whom we can infer linguistic information, we find over a dozen languages represented. Interestingly, no one language was in the majority numerically. Yet, in spite of the small number of English native speakers, we find in multiple sources (Taylor 1855; Collinson 1889; King 1898; Ōkuma 1966; discussed in section 3.6) that both first-generation settlers and subsequent island-born generations spoke "English," or more specifically an English-based contact language. Moreover, the evidence indicates that this "English" was the common means of communication for all but a few islanders, as indicated by Russell Robertson (1876, 138), who writes, "I have not before noted that English is spoken by all the settlers, unless I except some half dozen from the Kingsmill group [Gilbert Islands of Kiribati], who speak their own language."

Although one of the major subgroups among the European settlers were those from Portuguese-speaking areas, we have almost no definitive evidence of these settlers' contribution to the Bonin community language. However, the role of the Portuguese language and of Portuguese speakers in the genesis of many modern European-based contact languages is well researched and documented, regardless of whether one subscribes to the monogenesis theory of pidgins or not (Sebba 1997, 72–76). This intriguing connection makes a closer examination of these settlers worthwhile.

In 1837, HMS *Raleigh* visited Chichijima (known then as Peel Island). In his report to the Admiralty, Captain Michael Quin describes the islanders. In addition to the 25 "first settlers," he records there were 11 "later settlers." (Table 3.1 is based on the detailed records he kept of island arrivals.)

There were many transients or short-term residents on the islands about whom we have little information, linguistic or otherwise. These were people who, although often staying for extended periods, did not settle there permanently. For example, Quin (1856, 232–33) gives accounts of the number of people who jumped ship on the island from 1830 to 1837, with numbers totaling 45. Yet, he

TABLE 3.1
Numbers of People Disembarking on the Bonins
(Quin 1856, 232–33)

| | | Original | Later |
|---|---|---|---|
| 1830 | Schooner with original settlers | 20 | |
| 1830 | Deserters from a schooner | 3 | |
| 1830 | Arrivals of unknown mode | 2 | |
| 1831 | English ship, *Partridge* | | 7 |
| 1832 | English bark, *Walmer* | | 1 |
| 1833 | English whaler, *Amelia Wilson* | | 4 |
| 1833 | English whaler, *Cadmus* | | 14 |
| 1834 | English bark, *Fawn* | | 2 |
| 1834 | English ship, *Corsair* | | 2 |
| 1834 | American ship, *Howard* | | 1 |
| 1834 | English bark, *Rochester* | | 1 |
| 1835 | American ship, *Amazon* | | 4 |
| 1835 | English bark, *John Palmer* | | 2 |
| 1836 | American ship, *Peacock* | | 2 |
| 1836 | American schooner, *Enterprise* | | 1 |
| 1837 | English bark, *Rochester* | | 2 |
| 1837 | English bark, *Caroline* | | 1 |
| 1837 | English bark, *Admiral Cockburn* | | 1 |
| | TOTAL ARRIVALS | 25 | 45 |

reports that the number of "after-settlers" (those who arrived after the original 1830 band) numbered only 11 adults. The 34 people that this leaves unaccounted for are thought to be transients. Although the possible linguistic effects that these individuals may have had on the development of a community language are strictly speculative, this is a possibility which should not be ignored.

## 3.2. LINGUISTICALLY MIXED HOUSEHOLDS

After determining that the population of the Bonin Islands prior to the arrival of the Japanese was linguistically diverse, we must next turn to the question of what language or languages these people used to communicate with each other, both within the community and more importantly within the home where they were raising the second generation of Bonin Islanders.

There are references that indicate the settlers did not communicate very much with each other, and they should not be ignored since there are so few records regarding communication on the islands at all. The following extracts from Bayard Taylor's (1855) account of the Perry Expedition refer to Thomas Webb, an English seaman who, although he did not arrive on the island until 1847, went on to become one of the most influential settlers.

[Webb] was civil and respectful, though silent, rarely speaking unless in answer to our questions. [392]

The Englishman [Webb] stated that he had been seven years on the island. There was a kind of hesitation in his manner of speaking, which I fancied arose from an absence of intercourse with civilized society, as he seemed to be a man of average intelligence. There was, apparently, little association among the settlers. [393]

However, Webb's lack of verbosity in front of visitors notwithstanding, it is still very difficult to imagine a society in which the people did not communicate with each other at all. According to the records of visitors to the islands, we know that the populations of Chichijima and Hahajima combined ranged in the dozens during the mid-nineteenth century. From the smallness of the total population, it is virtually unthinkable that the settlers were not able to communicate with each other in some form or fashion.

Indeed, most of the available evidence contradicts Taylor's impressions and does suggest the tiny, ethnically diverse community of fewer than 50 people was not a segregated one. From various records we know that most of the men on the island were Westerners. Although some of the original Kanaka men such as Harry Bolla Otaheite and John "Judge" Marquese (mentioned earlier) remained on the island and were central to the community, many apparently did not stay on the island for long (Head and Daws 1968, 63).

Of the women who came to the island, we know of none for whom English was a native language. If a Western man on the island had a female companion, she was without exception a

Pacific Islander. Thus, the children born on the island were all raised either by mothers whose first languages were Austronesian or by second-generation women born on the island, themselves raised by such women. Nevertheless, we can assume that most or all of these women had some command of a pidginized English in order to communicate with their husbands and others in the society. Furthermore, as we discuss below, children raised on the island are reported to have been able to communicate in English, a factor which strengthens the hypothesis that their mothers knew some English-related variety as well.

Our knowledge of the ethnically mixed households during this period comes from twentieth-century studies such as Goldschmidt (1927) and Wagenseil (1962), but we also have firsthand records of domestic aspects of life on the island in the early nineteenth century. Dr. William Samuel Waithman Ruschenberger (1838), who subsequently became the fleet surgeon to the British East India Squadron and eventually the senior medical officer of the Navy, recorded the following upon his visit to Peel Island as a Navy surgeon in 1836.

Most of the white men have one or two wives, natives of the Sandwich Islands. In all, there are nineteen women on the island, among whom infanticide and infidelity, which they are at no pains to conceal from their husbands, are common; and this is in a population not exceeding forty souls! [302]

Here Mr. Mazarra [*sic*] met us, and led us toward the little village, at the entrance of which are several broad-leafed trees. Several Sandwich islanders, men and women, were lounging on some rough hewn logs, beneath their shade. We halted here for a moment, and Mr. Chapin and an Englishman came forward to welcome us. [305]

We were now led through the village, consisting of half a dozen comfortable huts, each fenced in with vertical posts of cabbage-tree, including a small garden in front. We were conducted to the dwelling of Mr. Chapin.... A door between the beds communicated with two inner apartments, half the size of the first, in which women were engaged in affairs of the household.... Such is the general style of the huts of this new settlement, which is called Clarkston [Blossom Village or Susaki]. [306–7]

We can see from this and other passages that the Westerners and Pacific Islanders on Peel Island did not live in segregated societies and that the households on the island were linguistically mixed ones.

In order to get an idea of the linguistic situation of households in the early and mid-nineteenth century, let us look at table 3.2. It shows the known early male settlers, the languages they spoke, and the period they are known to have lived on the island. Female islanders are listed here only as the spouses to illustrate the point about households, but also because the scarcity of information regarding females makes individual listings for them impractical.

As the last column in this table shows, there are many islanders for whom we have no evidence of offspring. It is possible that some of these men had children but their last names have not remained because their children (or grandchildren) were all female. Another possibility is that they had male children who remained bachelors or died before reaching adulthood. Nonetheless, it is important not to discount the contributions that childless islanders may have made to the construction and maintenance of a community language in that they formed a part of the linguistic community in which all island children grew up. (See section 5.3.4 on the influence of individuals in small communities.)

The overwhelming majority of households on the Bonins in this period did not share a common native language and thus would have had to use a nonnative pidginized form of language to communicate. This means that tertiary hybridization occurred, and this is the main mechanism leading to the stabilization of a pidgin (Holm 1988, 5; Sebba 1997, 103).

## 3.3. ABSENCE OF FORMAL EDUCATION

When considering the nature of the English language variety used on the Bonins, we should consider literacy, education, and other social factors that usually facilitate standard language usage. Literacy often tends to support or to strengthen concepts of language norms, but in the linguistic history of the islands, we do not have to deal much with these complications, because the available evi-

TABLE 3.2
Early Settlers on the Island

| Head of Household's Name | Arrived | Departed/Died | Native Language (Country of Origin) | Spouse's Language | Descendants |
|---|---|---|---|---|---|
| Nathaniel Savory | 1830 | 1874 | U.S. English (Massachusetts) | 1st Portuguese-Hawaiian, 2nd Chamorro (Maria delos Santos, widow of Mazarro) | yes |
| Richard J. Millinchamp | 1830 | gone by 1853 | U.K. English (left Bonins for Guam) | 1st Hawaiian, 2nd Chamorro (Joacquina de la Cruz) | |
| Matteo Mazarro | 1830 | 1848 | Italian (Genoa) | Chamorro (Maria delos Santos) | yes |
| Aldin B. Chapin | 1830 | 1852 | U.S. English (Boston) | (unmarried) | no |
| Charles Johnson | 1830 | after 1838 | Danish | | no? |
| Harry Bolla (aka Harry Otaheite) | 1830 | after 1853 | Tahitian | | |
| John "Judge" Marquese | 1830 | by 1875 | North Marquesan (Nuku-hiva) | Carolinian (Pidear; Agrihan Island, Northern Marianas) 1831–36 | |
| Joachim Gonzales (John Bravo) | 1831 | 1885 | Portuguese (Brava Island, Cape Verde) | Hawaiian (Mary) | yes |
| Joe Cullins (aka Joseph Freeman) | 1831 | 1874 | U.K. English | Kanaka (Betty) (?–1881) | |
| William Penn Gilley | 1832 | 1863 | U.K. English (murdered in Arctic) | Hawaiian (Tineree) 1855–62 | yes |
| Joseph Antonio | 1833 | | Brazilian Portuguese | | |
| John Roberts | 1833 | | Portuguese (Lisbon) | | |
| Francis Silva (Silver) | 1836 | | Portuguese (Azores, Faial Island) | | |
| Thomas Bailey | 1835 | | English (Hawaii) | | |
| Thomas Davis | 1841 | 1874 | Hawaiian? | | |
| George Augustine Washington | 1843? | 1880 | Malagasy (Madagascar; shot on Anijima) | Bonin Islander (Esther Savory, daughter of Nathaniel) | yes |
| James Motley | 1846 | 1866 | U.K. English (London) (lived on Bailey Islands) | Kanaka (Kitty) 1860–87 | |
| Thomas H. Webb | 1847 | 1881 | U.K. English (Surrey) (murdered by Kanakas) | Bonin Islander (Caroline Robinson, half Ponapean, raised on Haha) 1847–80 | yes |
| | | | | (Webb's mother) | |

TABLE CONTINUED ON NEXT PAGE

TABLE 3.2 (CONTINUED)
Early Settlers on the Island

| Head of Household's Name | Arrived | Departed/Died | Native Language (Country of Origin) | Spouse's Language | Descendants |
| --- | --- | --- | --- | --- | --- |
| Bill Mann | 1847 | | | Ponapean (Hypa) | no? |
| George Robinson | 1847 | 1861 | U.K. English (left Bonin Islands for Hawaii) | Ponapean (Teapa) 1847–60 | yes |
| Frederick Rohlfs (Rose) | 1852 | 1898 | German (Bremen) | 1st Kanaka (Kitty, widow of Motley) 1860–87; 2nd Japanese | yes |
| George Horton | 1853 | 1862 | U.K. English (died in Yokohama prison) | | no? |
| Louis Leseur | 1862 | 1885 | French (Brittany) | Carolinian (Pidear; Agrihan Island, Northern Marianas; widow of Marquese) | yes |
| William Allen | 1862 | 1882 | German (Bremen) | Hawaiian (Poconoi) ?–1875 | |
| Benjamin Pease | 1864 | 1874 | U.K. English (killed by Spencer) | Bonin Islander (Susan Robinson, half Ponapean) | yes |
| Robert S. Myers (Morris?) | 1874 | 1883 | Bermudan English (Negro) | Japanese (Yoshi from Yokohama) 1875–79 | |
| J. Spencer | | 1875 | Bermudan English? (Negro? Gay-head Indian? Kanaka?) (murdered) | Bonin Islander (Susan Robinson, half Ponapean, Pease widow) | yes |
| John Tewcrab | 1874 | 1882 | ? Kiribati (attended Tokyo school) | Japanese | yes |
| W. Tewcrab | 1874 | 1882 | ? Kiribati | | |
| Thomas Tewcrab | 1874 | 1882 | ? Kiribati | Wellington Island (Mokil; Boasin or Bosan) 1860–? | |
| Sino (Lerao Lucino) | ?by 1877 | | ? Tagalog (Manila, Philippines) | Japanese (Ishii Katsu) | |
| Bill Boles | | | Bougainville (between Solomons and Papua) | Kanaka (Sabess) | yes |
| John Ackerman | | | Tahitian | | yes |
| Charlie Papaya | ?by 1877 | 1877 | Hawaiian | | |
| Copepe | ?by 1877 | | Nonouti Island (Kiribati) | 1st Japanese; 2nd ? (Depes) | yes |

dence shows that most of the first-generation settlers and probably most of the second-generation islanders were illiterate.

In the absence of opportunities for formal training in English, all of the nonnative users of English on the island are assumed to have acquired the language through simple day-to-day contact and "natural acquisition." This situation would certainly have facilitated the development of a pidginized form of English. The power relationships among the various linguistic groups on the island indicate that the European and Pacific Island settlers had sufficient motivation for acquiring English. The original colony itself was established in the name of Great Britain by a leader who claimed British citizenship (Mazarro) and three native English speakers.

It is unreasonable, however, to believe that the early Pacific Islander settlers had any formal training in English. Western schools were only established in the Sandwich Islands in 1820, and for several decades the focus was on reading and writing in the Hawaiian language, not English (Carr 1972, 4). Hawaiian occupied a firm position as the language of formal situations (Reinecke 1969). Although Hawaiian Pidgin English, as an identifiable variety, did not develop until Asian workers arrived in the 1870s (Sebba 1997, 171), the existence in Hawaii of early Pacific pidgin words is documented as early as 1791 (Carr 1972, 4).

We know that Nathaniel Savory was highly literate from the correspondence he carried on with his family in Massachusetts (Cholmondeley 1915, 43–88, has numerous examples of these). He also kept a diary every day after arriving on the island, but it was lost in the big tsunami of 1872 (126).

Aldin Chapin (another of the original 1830 settlers) also appears to have been highly literate. Ruschenberger (1838, 306) writes of his 1836 visit:

A table, covered with newspapers and writing materials, and over it, upon the wall, hung a spy glass, and a thin manuscript, headed 'Laws of the Bonin Isles.' A sea chest stood on each side of the room, and a bed, with calico curtains, filled each corner. A few French prints, and a shelf of fifty or sixty miscellaneous volumes, occupied rather than adorned the walls.

Captain Richard Collinson of HMS *Enterprise* also attests to Chapin's literacy in a record of his 1851 visit.

I also had the gratification of increasing Mr. Chapin's library, which I have little doubt affords the old patriarch some gratification, and may possibly be useful to the rising generation. [Collinson 1889, 118]

As for the literacy of the other original and early settlers, it appears only one other person was literate, as we see in the following.

Chapin was the most literate man at Port Lloyd, a natural keeper of the 'laws.' The settlers' code was simple enough, suitable to a colony where only three men (including Savory and Chapin but not Mazarro) could write their names. [Head and Daws 1968, 63]

Subsequent decades saw the addition of only one prominent literate settler to the population in the person of Thomas Webb, who did not come to the island until almost two decades after the initial settlers' arrival. Russell Robertson, a British official living in Yokohama who visited Chichijima in November 1875, reports the following.

Of books, with the exception of a few I saw in Webb's house, there are none, and, Webb excepted, no one on the Islands can either read or write. [Robertson 1876, 133]

When Englishman Lionel Berners Cholmondeley made his visits to the island between 1894 and 1897, the Japanese had already begun bilingual education (section 4.5), but his description of the island society in the aftermath of Savory's death in 1874 does not indicate that any of the settlers were literate at the time except Webb.

Thomas Webb, after Nathaniel Savory, was the man of greatest consequence on the island. He had the advantage of being a scholar; and, being the possessor of a Bible and perhaps of an English Prayer Book, was generally called on to perform rites of baptism and burial. [Cholmondeley 1915, 122]

Since there was no school or formal education of any kind on the island, as far as is known, most of the subsequent generations were illiterate until the Japanese initiated bilingual education in the 1870s. Robertson's blanket statement of islander illiteracy indicates that Webb did not pass his reading and writing skills on even to his own children. As for Savory, Cholmondeley makes it clear that he made no effort to pass along his knowledge to his offspring.

The question we may now turn to consider is, how Nathaniel played the part of a father to his children. In the matter of education—so far as teaching them to read and write—it may be said at once that he faced a problem that fairly baffled him. He was no schoolmaster; their mother could do nothing; there was nobody else to whom he could turn, and he gave the problem up. [Cholmondeley 1915, 158]

### 3.4. REPORTS FROM SHIPWRECKED JAPANESE SEAMEN (1840)

Japanese records give us a glimpse into the type of language being used on the islands during the first decade of settlement. A word list compiled by shipwrecked Japanese seamen contains concrete evidence of language contact on the Bonins at the time. In addition to the words of obvious Hawaiian or English origin in the list, there are others that cannot be readily accounted for and indicate the effects of other languages, as well as possible evidence of the reduplication of English words, a process often observed in Pacific pidgins.

In 1840, a small Japanese fishing vessel, the *Chūkichi-maru*, from Otomoura in Kesen-gun, Rikuoku (present-day Otomo-chō in Rikuzen Takata-shi, Iwate Prefecture), was caught in a storm and badly damaged. The seamen were blown drastically off course and drifted until being rescued by the inhabitants of an island who they found spoke a strange and unfamiliar language. They lived on the island for 63 days, repaired their boat with the aid of the islanders who had befriended them, and made their way back to the Japanese mainland on their own. For years there was disagreement about the actual location of the islands. It was even suggested that these islands might have been Hawaii, but from the late nineteenth century, it has been clear that these islands were Hahajima and Chichijima of the Ogasawara Group. According to the seamen, the islanders numbered 38 (25 males, 13 females; including 8 children). This number roughly matches the figures (36 people) given by Quin in 1837. Although we cannot be certain whether the seamen interacted to the same extent with all the islanders, we can see from the numbers that they were aware of all the people on the islands at the time.

Upon returning to the Japanese mainland, the seamen were interrogated by government officials. (In this era, leaving the country or fraternizing with foreigners was punishable by death in Japan.) The complete record of the details they gave of the island and its inhabitants includes a list of 53 words and phrases that the Japanese seamen recalled the native islanders using.

Until recently there was little academic concern for this list, with Ogasawara scholars making only vague comments that it contained words identifiable as both Hawaiian and English. Recently, Ogasawara resident and local language scholar Fuyuo Nobushima (1997) has written an excellent paper on the nature of each individual word in the list. Table 3.3 contains words and phrases reported to have been in use on the islands where the Japanese seamen were shipwrecked.

The etymologies are based on Nobushima's, with several alterations made by myself. An analysis of the 53 expressions shows that 11 are English, 36 are Hawaiian, and 6 are of unclear origin. Some of the etymological claims are conjecture, but overall they reflect linguistic principles regarding borrowings, phonological changes, and semantic shifts, as well as the pragmatic problems associated with language contact.

Most of the dissimilarities between words reported and those proposed for their sources can be explained by regular sound correspondences. Many of these (the voicing of some voiceless consonants, between /i/ and /e/, for example) seem to reflect characteristics of the dialect of the Japanese seamen's home region.

There is one thing that no analysis of the list alone can tell us: Were the Hawaiian words used only by the Hawaiians and the

TABLE 3.3

Words Reported in Use on Island by Shipwrecked Japanese Seamen

| Reported Word (romanized) | Reported Meaning | Proposed Language of Origin | Proposed Original Form | Sound Correspondence, etc. |
|---|---|---|---|---|
| *noushi* | 'nose' | English | *nose* | |
| *maufu* | 'mouth' | English | *mouth* | |
| *bare* | 'hand' | Hawaiian | *pale* 'to ward off, thrust aside' | object/action confusion |
| *neie* | 'leg, foot' | Hawaiian | *ne'e* 'to step, march, creep' | object/action confusion |
| *neho* | 'tooth' | Hawaiian | *niho* | *e/i* |
| *heiheiiyao* | 'ear' | Hawaiian | *pepeiao* | *h/p* |
| *bou* | 'head' | Hawaiian | *po'o* | *b/p* |
| *wayou* | 'breast' | Hawaiian | *waiū* | |
| *raho* | 'scrotum' | Hawaiian | *laho* | |
| *wobowo* | 'belly' | Hawaiian | *'ōpū* | *wo/'ō; b/p* |
| *woure* | 'penis' | Hawaiian | *ule* | *wo/ø* |
| *wokore* | 'buttocks' | Hawaiian | *'ōkole* | *wo/'ō* |
| *towohe* | 'vagina' | Hawaiian | *kohe* | *t/k* |
| *teuha* | 'back' | Hawaiian | *kua* | *t/k* |
| *wowara* | 'white potato' | Hawaiian | *'uala* | *wo/ø* |
| *roshiu* | 'red potato' | English | *radish* | |
| *yeyama* | 'black potato' | English | *yam* | |
| *bakeke* | 'dried bonito fish' | Hawaiian | *pākeke* 'sweet potato' | |
| *tei* | 'tea' | English | *tea* | *e/i* |
| *aiboboka* | 'tobacco' | Hawaiian | *ipu paka (baka)* 'tobacco pipe' | *b/p* |
| *ibaka* | 'tobacco' | Hawaiian | *paka (baka)* | *i/ø; b/p* |
| *ikaha* | 'clothing' | Hawaiian | *kappa* | *i/ø; h/p* |
| *babare* | 'straw hat' | Hawaiian | *pāpale* | *b/p* |
| *gama* | 'sandals' | Hawaiian | *kāma'a* | |
| *borome* | 'broom' | Hawaiian | *pūlumi (burumi)*; Tahitian *poromu* | *b/p; e/i* |
| *bou* | 'rifle' | Hawaiian | *pū* | *b/p; ou/ū* |
| *baahei* | 'knife' | Hawaiian | *pahi* | *b/p; e/i* |
| *baahe* | 'small sword' | Hawaiian | *pahi* | *b/p* |
| *haheyoro* | 'a saw' | Hawaiian | *pahi olo* | *h/p; e/i* |
| *bora* | 'cup' | Hawaiian | *pola (bola)* | *b/p* |
| *baba* | 'table' | Hawaiian | *papa* | *b/p* |
| *aibohawo* | 'tea kettle' | Hawaiian | *ipu hao* | *a/ø; b/p* |
| *hawo* | 'kettle' | Hawaiian | *hao* 'metal tool' | *wo/o* |
| *bakete* | 'bucket' | Hawaiian | *bakete* | *b/p* |
| *keite* | 'small bucket' | Hawaiian | *bakete* | *b/p* |
| *huha* | 'pig' | Hawaiian | *pua'a* | *h/p* |
| *motsukou* | 'mother ship' | Hawaiian | *moku* 'boat' | |

TABLE CONTINUED ON NEXT PAGE

TABLE 3.3 (CONTINUED)
Words Reported in Use on Island by Shipwrecked Japanese Seamen

| Reported Word (romanized) | Reported Meaning | Proposed Language of Origin | Proposed Original Form | Sound Correspondence, etc. |
|---|---|---|---|---|
| *batsubatsu* | 'lighter, jolly (boat)' | English | *boat* | *b/p*; *t/k* (reduplication of *boat*) |
| *woshiyubu* | 'passenger ship' | English | *ship* | *wo/ø*; *b/p* |
| *kanbashi* | 'compass needle' | English | *compass* | *b/p* |
| *kaiton* | 'captain' | Portuguese | *capitão*; English *captain* | |
| *maiten* | 'boss' | ? | ? | |
| *koukou* | 'a cook' | | Tahitian *tutu?*; reduplication of English *cook?* | *ou/u* |
| *wowaka* | 'water' | English | *water* | *wo/ø*; *k/t* |
| *hayahaya* | 'fire' | English | *fire* | reduplication |
| *you* | 'man' | English | *you* | *ou/u* |
| *mei* | 'woman' | English | *me* | *ei/e* |
| *kaukau* | 'eat' | Hawaiian Pidgin | *kaukau* | |
| *imoyai* | 'sleep' | Hawaiian | *hiamoe, moe* | *i/e* |
| *banebane* | 'copulation, sex' | Hawaiian | *panipani* | *b/p*; *e/i* |
| *nao nao* | used when refusing something | English | *no, no*; Port. *nao* | |
| *arouha* | said placing right hand above eye to people coming in from outside or to those returning | Hawaiian | *aloha* | |
| *aina* | name of this island used by islanders | Hawaiian | *'āina* 'land' | |

English ones used only by the English speakers, or were all of these words being used by all of the islanders? One aspect that does indeed suggest the development of a pidgin is the reduplication of English words. The forms the Japanese recorded as *koukou* (from the English *cook*), *batsubatsu* (from *boat*), and *hayahaya* (from *fire*) are (according to Nobushima's analysis) examples of this.

The seamen record *kaukau* (not *kaikai*, the word found in contact languages throughout the Pacific) to mean 'eating'. *Kaukau* is a word used in Hawaiian Pidgin (not Hawaiian), thought to have originated in Coastal Chinese Pidgin, but recorded in use in Hawaii in 1791 and again in 1820 (Carr 1972, 98). This term is probably related to *kaikai* used in contact languages throughout the Pacific (see section 3.9).

Another point of interest is the word *wowaka*. If this does indeed derive from *water*, then the *t/k* alteration indicates the usage of English words by the Polynesian settlers, speakers for whom these sounds would have had some phonological correspondence. There is no linguistic reason to believe that this substitution is attributable to the Japanese seamen.

Considering both the population of the island and the contents of the word list in table 3.3 (as well as fragmentary evidence from other sources discussed in section 3.6 below), it is possible to speculate that the common means of communication on the island contained linguistic elements from both Hawaiian and English and possibly from other languages.

## 3.5. PACIFIC INFLUENCES

Pacific languages had their influence on the early Bonins. Nonlinguistic contributions by Oceanic cultures to the coalescing island culture of this era are apparent as well. The shipwrecked Japanese made sketches of Caucasian-looking men (note the beards and bottons on their shirts) fishing from outrigger canoes (figure 3.2).

In the following decade, lithographs and texts created by Commodore Perry's crew recorded the mixture of Pacific and Western cultures. In the early Meiji period (1870s and 1880s), Japanese scholars and photographers documented the life of the Bonin Islanders living in houses constructed of palm leaves and wearing loose-fitting white clothes resembling those common in the Hawaiian islands in that day. These photographs show that Westerners still fished in outrigger canoes using tools and methods which they or their parents and grandparents had brought from Oceania. They hunted the fauna and gathered the flora that naturally more closely resembled that of Polynesia and Micronesia than mainland Japan, and these similarities are reflected in the borrowed vocabulary used in the terminology related to these things (section 3.7).

FIGURE 3.2
Sketch of Western Bonin Islanders Fishing from Outrigger Canoe (1840s)
(Kurata 1983, 15)

The language and culture of the Bonin Islands is typically portrayed as a mixture of English (Western) and Japanese. But it is important to emphasize that the influence of Pacific languages on the Bonins was not a single event at the beginning of this community's history, but rather a recurring factor throughout two centuries. We will see in sections 4.7 and 8.5 that Pacific Island languages and culture have contributed significantly to the multiethnic community of the Bonins.

## 3.6. ISLANDERS' LINGUISTIC CONTACT WITH OUTSIDERS

3.6.1. FIRST-GENERATION SETTLERS' EXPERIENCES PRIOR TO SETTLING ON THE ISLANDS. Circumstantial evidence would indicate that the first-generation settlers had exposure to Pacific contact languages (probably English-based) prior to their arrival on the island. As far as is known, every one of the Pacific Islander settlers reached Chichijima on the ships of Westerners. This presupposes at least some command of a European tongue, probably a contact variety of English. We must also recall that many of the Western male settlers, including Savory and Webb, were originally seamen, so we can assume they too had had ample exposure to early Pacific contact varieties before their arrival on the island.

Even for those who had not been seamen, simply getting to the island would have required a great deal of time for Westerners, and we know that many had been living on other Pacific Islands prior to their migration to the Bonins. These include the original group of settlers, who sailed from Honolulu; the patriarch of the Gilley clan, William Penn Gilley, who appears to have spent time in Hawaii as a boy; and George Robinson, who arrived from the Caroline Islands (Shepardson 1998, chapters 1 and 11). Settlers such as these would already have had exposure to early Pacific pidgins there before ever arriving on Peel Island.

Furthermore, several of the settlers were natives of regions in which Atlantic contact languages would have been in wide usage. Joachim Gonzales's home, Cape Verde, figures very prominently in the history of European-based contact languages worldwide. Francis Silva, mentioned in early records, was from Faial Island in the Azores. J. Spencer, who arrived years later, is described as a "Negro from Bermuda," as is Robert Morris (or Myers). It is possible that these men encountered Atlantic contact languages on their voyages.[1]

3.6.2. ISLANDER OPPORTUNITIES FOR CONTACT WITH VISITORS. A common impression of the Bonin Islands settlers is that they were isolated in the middle of the Pacific, and this is largely true. However, we know that several ships a year entered Port Lloyd (the port at Chichijima, now known as Futami-wan [二見湾]). According to a report by Nathaniel Savory, 24 ships (22 of them whalers) put into port during the 31 months between January 1, 1833, and July 1, 1835 (Clement 1905, 190). After this, we also know that ships arrived at least frequently enough to enable Savory to correspond with his relatives in Massachusetts (Cholmondeley 1915, 43–88).

The pace of visitors had grown by 1838, when Captain P. I. Blake of the HMS *Larne* records the following in a report he filed to the authorities in Great Britain:

During the last season, about twelve or fourteen of these ships, English and American, called at Port Lloyd for refreshments on an average each of them consumed there and took away produce and Stock to the amount of from five to six hundred dollars, part of which is generally settled for by barter, especially in tobacco and spirits, which are apparently both of them much in demand throughout the Pacific. One Whaler I was informed, took away between sixty and seventy hogs, with a proportionate quantity of yams, sweet potatoes, maize, etc. In addition to those that have entered the harbour (a list of which is noted in the annexed paper no. 2) several have called off, and sent in their boats with trusty crews for supplies (which have been frequently done at great hazard) from the fear of their crews deserting should they enter the Port and this it appears is the greatest evil complained of. [Blake 1838, 115]

In his "annexed" (appended) list entitled "A List of Whalers, English and American that called at Port Loyd, Bonin Islands for refreshments etc, during the last season—viz between April and September 1838," he lists seven English ships by name and notes "Three or four more called off, and received supplies, but did not enter the harbour. Names not remembered." He lists four American ships by name and notes that two others stopped as well (Blake 1838, 124–25). This totals 16 or 17 ships within a six-month period. The islands were becoming an important stop for ships crossing the Pacific.

We can see from this report that Bonin Islanders not only had frequent visitors, with whom they bartered and traded, but also that they had outsider "guests" in the form of deserters, a few of whom stayed on the island permanently but many of whom moved on.

Passengers on these ships occasionally stayed on the Bonins for varying periods of time. We saw previously (table 3.1) that Michael Quin's 1837 records indicate there was a relatively large number of short-term island residents. The presence of such transients comes as no surprise; other islands in the Pacific were peopled with such beachcombers in this era. The research site Micronesian Seminar has an archive with 542 documented cases of beachcombers on

Chuuk, Kosrae, Palau, Pohnpei, Yap, and the Marshall Islands during the nineteenth century (Hezel 2006). The flow of transients into the Bonins would have added further variety to the islands' linguistic mixture.

The ships that sailed the Pacific in the nineteenth century (and before) had crews from various linguistic backgrounds. The often-quoted figure that the crew of Lord Nelson's flagship, HMS *Victory*, contained no fewer than 14 different nationalities, whether entirely accurate or not, nonetheless typifies the linguistic variation of ships' crews. These men often communicated with one another, as well as with the various peoples they encountered in various ports of call, through the means of a nautical jargon, often called South Seas Jargon or Pacific Jargon English.

The ships that put into port at Chichijima provided an opportunity for the islanders to come in contact with this language variety. Although these contacts were temporary, they did nonetheless last for days or weeks at a time (particularly if ships were making repairs). Moreover, we know from various firsthand accounts that these contacts were between whole crews of the ships and a large portion of the islanders, and not simply formal interactions between the captain and a local leader.

3.6.3. FIRST-GENERATION PACIFIC ISLANDER SETTLERS' COMMUNICATIONS WITH OUTSIDERS. When ships visited the Bonins, the captains frequently mentioned their experiences communicating with the Bonin Islanders in their logs. Table 3.4 lists all such logs which are known to mention contact with the islands.

Many stated that, although the islanders were able to communicate with them, the islanders' English was poor. These descriptions support the interpretation of the islanders' language as a contact variety of English, and indeed other factors support this theory as well.

In the record of his visit to Peel Island in 1836, Ruschenberger mentions communicating with a Pacific Islander settler.

A canoe loaded with melons and pumpkins floated on its [the stream's] surface; and a Sandwich Islander, asleep in the shade of a rock hard by, declared it to lead to some habitation or cultivated ground. [1838, 309]

TABLE 3.4
Early Written Records by Visitors to the Bonins

| Year of Visit | Visitor | Ship | Sources |
|---|---|---|---|
| 1823 | Capt. James J. Coffin | American whaler *Transit* | Cholmondeley (1915) |
| 1827 | Capt. Frederick William Beechey | HMS *Blossom* | Beechey (1831) |
| 1827 | Lt. George Peard | HMS *Blossom* | Peard (1973) |
| 1828 | Frédéric Lütke (Fedor Petrovich Litke) | Corvette *Senëüavin* (*Seniavine*) | Lütke (1835) |
| 1836 | Navy surgeon Dr. William Samuel Waithman Ruschenberger | American barque *Volunteer* | Ruschenberger (1838) |
| 1837 | Capt. Michael Quin | HMS *Raleigh* | Quin (1837, 1856) |
| 1840 | Surgeon John Wilson | *Gipsy* | Forster (1991) |
| 1851 | Capt. Richard Collinson | HMS *Enterprise* | Collinson (1852, 1889) |
| 1853 | Bayard Taylor (Perry) | USS *Susquehanna* | Taylor (1855) |
| 1853 | Samuel Williams, Chinese Interpreter (Perry) | USS *Saratoga* | Williams (1910) |
| 1853 | Francis L. Hawks (Perry) | USS *Powhatan* | Hawks (1856) |
| 1853 | John S. Sewall, Captain's Clerk (Perry) | USS *Powhatan* | Sewall (1905) |
| 1854 | John Sproston, Midshipman (Perry) | USS *Macedonian* | Sakanishi (1940) |

In the records of Collinson, mentioned previously, we find the following record of the communication between the visiting English speakers and the Pacific Islander settlers in 1851.

As we drew in, a canoe under sail crossed our bows, the sole occupant of which was soon on board. He had but small clothing, and less English, but managed, however, to let us know that his name was Harry, that he was a pilot, and that he had pigs, turtles, yams and onions for sale. [1889, 112]

This passage does indeed provide bits of information about the linguistic situation. While the man's English is characterized as limited, he nonetheless manages to convey his name, his ability to pilot ships, and his desire to sell goods.

Bayard Taylor (1855) also writes of his party's experiences communicating with the Pacific Islander settlers on Chichijima on June 14, 1853. These episodes, as with the ones we just saw, verify that non-Western inhabitants of the island did indeed have some control over an English-based language variety.

Presently a South-Sea Islander, in a coarse cotton shirt and pantaloons, and with one half of his face tattooed a light blue, made his appearance. He said he was a native of Nukaheva, in the Marquesas, and his name was "Judge." He conducted us around the corner of the mountain, where the valley opened westward to the sea.... I asked him to accompany us to the southern extremity of the island, which he said was about three or four miles distant. There was no path, and he did not seem inclined to go, but he sent his boy after a companion, who, he said, could pilot us over the hills. The latter was a tawny native of Otaheite [Tahiti], and spoke very little English. He confessed that he knew the way, as well as the wild-boar haunts in the woods, but refused to go without the Judge. As it was next to impossible to find our way without a guide, I settled the matter by taking both. [401–2]

The Tahitian here is the "Harry" mentioned by Collinson. The following pages contain more of Taylor's (1855) references to this intercultural encounter.

The Otaheitan informed us we were in the neighborhood of wild boars. [403]

The Otaheitan professed to know the way. [404]

The guides called the place "Southeast Bay." They stated that it was frequently visited by whalers for food and water.... The natives said that there was no other way of returning except the ravine by which we came. [406]

He [the Judge] declared that this was the usual road. [407]

We see from these detailed firsthand reports that Judge was able to convey that (1) he was from Nukaheva, (2) his name was Judge, (3) the distance to the tip of the island was 3 to 4 miles, and (4) he was sending for someone who could guide them. Harry conveyed that he (1) knew the way to the tip of the island, (2) knew where boars were, and (3) would not go unless Judge accompanied them. One or both of the men conveyed that (1) they were a half mile from the sea, (2) the place was called "Southeast Bay," (3) whalers often came looking for water or food, and (4) the only way to return was through the ravine whence they came.

The information conveyed here is much more abstract and complex than the sort of "here and now" facts transmitted in, for example, a contact situation where the interlocutors point to objects and ask their names. We can conclude that the islander(s) had the English communication abilities to relate information to English speakers whom they had just met (and by implication to comprehend the Americans' utterances as well). In spite of this rather high level of information exchange, we find Harry's speech characterized as poor English. This seeming contradiction suggests the use of a contact language.

3.6.4. ISLAND-BORN SECOND-GENERATION SPEAKERS' COMMUNICATION WITH VISITORS. The original European settlers almost all bore children with Polynesian wives. Not only did these Polynesian women not speak English as their native language, but neither did the overwhelming majority of the men. If these couples used a pidginized form of English to communicate with each other inside the home and to communicate with their neighbors, then it would have been this language to which their children were exposed. Thus, circumstances would have been highly conducive to the acquisition by native speakers of a pidgin, in other words for creolization to occur. However, as we shall see, what developed was not a full-fledged creole but a creoloid.

Samuel Williams, the Chinese interpreter for Perry aboard the USS *Saratoga*, left a journal of his experiences. He describes his party's first encounter with a Chichijima resident on their first arrival on the morning of June 14, 1853.

A Hawaiian—a youth born on the island came off to pilot us if needed, and about nine o'clock [in the morning] we anchored. [Williams 1910, 29]

The night of his arrival, Williams visits the homes of several settlers, and we discover that this "Hawaiian" youth is actually one of the Gonzales children.

One of them was occupied by a Portuguese who had lived here twenty-one years and has had ten children, only one (our pilot erewhile) of whom now lives with him. [29]

The Gonzales boy who acted as the Americans' guide was born of a Portuguese-speaking father and a Hawaiian-speaking mother. Nonetheless, he was able to communicate with the American visitors to the extent that he served as their guide in spite of the fact that he was still living with his parents and presumably had not yet had any of the off-island experiences (education in Oahu, work on a seagoing vessel) that his fellow islanders had. In view of the lack of opportunities for formal English training and in light of our knowledge about the linguistic makeup of the island population (the extremely few native speakers of English), we can only assume that this youth spoke a naturally acquired contact variety of English.

3.6.5. FIRST-GENERATION SETTLERS' OFF-ISLAND EXPERIENCES. In spite of the fact that the Bonins were largely isolated from the outside world during the early decades of their settlement, Bonin Islanders did nonetheless maintain links with Polynesia and Micronesia. Historical records tell us that several of the first-generation European settlers traveled back and forth to Guam (and less often to Hawaii) in the almost half century between their arrival in the 1830s and the arrival of the Japanese in the 1870s (Cholmondeley 1915, 18, 19, 33, 115, 121, etc.). We may assume they encountered both Pacific languages as well as Pacific contact varieties of English. USS *Macedonian* Midshipman John Sproston, who visited Peel Island as part of Commodore Perry's fleet, left the following journal entry for April 20, 1854:

Collins [Joseph Cullens], Webb and Bravo are the names of three other old settlers. Webb has gone in the Am[erican] whale-ship, Bowditch, as first mate, but will return again. [Sakanishi 1940, 27]

Thomas Webb was, along with Nathaniel Savory and Joachim Gonzales, one of the most influential of the early settlers and one who left his mark on the island in the form of descendants. It is not unlikely that islanders like Webb who had worked on ships came in contact with nautical pidgins (see Clark 1979).

We know that in later years Webb had to intercede between the newly arrived Japanese officials and the islanders. Webb could not speak Japanese; the Japanese had brought their own Japanese-English translators. However, from the evidence we have examined thus far, it follows that the islanders may not have understood mainstream English because they spoke a contact variety. In this case, it would have been necessary for someone such as Webb, who understood both the islanders' contact variety of English and the standard English spoken by the Japanese officials, to translate between the two.

3.6.6. SECOND-GENERATION ISLANDERS' OFF-ISLAND STUDY AND WORK EXPERIENCES. In addition to their contacts with visiting seamen, many of the second-generation islanders lived away from the island for extended periods. This further increased the possibilities for their coming into contact with other languages, particularly Pacific varieties of contact language.

In 1851, Collinson recorded the following when visiting Chichijima:

> Since the isle has been settled (about twenty-one years), there have been born on the isle twenty-six children, of which twenty-one were boys and five girls; twelve children have died, ten boys and two girls; and also eight male adults and six females. Some of the men have been left here sick from the ships; the greater part of the boys, all but four are gone away on board different ships; and two of the girls are gone to Oahu for their education. [1889, 114]

Of the 11 island-born boys still alive at the time, no fewer than seven (two-thirds) were living away aboard ships. Two of the three female children were also receiving their educations in Hawaii.

The observation made in 1851 that two of the island girls were in Oahu being educated seems to contradict Robertson's 1875 report (mentioned in section 3.3) that Webb was the only literate person on the island. We may speculate on several possible explanations for this. (1) The girls, for various reasons, may not have returned from Hawaii, in which case they would not have brought outside language varieties back to the island as I suggest. (2) They may indeed have returned from Hawaii in the 1850s, but moved away again or died by the time of Robertson's visit two decades later. (3) They may have received educations which did not include

literacy (e.g., learning manners, to sew), or they may have learned
to read and write only Hawaiian and Robertson may not have considered this knowledge "literacy."

The boys were most certainly surrounded by speakers of ship
jargon or Pacific English Pidgin, and the girls were most likely living in an environment of Hawaiian and a Hawaiian-influenced variety of English.

Thus, we find that the islanders did not live in complete isolation during the decades before the arrival of the Japanese in the
latter half of the nineteenth century. Rather, they experienced
repeated language contact not only in dealing with their fellow
settlers, but with visitors to the island and in their own off-island
experiences. In this way, younger islanders would have had numerous and extended opportunities to hear other Pacific languages,
Pacific contact languages, and other varieties of English.

Hawaiian Pidgin English is not thought to have developed until Asian and Latin workers arrived the 1870s. Nonetheless, as Carr
(1972, 5) points out, "The fact is that even during the decades
when the major linguistic contact in the Island was confined to two
languages, Hawaiian and English, the learning problems were for-
midable, and the indigenous language had a marked effect upon
the spoken English."

## 3.7. NON-ENGLISH LEXICAL ITEMS

Many words in use on the Bonins even in the late twentieth century are thought to be derived from the contact with Pacific Island
languages that occurred from the 1830s until the end of the nineteenth century. Today these lexemes are used not only in the English of the Bonins, but in Ogasawara Japanese and the Ogasawara
Mixed Language as well. Hawaiian words form the majority of the
Oceanic-language words we find on the Bonins. Since Polynesian
migration to the islands occurred only in the early history of the
settlement, it seems clear that most of these words came to the
island during the first half of the nineteenth century, so in spite of
their continued usage in the twentieth century, they are discussed
in this chapter.

Much of the information about these comes from Fuyuo Nobushima (1998), who actively works, with no academic affiliation,
collecting island words and researching their etymologies. Additional words (and some alternative etymologies) have come from
my own fieldwork and research.

Words from Oceanic languages are particularly prevalent in
plant and animal names. In table 3.5, I show the Bonin word form
(with alternate pronunciations), followed by its meaning on the
Bonins, and its proposed etymology (language of origin, original
word form, and original meaning if different from the Bonins).

Many place-names of Oceanic-language origin exist on the Bonins as well, including *Pukunui* (from Haw. *puka nui* 'big hole'),
*Puhi Island*, and *Holey Point* (because the respective fish can be
found at these places). The place name *Aki* is said by islanders to be
of Hawaiian origin, but there is no strong and clear theory about
the actual etymology of the name.

The Bonin Island tree *biide-biide* is universally known on the
island. The word was used as the title of a verse by the popular Japanese writer Hakushū Kitahara (北原白秋) in 1929 and has reached
symbolic proportions on the islands. It is used as the name of a bar,
as the name of the school's annual Cultural Festival, and in the title
of a series of writings produced by the high school.

Even more interesting to linguists, however, is the mystery of
how the Bonin word *biide-biide*, also recorded as *uri-uri* and *ude-ude*,
could have derived from the Hawaiian *wili-wili*. In order to explain
why Japanese in the early Meiji period heard pronunciations that
to them sounded as divergent as *biide-biide* and *uri-uri*, we must conclude that the non-Japanese islanders at the time were still using
BOTH the pronunciations *vili-vili* and *wili-wili*. First, *uri-uri* and *ude-
ude* are easily linked because in many dialects of Japanese there is
confusion between /d/ and /r/ as well as between /e/ and /i/. That
the Bonins /u/ derived from the Hawaiian /wi/ is also predictable
because the sequence /wi/ is impossible in Japanese phonology and
/ui/ or simply /u/ would be a likely substitution for those sounds.
The same goes for the substitution of the Japanese flap [ɾ] for the
Hawaiian lateral approximant [l]. As discussed later in this book,
Bonin Islanders well into the twentieth century displayed variation

TABLE 3.5

## Oceanic Words Thought to Have Entered Ogasawara Speech in the Early to Mid-Nineteenth Century

| Bonin Word Form | Meaning on the Bonins | Proposed Etymology (Original Meaning When Different) |
|---|---|---|
| *arahii* (*arihii*) | 'goldlined sea bream, *Gnathodentex aurolineatu*' | Haw. *ala'ihi* 'squirrelfish, *Flammeo scythrops*' |
| *biide-biide* (*bari-bari, uri-uri, ude-ude*) | 'leguminous tree, *Erythrina boninensis*' | Haw. *wiliwili* '*Erythrina sandwicensis*' |
| *hōrei* (*hōresu*) | 'yellow variety of gray chub, *Kyphosus bigibbus*' | Haw. *hōlei* 'yellow tree used for dyeing, *Ochrosia compta*' |
| *Holey Point* | place-name | " |
| *kopepe* | 'uncivilized' | ?Mokilese, *koahpehpe* 'driftwood' |
| *kopepe kasago* | 'variety of grouper, *Epinephelus merra*' | " |
| *Kopepe-yashiki* (lit. 'shack') | place-name | " |
| *Kopepe-hama* ('beach') | place-name | " |
| *Kopepe-kaigan* ('shore') | place-name | " |
| *moe-moe* (*moi-moi*) | 'sex, copulation' | Haw. *moe* 'sleep' |
| *nuku-mome* | 'young striped jack *Pseudo-caranx dentex*' | Haw. *nuku mone'u* 'jackfish, *Caranx melampygus*' |
| *piimaka* | 'raw fish dish made with vinegar' | Haw. *pinika* 'vinegar' |
| *puhi* | 'moray eel, *Gymnothorax kidako*, etc.' | Haw. *puhi* 'eel' |
| *Puhi Island* | place-name | " |
| *Pukunui* | place-name | Haw. *puka nui* 'big hole' |
| *rahaina* | 'sugar cane' | Haw. *lahaina* 'sugar cane' |
| *rawara* (*rawarawa, rauhara, rowara, rohara, raharo, rūwara, rohawo, lohala*) | 'pandanus tree, *Pandanus odoratissimus*' | Haw. *lau hala* 'pandanus leaf' |
| *tahara* | 'spangled emperor, *Lethrinus nebulosus*' | ?Haw. *kahala, tahala* 'amberjack, yellowtail, *Seriola dumerilii*' |
| *tamana* (*tamena, tremana*) | 'hardwood tree *Calophyllum inophyllum*' | Haw. *kamani, tamani* |
| *Tani* | an islander's nickname, said to be "the Kanaka word for 'big, strong'" | Haw. *tane* (or *kane*) 'man, masculine' |
| *ūfū* (*uhu*) | 'parrotfish, Family Scaridae' | Haw. *uhu* 'parrotfish, *Scarus perspicillatus*' |

between [w] and [v], and this variation is inherent in the Hawaiian language as well. These etymological relationships are shown in figure 3.3.

The Ogasawara terms *biide-biide* and *uri-uri* (*ude-ude*) appear unrelated (and indeed unrelatable). This lack of connection is shown in the break in figure 3.3. The arrows show that *biide-biide* derived from *vili-vili* as *uri-uri* (*ude-ude*) derived from *wili-wili* (or more accurately are the orthographic representations of the way this word sounded to early Japanese hearers). Lines between *vili-vili* and *wili-wili* show the connection between these two forms (phonological variants).

In table 3.5, we have seen numerous examples of Hawaiian words, but those of Micronesian origin are much harder to find. The available information regarding the homelands of the Pacific Islander settlers shows that Polynesians outnumbered the Micronesians among the early arrivals, but that after the 1840s most of the men and women who arrived came from Micronesia. This fact indicates that the Hawaiian-origin vocabulary dates back to the earliest years of the settlement. As traffic back and forth between Hawaii decreased in the mid-nineteenth century, contacts with Guam and Saipan increased. There was also contact with Saipan from the 1920s until World War II and with Guam during the Navy Era. So the few words of Chamorro origin may have come in during the nineteenth or twentieth centuries.

The comparative rarity of words indicating the more recent contacts with Micronesia might seem strange; in one sense one might expect the older Polynesian words to have died out, perhaps being replaced by more recent Micronesian words. But this is not how language works; we must look at things from a differ-

FIGURE 3.3
The Hawaiian Origin of *biide-biide*

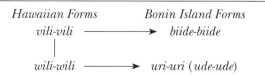

| Hawaiian Forms | Bonin Island Forms |
|---|---|
| vili-vili ⟶ | biide-biide |
| ⎮ | |
| wili-wili ⟶ | uri-uri (ude-ude) |

ent perspective. Mufwene (1996) has written about the "Founder Principle," which revolves around the notion that the earliest contributors to a language mixture situation have deeper effects than subsequent ones; perhaps the plethora of Hawaiian words is explainable by this principle.

One example of the influence of a European language (other than English) on the language of the island may be found in the word *borras*. In the 1890s when Cholmondeley visited the island, he recorded the following about the 1872 tsunami, which devastated the island.

I must give brief account of a tidal wave, or "borras" as the Bonin settlers term it. [1915, 125]

The word probably derives from a European word. The Greek god of the north wind, Boreas, is the source of eponyms in various European languages meaning 'storm at sea'. In Portuguese the term *borrasca* means 'storm'. A nineteenth-century English-based mariner pidgin used in Southeast Asian ports also had the word *bora* for 'north wind'. Considering the great influence on the island of the Portuguese Gonzales family (and the presence of other Portuguese-speaking island residents), as well as the continued contacts with ships' crews and islanders' experiences signing on for long north Pacific voyages, there could be multiple routes for the term's passage to the Bonins.

The above examples are lexical items, not grammatical influences, so they shed little light on the question of what a nineteenth-century Bonin Pidgin English might have sounded like, but they do serve as demonstrations of the influence that Pacific Islanders had on one aspect (the lexical one) of island language life and allow us to speculate about their influences on the more structural aspects of language contact on the islands.

## 3.8. EPONYMS

There are several interesting cases involving people's names (eponyms) and Oceanic-language words on the Bonins. In some cases, common nouns became people's (nick)names; in other cases, people's names became common nouns or place-names.

*Tani* was the nickname of an islander born in the early twentieth century, but since it is said to have been given him by a grandparent and it seems to be Hawaiian in origin, its usage on the Bonins must date from the early settlers. Arima (1990, 217) records that the nickname *Tani* was reported to her as the "Kanaka word for big, strong," and Tsuda (1988, 282) reports that this nickname was bestowed upon the man by his grandfather. *Tane* (or *kane*) means 'man, masculine' in Hawaiian.

A nineteenth-century settler of unknown origin called Kopepe is the source of multiple place-names, such as *Kopepe-kaigan* 'shore', *Kopepe-hama* 'beach', and *Kopepe-yashiki* 'lit. shack'. His name is also given to the fish *kopepe kasago* 'a variety of grouper'. Before the war, the Westerners of Ogasawara used the eponymic term *kopepe* to refer to someone who lived outside of civilized society (since the original Kopepe was a subsistence fisherman who had limited contact with either Japanese or Western islanders). On the Bonins, the man Kopepe is variously said to have come from places as far apart as Nonouti (Kiribati) and Buka (Papua New Guinea) and Ngatik (Caroline Islands). Recent evidence suggests he was from Mokil Atoll near Ponape. As indicated by the place-names, he moved about quite often, even within the Bonins, and in an interview, his daughter speaks of him as a drifter (Segawa 1931). In Mokilese, *koahpehpe* means 'driftwood'. If this is the accurate etymology, then we can add Mokilese to the list of languages that contributed words to the Bonin Islands. (For more on personal names, see section 6.3.)

Not all eponyms from Oceanic languages are concrete nouns. *Kopepe* can to be a term for anyone 'uncivilized'. The attribute *laukau* 'crazy' comes from the name of an island-born woman whose father came from Rotuma Island (Fiji). Mühlhäusler (1998) shows that eponyms are common in other isolated island communities.

While we are on the subject of eponyms, let me diverge from the topic of Oceanic-language words and examine some examples from English and Japanese. *Ponchan* or *ponsuke* 'simpleminded' comes from the nickname of a Japanese boy sentenced to the reform school on the island in the early twentieth century and fits in with the unflattering attribute eponyms seen above.

In the vein of the *kopepe kasago* example above, we have English and Japanese names being attached to plants and animals. One example is the *Savory palm 'Clinostigma savoryana'*. An alternate form of the fish name *hōrei*, examined above, is *hōresu* 'gray chub', which comes with its own alternative etymology. It is said to be named for Horace Savory, although this is probably a folk etymology. Another fish name (assigned alternately to a type of wrasse or parrotfish) is the *eizō*, said to be named for a Japanese man.

There are place-names like *Savory Rock, Jackson Beach, Perry Hole*, and *Jack William* (a bay), named for Euro-American settlers. Since it was common practice to give islanders with "foreign" names English nicknames, even place-names like *Washington Beach, Brava Point, John Beach*, and *Bill Beach*, while English-sounding, are actually named for settlers who did not speak English as their native language. Their existence then demonstrates a more indirect influence of non-English-speaking settlers to the overall linguistic landscape of the island. This is just a small sampling of places named by islanders for islanders; I have not included the many toponyms given by visiting ships' captains to commemorate their patrons back home or themselves.

## 3.9. SIMILAR LANGUAGE CONTACT SITUATIONS

There are cases remarkably similar to the Bonins in which Western men took small numbers of Pacific Islanders and settled hitherto uninhabited islands. In some cases, English-based pidgins developed as the common means of communication between the two groups, as on Pitcairn Island (Ross and Moverley 1964; see also Mühlhäusler 1998). These pidgins were typically creolized in the second-generation speakers born on the island, as in the case of Palmerston Island (Ehrhart-Kneher 1996). Laycock (1989) contends that the modern-day Pitcairn language draws on the pidgin English spoken by the original settlers and is not a true creole, even though it exhibits "creole-like features."

Unlike many Pacific island language contact situations of the
nineteenth century, the Bonins language situation developed
largely in isolation from other Pacific contact varieties. South Seas
Jargon is thought to have been still in its early stages of development and diffusion in 1830, and the interrelated varieties of Pacific pidgins and creoles that derived from it did not reach their
peak until decades later.

Clark (1979) examines the use of 30 grammatical and lexical features common to many Pacific contact languages and determines that Pitcairn uses only 7 of these, and furthermore that
those 7 are all features used outside the Pacific region in pidgins
and creoles globally. He concludes that the unique position which
Pitcairn occupies within the context of Pacific contact languages
owes much to the early date of its development (late eighteenth
and early nineteenth century) and to its relative lack of contact
with other contact languages during important periods in its development.

So, if we examine the language of a community and it does
NOT have typically contact-language features, that does not necessarily rule out the possibility of a past contact variety; it just means
that (as was the case on Pitcairn) that contact variety developed
with relatively little influence from other contact languages.

The Bonins were similarly isolated and MOST of the features
that Clark (1979) lists as Pan-Pacific or even global features of pidgins and creoles (*been, fellow, kaikai, piccaninny, savvy*, etc.) are NOT
found in the Bonins today, and we have no particular reason to
think that they were used there in the past either. (However, see
section 3.4 for evidence that *kaukau* was used there in the mid-
nineteenth century.) There is some evidence for the use of some
other features, however, like adverbial *by and by*, past marker *been*,
and quantifier *plenty* (examined in section 5.7), but the examples
we do have of these usages are scant and vague (i.e., also interpre-
table as mainstream English). The Bonins share hardly any of the
Pan-Pacific contact languages' features, so we can conclude that a
contact language DID develop on the nineteenth-century Bonins
but that it was not a typical Pacific Pidgin English. It was atypical
for its lack of contact with, and similarities to, other Pacific pidgins,

but also because it seems to have had continued contact with mainstream (native) varieties of English (and thus not led to the drastic grammatical restructuring of other pidgins and creoles).

## 3.10. A PIDGINIZED ENGLISH VARIETY USED AMONG FIRST-GENERATION SETTLERS

This chapter has examined various kinds of evidence, which (although only fragmentary when seen individually) come together to form a picture of a society creating and developing an English-based contact language. There is ample circumstantial, descriptive,

FIGURE 3.4

Schematic Summary of the Formation of Two Contact Languages on Ogasawara in the Nineteenth and Twentieth Centuries

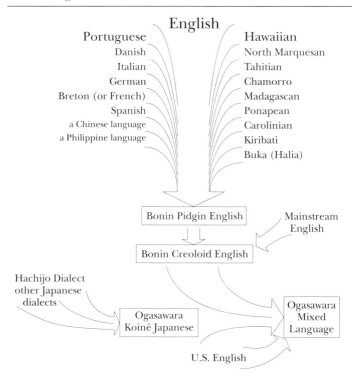

and theoretical evidence to assume that an English-based pidgin originated on Chichijima in the nineteenth century. Look at the top portion of figure 3.4. This is a schematic summary of the influences upon this early pidginized English, with English as the superstratum and various Pacific and European languages forming the substratum.

We do have evidence that nonnative varieties of English were used on the Bonins during the nineteenth century. We do not have evidence that they coalesced into a single homogeneous stable pidgin, the type where we could bring up a grammatical feature and ask, "Is this grammatical or ungrammatical in Bonin Pidgin English?" and arrive at a clear consensus. Furthermore, there were constant streams of newly arriving settlers well into the 1870s who brought with them varying types of nonnative English, adding to the heterogeneity of the English used on the Bonins during the nineteenth century.

At the same time, circumstantial factors do indicate that some degree of homogeneity would have developed. Some of the early first-generation settlers survived into the latter part of the nineteenth century. The restrictions of communication tell us that their individual varieties of English would have come to resemble one another over the decades. The degree of isolation (from the outside) we have discussed would only have made contacts within the island more frequent, more vital, and thus more intense.

Our best guess then (given the lack of evidence, an educated guess is our only choice) is that many nonnative varieties of English coalesced with a few native varieties to form an unstable pidginized variety that we will call Bonin Pidgin English.

## 3.11. A CREOLOID ENGLISH VARIETY USED AMONG ISLAND-BORN SPEAKERS

We have precious little data about the language varieties used by the first-generation settlers and little more about the type of English spoken by second-generation (island-born) speakers. We have tape recordings of third-generation speakers, which we analyze in chapter 5.

What can we deduce about the language variety used by is-land-born speakers? First of all, we know it was English-based. The children of speakers of Hawaiian, Portuguese, Kiribati, and so on did not pass down their native tongues to their children. English-based, however, does not mean native English. The circumstantial evidence suggest little possibility of this. The number of native English speakers on the island was low (single digits), meaning they would have accounted for less than one-tenth of the population.

Many nonnative features appear in the English of subsequent generations, and when we strain out the features that are Japanese or Japanese-influenced, we are left with features inherited from the nineteenth-century pre-Japanese lingua franca of the island. These features include *th*-stopping, nonnative usage (the absence of or misuse) of definite and indefinite articles, the singular-plural dis-tinction, subject-verb concord, imperative expressions, past-tense verb forms, contrastive constructions, and so on (see sections 4.5, 5.7, 5.9).

These features are creole-like in that they are persistent fea-tures that retain evidence of earlier nonnative influences, but they do not exhibit the kind of drastic grammatical restructuring of the language system which is definitive of a creole. This type of language variety has been called a creoloid. The fact that the lan-guage of island-born speakers, while showing creole-like nonnative features, is relatively similar to the structure of mainstream varie-ties of English is probably due to the fact that mainstream varieties of English have coexisted alongside island-grown contact varieties throughout much of the islands' history.

We must consider the short time span between the arrival of the first generation of settlers and the birth of the island-born second generation. The pidginized speech of the first-generation speakers would not have had time to become a stable pidgin be-fore the first generation of children began to be born on the is-lands. This implies that Bonin Creoloid English formed through the "abrupt creolization" processes described by Thomason and Kaufmann (1988).

Why did the Bonins develop a creoloid and not a fullblown creole? The reasons seem to lie in the central role played by native English-speaking islanders like Nathaniel Savory and Thomas Webb and the influence they exerted (in spite of their minority numbers) on the island children. Another reason probably lies in the opportunities youngsters had to live off-island or at least communicate with outsiders.

## 3.12. REFERENCES TO A CONTACT LANGUAGE

There are a few firsthand accounts of island-born speakers using a contact variety of English. These accounts are from the late nineteenth century after the Japanese took over (and in that sense could be placed in the next chapter), but they describe speakers who had acquired language before the influence of Japanese, so I will offer them for consideration here.

The following passage was written by a British missionary who visited the islands in 1895 and 1898. It concerns Hypa, the Micronesian nursemaid (born on Imofek Island, 1785) of the Robinson family, who lived on Hahajima.

We must remember that Hypa was not only now far advanced in extreme old age, but had never acquired sufficient knowledge of English to understand any except the simplest sentences, and only those who had been brought up by her or had lived in the same house with her could understand her broken language, half English, half Kanaka. [King 1898, 420]

From this description, we learn not only that Hypa communicated in a simplified variety of English, but that the adults in the Robinson household and their children whom she had raised were able to comprehend this language as well. From information we have concerning the effects of servant nannies on the children in their care (Dillard 1976, chapter 5; see also Roberts 1997 on the linguistic influence of caregivers) and from the knowledge that the Robinson children were surrounded almost exclusively by other Pacific Islanders in their father's employ, we can easily hypothesize that the children grew up not only understanding but also speaking the contact variety of English used by the servants and laborers around them.

Moreover, there are references to the use of a contact language among schoolchildren in the 1870s, at the dawn of Japanese colonization, strongly indicating that a creoloid was the native tongue of the children born and raised on the island. We find the following report in a text by Ryōichi Ōkuma, author of 17 articles and books about the history of Ogasawara.

Many of the students in those days [1878, the beginning of Japanese education on the island] used a language which was a mixture of English and the Kanakan tongue. [Ōkuma 1966, 238; my translation]

Disappointingly, Ōkuma cites no references for this statement, and subsequent searching on my part has turned up nothing. It is nonetheless intriguing that he mentions not only the English and "Kanakan" tongues being used (referring to Pacific island languages) but their being mixed together. We will discuss various types of language mixing on the Bonins subsequently in section 4.6 and chapters 7 and 10.

## 3.13. LATE NINETEENTH-CENTURY BONIN ENGLISH IN REPORTED SPEECH

One of the only references we have to the speech of a second-generation speaker is the following story, quoted as it was told by Horace Savory (1855–1930), eldest son of the original settler Nathaniel.

The ole man mos' allus let us off if we spoke up and didn't try to hide what we done. I remember once when Jane was a youngster. We used to get our drinking-water in a demi-john, them bottles what have got like a basket outside o' 'm. Big heavy things, they was. Well, one day Jane, she goes to get water from the river and somehow lets the demi-john slip out of her hands so that, of course, it got all broke up. "Never yer say noding," ses she, "I shan't say who done it," she ses, and she tooken it home, and put it in the middle of the table same as allers. Yer see being it had the basket outside, yer couldn't tell as the bottle inside were all broke. Then she goes to the sleeping room and puts on every dress she had, one over de oder, till she looked round as a ball—everything she had. Then she went to hide for she know'd the ole man 'd spank her when he found out what she'd done.

By-'n-bye he com'd in; straight he goes to the demi-john to get some water. "Who done this?" he ses. "I'll give you such a whipping," he ses. "Come on!" Jane see'd it wasn't no sort of good to hide so she com'd out with all those clothes on. She know'd she couldn't feel the stick much. By jingo, I wonder the ole man didn't laugh!

"Did you done it?" he ses. "If yer tell me a lie about it," he ses, "yer'd better be keerful," he ses, "but if yer owns up I won't say no more about it."

Jane got off that time, but my father, he ses "Don't yer never try to hide anything," he ses. "Come and tell me at once and I forgie ye." But I shan't never furget how Jane looked she were that round!" [Cholmondeley 1915, 159–60]

The author of the book in which this passage appears gives us very little information about the origin and transmission of this story. He says, "It [this tale] was taken down, as he told it, from the lips of his [Nathaniel's] eldest son Horace Perry by Miss Black to whom reference has been made in the introduction" (Cholmondeley 1915, 159).

The identity of this Miss Black is not clarified in Cholmondeley's book. In the acknowledgments in the introduction, the author says, "To Miss Black of Tokyo, who has also been a visitor to the islands with her widowed mother, and from whose graphic story of her visit (not published), I have given a short extract in chapter 10, I am also greatly indebted for much kindly help" (5). The author notes, "Mrs. and Miss Black visited the Islands in December 1894, and stayed on till April 1895, doing all kinds of useful Christian work" (vii).

These women were Mrs. Elizabeth Black (1829–1922) and her daughter Pauline (1869–?). They were members of a family prominent in the Westerner community in Japan of this day. Husband/father John Reddie Black (1827–80) was a prominent newspaper publisher in Tokyo and a pioneer in the field. Son/brother Henry James Black (1858–1923) is famous as Kairakutei Burakku, whose Japanese was so fluent he performed and produced phonograph recordings as a *rakugoka* or storytelling comedian (McArthur 2002).

We have virtually no way of knowing if the woman who wrote down the oral narrative altered it either to make it closer to standard English or perhaps conversely to exaggerate the degree of nonstandardness to give a rustic feel to the story. We do know that this is one of the very few extant records (flawed or otherwise) of how the first generation of people born and raised on the island spoke. In that respect, this narrative is too important to be tacitly ignored without consideration. But alas, the most we can say about this story is that the author was trying to convey the image that Horace Savory spoke a nonstandard variety of English. There are decidedly uncreolelike constructions (conditional sentences with *if*, negation constructions like *didn't*, complex tense-aspect expressions like *used to*), but also decidedly nonstandard features (nonstandard tense "what we done," "she tooken," "he com'd in," "did you done it?" "Jane see'd," "she know'd"; nonstandard concord "them bottles," "they was," etc.). The story is absent of features we can point to as clearly pidgin- or creole-like in nature. (It lacks, for example, any of the features that Clark 1979 lists as typical of Pacific contact languages.)

It is possible that the author made the story closer to standard English, either to make it easier for the reader to comprehend or to avoid embarrassing the storyteller or both. But, if that is the case, we do not know why she would have left (or possibly added) folksy English words and pronunciation spellings. We cannot put our faith in Miss Black's having accurately recorded the islander's usage of specific grammatical constructions. It does appear, however, that she was attempting to convey her impression of a man who spoke a variety of English that was nonstandard, but not necessarily creole in nature.

In chapter 5, we will take a closer look at the English used on the island by a third-generation speaker, but before that (in chapter 4), I will outline some historical background information about the language situation in the latter part of the nineteenth century.

# PART II
# AFTER THE ARRIVAL
# OF JAPANESE

# 4. SOCIOHISTORICAL OVERVIEW: ENGLISH DURING THE EARLY JAPANESE PERIOD

As we saw in chapter 3, evidence from various sources supports the claim that an "early pidgin" developed on the Bonins based on the native languages (European and Pacific Island languages) of the original settlers, lexified largely by English. In this chapter, I examine how English was affected by Japanese from the time of that language's arrival on the islands in the 1870s up to World War II, at which time the islands reverted once again to an English-dominant society.

## 4.1. THE BONIN ISLANDS WITHIN THE CONTEXT OF JAPANESE LANGUAGE EXPANSION

It is beneficial to understand the spread of the Japanese language to the Bonins within the context of its expansion throughout the Asian Pacific region. In order to understand the sociolinguistic environment in which Bonin English and its speakers found themselves and to put events described here in their historical context, we will first look at Japanese as an expanding language in the Pacific during the late nineteenth and early twentieth centuries. It is important to understand the spread of the Japanese language to the Bonins as a part of the larger-scale spread of the language into the Pacific; there are some similarities between the Japanese of the Bonins and the Japanese language that survives in the elderly speakers of other Pacific islands, such as Saipan, Palau, or the Federated States of Micronesia. It is partly because the Bonins were stepping-stones for Japanese en route to these "South Seas Islands" (南洋諸島). Several of the early traders were originally residents of the Bonins. A Japanese cattle farmer named Mizutani Shinroku (水谷新六) left the Bonins in 1887 and traded in Ponape, Mokil,

Pingelap, Truk, and Guam before returning two years later (Pe-attie 1988, 16). Others followed him. When the islands north of the equator from Palau to the Marshalls came under Japanese rule after World War I, contact between them and the Bonins became even more intense.

In section 1.3, we saw that the Bonins occupy an important role in the study of English (particularly in the study of its history and its variation) but occupy an equally large role in the history of Japanese. The Japanese language diaspora began over a millennium ago and has been an ongoing process (Inoue 2000, 56). In the eighth century, the Japanese language was used throughout western Japan. The Ainu, who spoke a language unrelated to Japanese, were linguistically and politically assimilated by the Japanese as that language spread to northeastern Honshu (the main island of Japan) and later to Hokkaido. The inhabitants on the Ryukyu Islands, who spoke a variety of dialects of Okinawan (a sister language to Japanese), underwent a similar assimilation.

After the cases of the Hokkaido Ainu and the Ryukyuans (Okinawans), the Bonins were the first colony of Japan. As such they represent one of the first attempts at colonial language education. They are also the only Japanese colony to have spoken English as their original language. They are (again, with the possible exception of Hokkaido or the Ryukyus, depending upon your interpretation of those situations) the only colony that Japan did not lose after World War II (see figure 4.1).

The Japanese language spread into the northern part of Honshu (the Tōhoku region on the main island of Japan) in the seventeenth century and into Hokkaido and the Ryukyu Islands in the late nineteenth century. Heretofore Hokkaido and Tōhoku had been the land of the various dialects of the Ainu language. Ryukyu was the home of various dialects of Ryukyuan, which may be considered either a sister language or a dialect of mainland varieties of Japanese, but the point remains that Ryukyuan is not mutually intelligible with mainland varieties of Japanese.

Other areas into which Japanese spread are not now politically part of Japan. The Japanese language spread to the colonies, Taiwan, Chosen (the Korean peninsula), the South Seas Islands man-

FIGURE 4.1

The Gradual Spread of the Japanese Language
from the Fourth Century to 1910 (after Inoue 2000, 56)

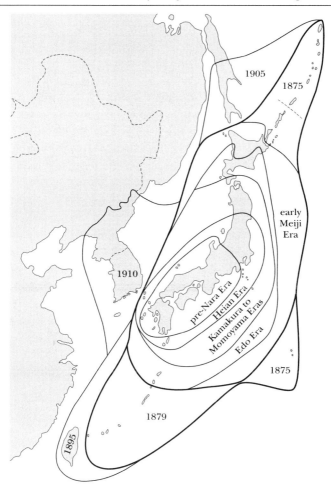

date (Micronesia), Manchuria, and so on, as these areas became
part of the Japanese empire, but Japanese has been steadily waning
in these areas since their independence. Others were never part of
Japan; the Japanese language spread into Canada, Hawaii, California, Brazil, and so on through emigration.

## 4.2. ISLANDERS' INITIAL CONTACT
## WITH JAPANESE

In the 1860s and 1870s, the Japanese language spread to the Ogasa-wara Islands—an area that had not used Japanese previously. In the initial contacts with the islanders, the Japanese brought translators with them who could speak English. In fact, the translator for the Kanrin-maru crew in 1861 was none other than Man-jirō Nakahama (中浜万次郎), known in the West as John Manjirō (Mizuno 1861; Tsuji 1995, 71, 82). As a child, he was shipwrecked at the age of 14, rescued by a U.S. ship, and educated in Massa-chesetts, later becoming a chief translator and negotiator for the Japanese shogunate government (Kawasumi 2003; Ishihara 2006). In 1868, an official named Kingo Toda (戸田謹吾) served as trans-lator (Tsuji 1995, 130).

It took the Japanese language only a short time to spread (geo-graphically) throughout Ogasawara. Chichijima and Hahajima were the only inhabited islands in the chain, and Japanese admin-istrative offices and bilingual English and Japanese schools were set up soon after Japanese in-migration began.

The spread of Japanese in the sociolinguistic sense of the word—the spread by domains—has been a much longer and pro-longed process. In other words, Japanese immediately became the language used by some islanders in almost all situations (domains) and by almost all islanders in at least some domains, but to this day Japanese is not used by all islanders in all domains. In this sense the use of Japanese on the Bonins differs significantly from that of other parts of present-day Japan.

On the main islands of Japan and even in the Ryukyus, it is true that various genetically related dialects of Japanese are used in dif-ferent domains, but the point is that these language varieties form both a geographic continuum and a code-switching continuum. With mainland Japan language varieties, there is a code-switching continuum in which speakers can speak "wholly in the local dia-lect," "speak a standardish form of the dialect," and so on. With Bonin English, there can obviously be no geographic continuum with Japanese language varieties. Ironically, however, the Bonins do have a type of code-switching continuum, because the Ogasawara

Mixed Language can be seen as the endpoint of not one linguistic continuum but two—one with English and one with Japanese—but we will examine this topic further in later chapters.

When the Japanese first came into the Bonin Islands, they established public education with both English and Japanese used as languages of instruction. In this way, for the non-Japanese settlers, education was one of the first domains in which Japanese was used. The written Japanese they learned was standard Japanese, but the spoken Japanese they heard most often was the Hachijō dialect, the variety spoken by the majority of the early Japanese settlers.

## 4.3. JOSEPH GONZALES AND ENGLISH EDUCATION IN THE LATE NINETEENTH CENTURY

Over the years much misinformation has been spread about the Bonins. One of the most common misconceptions is that English disappeared from the islands after the Japanese came in. Even more damaging are reports that ignore any trace of the Westerners whatsoever. A reference work claiming to be an encyclopedia of the Pacific Islands erroneously states:

In 1823 the islands were claimed by the United States, and in 1825 by Great Britain, but both claims were weak and not followed up with any settlements. [In] 1830 some Hawaiians attempted colonization but this effort failed. (Lal and Fortune 2000, 597–98)

During World War II, a small book concerning the Bonins was published in the United States. In it, we find the following statements made.

…men and women having the physical characteristics of the Caucasian and Polynesian races, yet with no speech or loyalty other than Japanese. [Gast 1944, 5]

Nothing but Japanese was taught in the schools and the English language was lost. [24]

Since several of the Western islanders served in the Japanese Imperial Army (at least two were killed), the judgment about their "loyalty" seems unavoidable. However, the statement that English was not taught in the schools, as well as the statement that the English language had disappeared, is false. Of course, the implication that the lack of a language's use as a medium of education would ipso facto lead to its disappearance is itself logic that linguists would find suspect.

From 1876, English was taught at the public school established at Ōgiura (on Chichijima). In 1902, there were English departments in all of the "high schools" in Ogasawara (Tsuji 1995, 207). Furthermore, as we saw in a previous citation, the Gonzaleses began teaching in the public schools in this era, a family tradition that continued at least through the end of the Meiji period. In addition to the public schools, Shimizu (1994, 6), writes, "The English school at this church was continued by Joseph Gonzales' son Josiah, who continued it until the outbreak of the Pacific War."

The view that the English language disappeared on Chichijima as a result of the colonization by the Japanese is not entirely accurate for the following reasons: (1) The English that was in use on the island at the time the Japanese arrived was most certainly not a variety like those used in Britain or the United States, but rather a variety unique to the island (an English-based creoloid evolved from the earlier pidgin). (2) Even after the island became Japanese territory, school education was conducted using not only Japanese, but also English as a medium of instruction. And (3) the first formal education in English reading and writing came ironically only after the Japanese took control. Before this, not only had there been no school education, but there had been no transmission of literacy whatsoever.

In the only English-language book devoted to the social aspects of the Ogasawara Islands, Cholmondeley's *The History of the Bonin Islands* (1915), we find the following passage:

Where I think the Japanese failed from the first in their duty towards the settlers was in making no provision for teaching their children the elements of English. This was a boon they might easily have conferred upon them. Latterly this defect was supplied by the opening of a mission school, presided over by Joseph Gonzales, and many of the Japanese were not slow to avail themselves of the opportunity thus offered for their own children.

To-day the children of our settlers go as a matter of course to the Japanese elementary school, but we must bear in mind that many of the men, Mr. Gonzales included, have married Japanese wives, and the children of such marriages are hardly distinguished from Japanese. [Cholmondeley 1915, 176]

We know there was indeed some attempt made in the early days to teach English in the public school, and since Cholmondeley's close personal friend Joseph Gonzales is the one the government hired to teach it, we can only assume the author's complaint here is with the short duration of such educational support. Cholmondeley visited the islands in 1894, 1896, and 1897, so apparently this bilingual education (at the public school level) did not last for many years.

Ōkuma (1966, 238) wrote the following about the language that served as a medium for education and about language education itself following the takeover of the islands by the Japanese in the nineteenth century:

The educational enterprise in Ogasawara, and this was primary school education, began with the setting up of a temporary school house at Ōgiura (Aki) on Chichijima in March, 1877, two years following the establishment the Ministry of the Interior outpost office on the islands. At first, the official of the outpost Toda Kingo doubled as teacher, and in April the following year [1878] a new school house was built. Since it was in this modest schoolhouse that the boy and girl islanders between 6 and 19 years of age received their education, it must have been tough. Many of the students in those days used a language which was a mixture of English and the Kanakan native tongue, and the government initially provided them with books and school supplies, instruct them in both Japanese and English. Then in 1884, when the Tokyo outpost office moved to Ōmura, the school was moved there as well, and at the dedication ceremony for the school, all the islanders were assembled and the Ministry of the Interior Outpost Manager conveyed his aim that education be conducted in Japanese and in English. It is interesting to recall that among the teachers were three of the Naturalized Islanders, including the Reverend Joseph Gonzales, who had been commissioned to teach. [translation mine][2]

Rev. Joseph Gonzales (1870–1943) was the grandson of the Portuguese settler known as John Bravo. Cholmondeley, who first visited the Bonins in 1894, seems to have taken Gonzales under his wing and helped to train him as a minister at St. Andrew's in Tokyo. When St. George Church was built in 1909, Gonzales was appointed minister, and in addition to his regular duties, taught English at a mission school on Chichijima. There is a biography of him in Japanese Christianity History Encyclopedia (日本キリスト教 歴史大事典). Ōkuma (1966) describes Gonzales in more detail.

Joseph Gonzales was born on April 15, 1871, at Yellow Beach on Chichi- jima. He went to Japan and graduated a Japan Anglican divinity school in Kobe, then returned to Ogasawara at the urging of William Awdry,[3] the Christian Pastor of Southern Tokyo District for the Anglican Church of Japan.... From early on, he was teaching English to the children or youth of the village, and for this sincere character, he was respected enormously by the villagers, elected and served as Ōmura representative in the village government, and contributed greatly to the social education enterprise on the island. [240; translation mine]

The foreign emigrants and their descendents all eventually became natu- ralized Japanese citizens (the last by 1882). The first person to bring the gospel to these people who were without religion up to that time, was Joseph Gonzales, graduate of an Anglican mission school in Kobe.... In August 1895, he was responsible for the opening of the first church on the island, the Ogasawara Church (later St. George's Church). He took a Japanese wife, was naturalized as a Japanese citizen, helped open a mission school, and acted in a supplementary role with mandatory elementary school education. [237; translation mine]

A man born and raised on Chichijima remembers taking Gonzales's classes in his privately published memoirs. He was born in 1900, which would make these reminiscences roughly around 1910.

At elementary school, we were taught English from this teacher [Joseph Gonzales]. It began in the fifth grade with the Kanda Reader. Aside from this was the church English school, where every Saturday in a British style classroom with three people lined up at each of those big slanted desks, we studied reading and writing. I don't recall how much the tuition was, but it was much higher than that for primary school. Everyone was there along with the Western youngsters, and Jose-sensei looking about with a whip in his hand. [Aono 1978, 144; translation mine]

From this passage, we see at this point (approximately 1910) there were still classes in English at both the public elementary school and the church. We also see that the church classes were for reading and writing and that they were attended by ethnic-Japanese as well as the Western children. As mentioned above, the fee for classes was more than that for Japanese public schools (which have a small fee). Nonetheless, tuition for classes was within the reach of middle-class Japanese families. Hachijokei islander Sueka Kikuchi (1913–2001) reports having paid 50 sen per month to attend Gonzales's English classes (interview, Feb. 1999).

## 4.4. THE BEGINNING OF BILINGUALISM AND DIGLOSSIA IN THE LATE NINETEENTH CENTURY

With the arrival of Japanese settlers and their schools in the 1870s came the Japanese language. The non-Japanese settlers, particularly the younger ones, began to acquire the Japanese language. Prior to the arrival of the Japanese, there had been no formal education on the island. Almost all of the islanders were illiterate, and there were no books. The Japanese immediately set up schools and encouraged all islanders—Japanese and otherwise—to send their children to them. Classes were held in Japanese AND in English. The local government hired two of the kikajin to assist as teachers. By the turn of the century, a few island children were sent to mainland Japan (Kobe and Yokohama) for an education in English mission schools there.

As the Japanese administration continued, more and more younger islanders became more and more proficient in Japanese, to the point of being bilingual. But they did not use these two languages haphazardly—in other words, it was not a situation sociolinguists would refer to as free variation. Rather, there was a tendency to use the two languages in different situations—or as sociolinguists would say, in different domains. Japanese was the language of school and the language of work if one worked in the Japanese cash economy. English was the language of home life and of church. So, in a sense, English was the language of private or low domains, and Japanese was the language used in public or high domains. This is a classic case of diglossia (a language community in which the usage of two different languages is determined by sociolinguistic domain). In these days Ogasawara had a diglossic situation in which English was the low language and Japanese the high language (figure 4.2).

Somewhat paradoxically, however, English was sometimes used in what we could call super-high domains. By this I mean, islanders used English as a means of communication with people even further from their inner circle. Occasionally, foreign ships would pull into port at Chichijima, and it was the Westerners with their command of English who could and did deal with these people. As I mentioned, many Westerners went to English-medium schools in mainland Japan. Many islanders signed on to work on sealing ships with international crews. They were on these ships for months on end after stopping in Hakodate, docking in the Aleutians, at Victoria, San Francisco, and Honolulu—places where their English came in handy.

So if we think of language usage domains in terms of concentric circles, the Westerners used English in their inner circle—as their community language. They used Japanese in a wider circle, when they communicated with their Japanese fellow islanders, or

FIGURE 4.2
Diglossia on the Bonins and Changes in It over Time

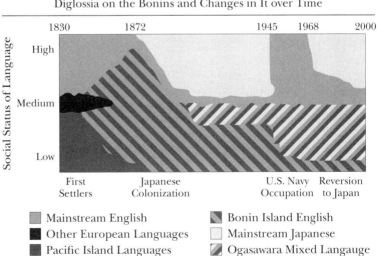

went to mainland Japan. And they again switched into English as an international language of communication.

## 4.5. EARLY EVIDENCE OF JAPANESE AND ENGLISH MIXING

There are snippets of remembered information about the language of second-generation speakers that are obviously problematic as data. But as we saw in section 4.3, a lack of information has never stopped people from speculating about the islands, so I contend that speculation based on sketchy evidence is preferable to speculation based on none at all.

I tape-recorded an interview with Irene Savory Lambert in Tokyo in June 11, 1999. She recalls stories about her great-grandfather Benjamin Savory (1866–1942) using "broken English," in phrases like *Fundoshi kusai. No sit down* '(your) loin cloth stinks, don't sit down'. (It was common for men doing manual labor to walk around wearing nothing else on their lower body. Benjamin thought them unseemly and refused to let people dressed this way sit in his house.) These memories (secondhand as they are) indicate that Benjamin was using a typical nonnative grammatical construction *no sit down* 'don't sit down', as we would expect from a speaker of Bonin Creoloid English. (For attestations of the negative construction "*no* + verb" in mid-nineteenth-century Micronesian and Polynesian contact varieties of English, see Clark 1979.) The Japanese portion of the utterance does not sound like a native construction. Since some functional elements may be omitted in colloquial Japanese, it is difficult to say this is unequivocally ungrammatical, but a sentence like *sono/omae no fundoshi wa kusai yo* 'that/your loin cloth TOP stinky PART' is more natural.

The report that Benjamin is mixing Japanese and English is interesting as well. However, it should not be construed that his "broken English" is the result of interference from Japanese; his descendants report that he was never able to achieve proficiency in Japanese. He was already 11 years old when the Japanese first established a school on the island, and classes were taught using both Japanese and English for at least seven years after that.

Furthermore, anecdotal reports from my own interviews (March 2002, Minoru Ikeda) indicate that at least some members of this generation (namely George Webb, 1870–1956) were never able to speak much Japanese. Historical evidence (as we will see in section 6.1) shows that Western children acquired English as their first language even into the generation of Benjamin's children.

Other islanders also recall stories that although Benjamin could not speak Japanese, he would sell chickens to the Japanese saying, "Kokekkō bata bata ten cents." The first two elements of this phrase are onomatopoeic, *kokekkō* the word for a 'rooster's crow', and *bata bata* the word meaning 'to run around'. This sentence is completely pidginized Japanese and (unlike the two-word utterance above) is incomprehensible out of context. On the one hand, the use of a long circumlocution to express the single noun 'chicken' falls in line with trends in other contact languages (such as the ubiquitous example: *this fella box you fight 'im he sing-out-out* for 'piano', Mühlhäusler 1986, 26). On the other hand, it is perplexing that he would have found this phrase easier to remember than the Japanese word *tori* 'chicken', which is only two syllables.

The mention of "cents" here even after the islands became part of Japan is intriguing and seems like a good point to diverge from linguistics matters and provide some additional sociohistorical background. Even in the days when the islands were part of no nation, islanders would use a currency referred to as "dollars" when they had transactions with outsiders, such as when passing ships paid them cash for goods. When specified, these are referred to as "Mexican dollars."

The American Philip C. Van Buskirk (1833–1903), both during his visit to the islands in the summer of 1881 and prior to that during a stay in Yokohama, uses a dollar sign ($) in his fastidious diary notations of expenses. In most cases it is unclear if he has paid for goods and services in dollars (and if so, if this means U.S. dollars) or if he is simply converting to a familiar currency, but in one case he specifically writes "June 14. Assessment Twenty Mexican Dollars" (Van Buskirk 1880–81, 1898).

Cholmondeley (1915, 22) reports that just before Nathaniel Savory made his voyage to the Bonins, he purchased supplies in

Honolulu on May 20, 1830, for a sum of $69.99, and "paid for them in Mexican dollars." The Mexican Dollar, a silver coin minted by the Mexican government, was commonly used as a trading currency in the Pacific Isles and in Chinese ports throughout the nineteenth century.

American and British seamen who visited the island also mention dollars, although it is often unclear if this means U.S. or not, and also unclear (after the Japanese takeover) is whether or not the seamen were exchanging their dollars somewhere before using them on the island. In 1893, a young seaman born John Griffith Chaney spent a few raucous and rowdy nights ashore on Chichijima, eventually waking up to find he had no dollars. Chaney published his experiences later under the pen name he made famous, Jack London. The following passage is worth quoting here.

And next, after the blackness, I open my eyes in the early dawn to see a Japanese woman, solicitously anxious, bending over me. She is the port pilot's wife and I am lying in her doorway. I am chilled and shivering, sick with the after-sickness of debauch. And I feel lightly clad. Those rascals of runaway apprentices! They have acquired the habit of running away. They have run away with my possessions. My watch is gone. My few dollars are gone. My coat is gone. So is my belt. And yes, my shoes. [London 1895]

In his journal entry for April 20, 1854, American seaman John Glendy Sproston writes of Nathaniel Savory, "The last time he was absent from the Island, nine years ago, a Chinese pirate came into the harbour, seized his wife and a daughter, also four thousand dollars and all his movables. This was told me by his present wife, a [Guamese] woman" (Sakanishi 1940). It is assumed that these were not U.S. dollars but Mexican Dollars.

## 4.6. WESTERN ISLANDERS EDUCATED IN MAINLAND JAPAN (1885–1920)

As we saw in chapter 3, many of the young islanders in the earlier part of the nineteenth century were sent off-island to be educated in Hawaii. After the Bonins were taken over by the Japanese, many of the young Westerners were sent to the Japanese mainland for their education. For example, Joseph Gonzales received his education in Kobe in English at a mission school.[4]

Other islanders went to mainland Japan to receive an education in English. One example is in a book by John S. Sewall, who visited the islands in 1853 as part of Perry's expedition. Writing about his experiences in a book published a half-century later, he states the following:

In all this half century since I have met but one person who has visited this out-of-the-way group. That was a former teacher in Yokohama, now the wife of a banker in America. On one of her voyages to Japan the ship in which she was a passenger was driven by a typhoon to take refuge in Port Lloyd. While there she made the acquaintance of the settlers, especially the house of Savory, and later a little granddaughter of the white chief was for some years a pupil in her school at Yokohama. At the time of her visit the Japanese government had assumed control and formed a colony; and there were then already some five hundred Japanese in residence. [1905, 137]

This provides yet another example of off-island schooling to follow up those examples we saw earlier of female children of the early settlers being sent to Honolulu for their education (prior to the arrival of the Japanese).

We cannot be sure when it was that this woman visited the island, but if the statement that the number of Japanese in residence numbered 500, then the date would be around 1885 or 1886. The Chichijima population is reported as 461 in 1885, 598 in 1886, exploding to a figure of 5,500 for all of the islands by the end of the century.

Japanese records also state that some of the islanders were in Yokohama or Kobe for schooling (Kamo 1889, 324). As port cities in which international communities (including international schools) have been established for well over a century, Yokohama and Kobe had a stronger foreign influence than, say, the larger cities of Tokyo or Osaka, and thus increase the possibility that the schools there were conducted in English instead of (or in addition to) Japanese.

Cholmondeley states that two of the Tewcrab men (boys?) were taken to mainland Japan by an English minister to study. We assume that at least part of their education was in English. Incidentally, we know that this trend to get English education on mainland Japan continued far into the twentieth century as well. We know that at least one other Savory descendent, Jerry Savory (born 1914), received an education in English at St. Joseph College, a complete secondary school now know as St. Joseph's International School, located in Yokohama. This trend continued further into the postwar period as well (section 8.1).

## 4.7. ENGLISH AND PACIFIC LANGUAGES IN CONTACT DURING THE EARLY JAPANESE PERIOD

At the time of Japanese colonization in the 1870s, firsthand accounts report that the islanders shared a common language. As noted in section 3.1, Russell Robertson (1876, 138) reports that "English is spoken by all the settlers, unless I except some half dozen from the Kingsmill group [Kiribati], who speak their own language."

Japanese reports also confirm the use of "English" ("An Outline of the Ogasawara" 1888, 121; Kamo 1889, 324). Japanese writers also mention the use of other languages, as in this quote from Ōkuma's book published a century later:

In addition to indigenous languages (the Kanakan language, etc.) it is true that English also had spread considerably among the inhabitants. [1966, 195–96; translation mine]

Robertson's observation about English usage among "all the settlers" clearly applies not only to the tiny number of English native speakers, but also to the first-generation settlers who spoke a language other than English and to their children and grandchildren, born and raised on the island. Nothing in these statements nor in other records, however, indicates that English used among the Bonin Islanders was a mainstream variety of English, such as those used in Britain or the United States. On the contrary, as outlined previously in chapter 3, all evidence—both direct (our knowledge of what happened on the Bonins) and indirect (our knowledge of the consequences of multiple language contact under similar circumstances on other islands)—strongly indicates the probability that an English-based contact language (creoloid) had developed among the islanders.

Even after the annexation of the islands by Japan and the influx of Japanese settlers in the 1870s, the Bonins still maintained linguistic ties with the Pacific. Settlers continued to arrive from Micronesia (Nonouti in Kiribati) and Melanesia (Bougainville). As early as 1887, a Japanese settler on the Bonins made his first journey to Ponape, Mokil, and Pingelap in the Caroline Islands and two years later journeyed to Guam and Truk (Peattie 1988, 16). When the League of Nations mandate gave the Japanese Empire control of Micronesia and Palau in 1919, Ogasawara was already well established as the gateway to the southern part of the empire (Peattie 1984, 177; 1988, 27–28). Both ethnic-Japanese and Westerner Ogasawarans traveled to the islands to trade or live. Songs ("Uwadorohi," "Gidai," "Urame," and "Afutaiwan" or "Aputairan") and dances (*Nan'yō Odori* 'South Seas dance') still performed on the island today were brought back to the Bonins by Westerner islanders working in Palau and the Carolines during this period (Konishi 2001). Several Westerners who lived in Guam or Saipan learned to speak the Chamorro language.

Table 4.1 presents two words that originated in Pacific languages but that are not found in nineteenth-century records and are believed to have entered the Bonin speech community during the prewar contact with the Nan'yō Islands (today's Palau, Commonwealth of Marianas, Federation of Micronesian States, Marshall Islands). (See also tables 3.5 and 8.1.)

TABLE 4.1
Oceanic Words Thought to Have Entered Ogasawara Speech
in the Late Nineteenth Century

| Bonin Word Form | Meaning on the Bonins | Proposed Etymology (Original Meaning When Different) |
| --- | --- | --- |
| fumpa | 'hermit crab' (Coenobita sp.) | Ponapean *mpwa* |
| kabobo | 'to promise (to marry); to have sex' | Palauan *kaubúch* 'to marry', *kabúb* 'to pair off' |

# 5. LATE-NINETEENTH-CENTURY BONIN ENGLISH

Coauthored with PETER TRUDGILL, *University of East Anglia*

IN ORDER TO GET A GLIMPSE of what the English of the Bonin Islands sounded like at the end of the nineteenth century, we examine the language system of a speaker who was born and raised on the island and who acquired language during this period. Charles "Uncle Charlie" Washington is by no means atypical of Bonin speakers of his generation and, in this sense, is an appropriate subject for our study. But we must be careful about the search for "the prototypical Bonin English speaker." Throughout the entire history of the islands, the population of English users has been minute. English speakers here have seldom been monolingual, and there has never been a high degree of uniformity or homogeneity among them. We might say that Uncle Charlie is A typical Bonin speaker of English from this period; not THE typical speaker. He had extensive off-island experiences that may well have influenced him linguistically, but again, for Bonin Islanders (of his and of other generations), off-island experiences were the rule rather than the exception.

I (Long) was able to analyze audio tape recordings made by an American anthropologist, Mary Shepardson, who tape-recorded field interviews among the Westerner islanders in late July 1971. In all we have data varying from only a minute in length to 1 hour 53 minutes from islanders Charles Washington, Martha Savory, Jesse Webb, Osute Webb, and Jerry Savory. These tapes (henceforth referred to as the Shepardson recordings) are the oldest sound recordings we have of Bonin Islanders.

The data used for the analysis below are from an interview with Charles Washington conducted by Shepardson (figure 5.1) and Blodwen Hammond. The recordings were made with the speaker's consent, and the tapes and some preliminary transcriptions made available to me (Long) by Beret Strong, Shepardson's grandniece and the executor of her Bonin research materials. The final transcriptions were performed by Yoshiyuki Asahi and Daniel Long. The transcriptions were published (with annotations and analysis) as Long (2001a). The sound recordings themselves were released on a CD included in a subsequent research report (Long 2002a). In this book, we refer to Charles Washington as Uncle Charlie, the term of respect by which he is known on the Bonins.

Here, we will outline some of the more salient (or in a few cases, quite subtle but nonetheless intriguing) features of English in the Bonin Islands. Due to the great individual differences in the linguistic repertoires of the islanders and also the great idiolectal differences among speakers, it is difficult to give a single description of Bonin English, but the characteristics below center on those that an English-speaking visitor to the islands would encounter in the present day, that is, on mid-twentieth-century-acquired Bonin Standard English. Where relevant, we mention characteristics that were present in the formal speech (Bonin Standard English) of speakers born in the late nineteenth century or indications we find in present-day language varieties of what the nineteenth-century contact varieties used on the islands sounded like.

## 5.1. ABOUT THE SPEAKER

Uncle Charlie Washington (1881–1972) was born on Chichijima in the Bonin Islands. Let us briefly examine his family background to get an idea of his linguistic influences. He was raised by his mother, Esther Savory Washington Gilley, and her second husband, George Gilley. His biological father, George Augustine Washington, was killed in an accident shortly after Charles's conception. Esther's father Nathaniel was from Massachusetts, and her mother probably spoke Chamorro. George Gilley was a third-generation Bonin Islander, whose paternal grandparents spoke English and Hawaiian, and whose mother, from Mokil Atoll near Ponape, spoke a Micronesian language.

Augustine Washington was a dark-skinned man, said to have been a cabin boy who jumped ship and remained on Chichijima. Augustine is mistakenly referred to as a "Negro from Bermuda" by a German anthropometrist (Goldschmidt 1927, 452), but this writer seems to be confusing Washington with another islander of the period, Robert Morris (or perhaps Robert Myers, difficult to determine from various Japanese katakana renderings of the name). This misinformation was subsequently repeated by other sources, namely a 1968 *National Geographic* article (Sampson 1968).

A firsthand written source from the late nineteenth century states the following: "Born in Mauritius Island, Seychelles. Came to the islands and ran away from his ship (in which Horace Savory was one of the shipmates) about 1872" (King 1898). Charlie himself told field researchers that Augustine was from Madagascar (Shepardson 1977, 102). Although Mauritius, the Seychelles, and Madagascar are far from being a single location, their historical relationship to each other makes this confusion understandable. We have no reason to doubt these older historical records, nor to doubt Charlie's verifiably accurate memories. All of the reliable evidence points to Augustine having been from one of these Indian Ocean islands.

At any rate, this point (however important to the Washington family on the Bonins today) bears little relevance to our search for clues into Charlie's linguistic upbringing because his father died months before he was born.

## 5.2. QUESTIONS TO BE POSED

5.2.1. INFORMATION TO BE GAINED FROM THESE INTERVIEWS. The interviews with Uncle Charlie give us important information about the history and everyday life of the island—the state of language education when he grew up, the lifestyles of the "Yankees," their experiences on mainland Japan during the war and with the South Sea Islanders on the islands when he was growing up—and the way he talked—the pronunciation, words, and expressions he used when he spoke English.

But the interviews tell us about more than simply the speech of one individual. Children do not acquire their native language in a vacuum; their speech is formed by the ways they hear the adults around them speaking. Thus, the way Uncle Charlie talks here in 1971 at age 90 allows us to make educated guesses about the language that was being used by adults on the island in the late nineteenth century. Since the actual recordings of these interviews exist and their sound quality is excellent, we can gain information not only about the words and expressions used by Bonin Islanders of this era, but about the pronunciation as well.

5.2.2. THE EFFECTS OF LIVING OFF ISLAND ON SHIP. Would not Uncle Charlie's English have been influenced by the long years he spent away from the island on ships at sea? Yes and no. His English definitely would have been influenced by his years away from the island. In fact, his way of speaking on these tapes, in particular, is a reflection of his ability to switch between his "at-home" style of local English and a more widely understood brand of English that he may have picked up at sea and used when talking to nonislanders.

There are two significant things to keep in mind here. First, people often pick up a new dialect, but that does not mean they lose the way they spoke growing up. For example, an American living in England a long time may, in day-to-day interactions, begin to substitute British ways of speaking for his native ones. But he may go back to his American way of talking when he returns to the United States. Secondly, there are limits to how much people can alter their speech. It is easy to pick up new vocabulary, a bit harder to modify the grammatical expressions one has used from childhood, and even more difficult to change one's pronunciation.

5.2.3. UNCLE CHARLIE'S ENGLISH AND "PIDGIN." Is Uncle Charlie's English "pidgin English"? No, significantly, it is not. It is much closer to the kinds of English spoken in the United States than we would have expected. There are similar islands in the Pacific where European or American men married Polynesian women and started relatively isolated communities. One well-known example is Pitcairn Island, where the descendants of the infamous mutineers from the HMS *Bounty* live today. Another is Palmerston Island, which linguistically has a similar history. On these islands, the people showed enormous adaptability and intelligence in creating their own new language from English and Polynesian languages. All of the evidence for the Bonins does indicate that such a Pidgin

English developed on these islands as well, but the English used by Uncle Charlie on these tapes is not a pidgin.

## 5.3. SEGMENTAL PHONOLOGY

5.3.1. VOWELS. Bonin Standard English retains most of the vowel distinctions of mainstream varieties. There are individual speaker differences, but the vowel system (see in figure 5.1) is clearly not the five cardinal vowel system we would expect from a Pacific contact variety of English or from English spoken by native speakers of Japanese.

What can we say about the origins of Uncle Charlie's English? There are many features that are American in origin, as we will see in the examination of his consonants below. But his English is also clearly conservative. He was born in 1881, but there are a number of features that are surprisingly old-fashioned even for a speaker with this birth date (in what follows we use the terminology and the system of key words introduced by Wells 1982).

1. He has no long mid diphthong (Wells 1982). The vowels of FACE and GOAT are pure (though not tense) monophthongs around [e:] and [o:].
2. He has no diphthong shift (Wells 1982). FLEECE and GOOSE are pure monophthongs, and GOOSE is a truly back [u:]. Similarly, PRICE has a front first element [aɪ], and MOUTH, a back first element [ɑʊ].

FIGURE 5.1
Vowel System of Bonin English

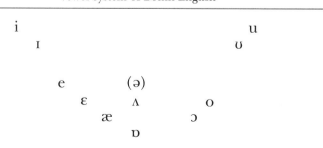

3. The vowel of FOOT shows no unrounding.
4. The vowel of STRUT is back, around cardinal [ʌ].
5. There is no HAPPY-tensing, i.e., the word-final vowel in *happy, money,* and *city* is [ɪ] and not [iː]. (Kenyon 1958 describes such tensing as an early twentieth-century innovation in the United States.)

Uncle Charlie's English is also somewhat dialectal. Note the following pronunciations:

| | |
|---|---|
| *sit* | /sɛt/ |
| *just* | /dʒɛst/ |
| *catch* | /kɛtʃ/ |
| *further* | /fʌðə/ |

He also lacks /oi/ except in *boy*; that is, words such as *hoist, join, joint,* and *point* have /aɪ/.

It is possible to pinpoint the geographical origins of Uncle Charlie's English phonology with considerable accuracy. The following all point in the direction of Eastern New England (ENE):

1. Words such as *foreign* have LOT and not NORTH. And LOT is rounded [ɒ].
2. The accent is nonrhotic.
   NEAR [ɪə]
   SQUARE [ɛə]
   CURE [ʊə]
   NURSE [ɜː] [ɜː ~ ɜ]
3. The vowel /aː/, which is phonetically very front, occurs not only in START, but also in PALM and a number of BATH words.

   *lance, chance, plant, commander*
   *can't, half*
   *father, Guam*

   Interestingly, words involving prevoiceless fricative environments, such as *after, mast,* and *ask,* mostly have /æ/ (see the discussion of variability in Boston in Wells 1982, 522–24).
4. Unstressed syllables in COMMA words tend to have [ɪ] rather than /ə/: *hoses* [hoːzɪz]. Wells (1982, 520) notes that "New England is well-known for the traditional tendency to use" this pronunciation.

5. The New England "short *o*" does not occur as such, but we see vestiges of it in that *broke* and *whole* are variably pronounced /bɾʊk, hʊl/ and *boat* is variably [bʊt].

6. The major nonrhotic accents of English around the world (Australian, New Zealand, South African, and English English) have merged the lexical sets of THOUGHT and NORTH/FORCE on /ɔː/, such that pairs like *court/caught, tort/taught, sort/sought, torque/talk, lord/laud, lore/law, more/maw,* and *Thor/thaw* are homophonous.

A number of rhotic accents, such as Scottish, Canadian, and, increasingly, a number of American accents, have the LOT/THOUGHT merger such that pairs like *cot/caught, tot/taught, knotty/naughty, rot/wrought, not/nought, Don/Dawn, hock/hawk, chock/chalk,* and *stock/stalk* are homophonous.

The English of ENE, however, is unique in combining both of these features. It is nonrhotic, with *stork* and *stalk* identical, but it also has the LOT/THOUGHT merger so that *stalk* is homophonous with *stock* as well. As far as we know, it is the only variety of English in the world in which the lexical set *stork/stock/stalk* are identical. However, there is a further complication: while most nonrhotic accents of English have merged the vowels of NORTH (from ME short /ɔ/ + /r/) and FORCE (from ME long /ɔː/ + /r/), as in *horse/hoarse, warn/worn, for/four,* ENE has not, preserving the opposition as /ɒ/ versus /ɔə/, as shown in table 5.1.

It is basically this ENE system that Uncle Charlie has preserved. He has /ɒ/ in *top, lot, caught, saw, north, short,* but /oə/ in *poor, door,*

TABLE 5.1
Comparison of Bonin English and Other English Vowel Systems

| | Conservative General American | Modern General American | Canadian | Scots | Conservative RP | Modern RP | Eastern New England | 19th-Century Bonin English | |
|---|---|---|---|---|---|---|---|---|---|
| LOT | ɑ | ɑ | ɑ | ɔ | ɒ | ɒ | ɒ | ɒ | *stock* |
| THOUGHT | ɔ | ɔ | ɑ | ɔː | ɔː | ɒ | ɒ | ɒ | *stalk* |
| NORTH | ɔr | ɔr | ɔr | ɔr | ɔː | ɔː | ɔə | ɒ | *stork* |
| FORCE | or | or | or | oə | ɔə | ɔə | oə | oə | *store* |

*four*, *course*, *(a)board*, and *(a)shore*. His phonetics, on the other hand, are not identical with (at least) modern ENE, given that *shore* and *show* are distinguished as /ʃoə/ versus /ʃoː/, the GOAT vowel being a pure monophthong.

Writers had commented on the "New England" pronunciation of Uncle Charlie. One such article was in the July 1968 *National Geographic*, wherein the author writes:

> Uncle Charlie...breezed along in fluent, colloquial English salted with traces of Massachusetts. He spoke of "cam" water, and of the "commahn-der" of the U.S. Navy base below. [Sampson 1968, 128]

Upon reading these comments—and before hearing actual sound recordings of Uncle Charlie—I (Long) was skeptical about the accuracy of this description and assumed that Sampson had simply heard a lack of postvocalic /r/ in Charlie's speech and attributed that to his Massachusetts heritage. I telephoned Sampson on December 23, 1997, to ask him about his memories of the interview. When I questioned him, he emphasized that his characterization had been of "traces" of Massachusetts pronunciations in Charlie's speech, that he had heard New England accents, but that Charlie did not have a perfect New England accent. At the time, I interpreted Sampson's comments as his trying to distance himself from his original characterization, but these recordings validate Sampson's observation.

5.3.2. CONSONANTS. As stated above, Uncle Charlie's English is clearly American in origin. Intervocalic /t/ as in *better* is most often, but not always, a voiced flap [ɾ]. He has yod-dropping after /t, d, n/; that is, there is no /j/ in *tune, during*, and *new*. His /l/ is relatively clear in all positions, and *h*-dropping does not occur.

His consonant system also differs greatly from the English used by speakers whose first language is Japanese. As seen in table 5.2, it contains consonant phonemes [ʔ, f, v, θ, ð, ʒ, ŋ, ɹ, l] which are not found in Japanese and often prove problematic for L2 learners of English.

Uncle Charlie shows variation in his *th* pronunciations. In addition to the fricative consonants [ð] and [θ] (as in *this* and *think*) of

TABLE 5.2
Consonant System of Bonin English

|  | Bilabial | Labiodental | Dental | Alveolar | Postalveolar | Palatal | Velar | Glottal |
|---|---|---|---|---|---|---|---|---|
| Stop | p  b |  |  | t  d |  |  | k  g | ʔ |
| Fricative | (ɸ) | f  v | θ  ð | s  z | ʃ  ʒ | (ç) |  | h |
| Affricate |  |  |  | (ts) | ʧ  ʤ |  |  |  |
| Nasal | m |  |  | n |  |  | ŋ |  |
| Flap |  |  |  | (ɾ) |  |  |  |  |
| Approximant | β̞ |  |  | ɹ |  |  |  |  |
| Lateral |  |  |  | l |  |  |  |  |
| Trill |  |  |  | r |  |  |  |  |

NOTE: When symbols appear in pairs, the one on the right represents the voiced consonant. Phonemes in parentheses are found only in words of Japanese origin.

standard English, he also uses the stops (or plosives) [t] and [d] resulting in pronunciations like [dis] and [tiŋk].

This is probably not the influence of Japanese on his speech. If this were the case, we would expect him to substitute the fricatives [s] or [z] for *th*, saying things like "zat" for *that* and "sank you" for *thank you* (phonologically the voiceless and voiced "th" before /i/ become [ʃ] and [ʤ], respectively). We do find [s] in his speech for /ð/ but in word-final position.

This "*th*-stopping" is found in many language-contact situations throughout the Pacific, and indeed the world in general. Similar correspondences are seen in Pitcairn (Källgård 1993), Ngatikese (Tryon 2000), and Palmerston (Ehrhart-Kneher 1996). The best explanation for this trait then seems to be that it results from the contact variety of English which developed on the island in the mid-nineteenth century among first-generation settlers. This is another feature of the Bonin Islands English that links it more closely with Pacific contact varieties of English than with Japanese-accented English.

We see that Uncle Charlie distinguishes four liquid phonemes as evidenced in the passages below. In (1) he is talking about the children of a settler from Bougainville Island (in present-day Papua New Guinea). He uses a trilled [r] the first time he says the name, but then repeats it using an English alveolar approximant [ɹ], apparently for the benefit of the American listener.

>    1. Was four daughters all told, what I remember. Yes, and they had a
>    son, name of Porrea [porea], Porrea [poɹea].

When pronouncing Japanese proper nouns, the speaker uses the Japanese flap [ɾ], but when speaking English he consistently distinguishes correctly between the alveolar approximant [ɹ] and the alveolar lateral approximant [l]. This supports the claim that English (or an English creoloid with an /l/-/r/ distinction) was his first language, as opposed to Japanese, which does not distinguish between two liquids. His phonological distinction is unmistakable in (2), in which he corrects the American interviewer, who has misunderstood a place-name supplied to her by a previous Japanese-speaking source.

>    2. SHEPARDSON: Now the place called Little Liver?
>    UNCLE CHARLIE: Little River. Small river.
>    SHEPARDSON: Oh really?
>    UNCLE CHARLIE: Little river, little river. Yeah, Little River, that's
>    beyond Pukunui. Little further on.

5.3.3. THE /v/ PHONEME AS [β] AND [v]. The English phoneme /v/ corresponds to three different variants in different varieties of English spoken on the Bonins, [v], [b], and [β ~ β̞].

The first variant, pronounced [v], is commonly found among speakers (middle-aged today) who grew up during the U.S. Navy's administration of the island, attended the Navy school, and, in many cases, advanced to high school in Guam. For these speakers, [v] is distinguished as a separate phoneme. The mid-twentieth-century infusion of American English into the community surely strengthened the usage of [v], but social circumstances in the later nineteenth century (mentioned below), indicate that [v] may have been used on the islands before World War II as well.

The parents of Navy-generation speakers sometimes produce [v], but often produce [b], especially those speakers who have undergone the greatest degree of Japanese influence. Speakers raised during the Navy Era usually produce the [v]. This is the second variant, pronounced as [b], representing a merger of /v/ and /b/. This variant is common among speakers (in their sixties and above today) whose English was acquired prior to World War II, when native speakers of Japanese formed the majority of the population. In this era, English was generally restricted to private situations, whereas Japanese was the language of wider communication, including formal education. Japanese has no /v/, and when English words like *vest* and *drive* are borrowed into Japanese, the [b] sound is substituted, yielding *besuto* and *doraibu*, respectively.

The third variant of /v/ is [β ~ β̞], a voiced bilabial approximant or a voiced bilabial fricative (henceforth [β̞]). It is clearly heard on tapes of Uncle Charlie, and this indicates that [β̞] predates [b] on the islands. The origin of this variant is more difficult to pin down to a single specific cause.

Upon closer inspection, we find Uncle Charlie has interesting variation in his use of the /v/ phoneme. He has [β̞] in the word-initial position, as in *visit*, *very*, and *village*, and intervocalically, as in *cover*, *government*, and *never*. He generally has [v] in the final position, as in *have*, *live*, and *you've*. He does occasionally have [v] in the intervocalic and preconsonantal positions as well, but these tend to be morpheme-final, as in *having*, *living*, *yourselves*, *leaves*, and *moved*.

Table 5.3 shows representative examples of the phonological distribution of the [β̞] for /v/.

5.3.4. ORIGIN OF THE [β̞] FOR /v/ PRONUNCIATION. Where did this pronunciation of /v/ as [β̞] come from? Below we will explore two possibilities. The first is that it results from the English spoken by the large number of Polynesian speakers living on the island in the nineteenth century. The second is that it arrived in the phonologies of native English-speaking settlers.

We know that many of the very first settlers—most of the women and a few of the men—were natives speakers of Polynesian

TABLE 5.3
Phonological Distribution of /v/ in the Speech of Charles Washington

|  |  | [β] | [v] |
|---|---|---|---|
| Initial | #v | *visit, very, village* |  |
| Prevocalic |  |  |  |
| single morpheme | VvV | *cover, never, provisions, evacuation, government* | *over* |
| multiple morpheme | Vv#V |  | *living, having, leaving* |
| Preconsonantal | Vv#C |  | *graves* |
| Final | Vv# | *believe* | *have, you've, wave, leave* |

languages like Hawaiian and Tahitian. Hawaiian has no contrast between /v/ and /w/: according to Elbert and Pukui (1979, 12–13), /w/ is [w] on Kaua'i and Ni'ihau, [v] on Hawaii, with [v] and [w] occurring as allophonic variants on the other Hawaiian islands. (Of course, [β ~ β] is a voiced bilabial approximant or a voiced bilabial fricative, whereas [w] is a voiced rounded labial-velar approximant, but these sounds all lack the labiodental contact of the [v] consonant.) There is evidence that this leads to confusion both ways between /v/ and /w/ in the English of Hawaiians and other Polynesians, but nothing to indicate the kind of complementary distribution found on the Bonins. Listening to the tapes, we do not find any indication that Uncle Charlie confuses /w/ and /v/ in the sense of using a [v] sound for /w/. On the contrary, he always pronounces English /w/ sounds as [w]. Consequently we turn to our second possibility.

We find the same kind of distribution in table 5.3 reported for native English varieties (see Trudgill et al. 2003), particularly in parts of southern England.

Two early settlers (both males) who exerted a tremendous degree of influence over the community were native speakers of English whose home regions we can pinpoint: Thomas Webb from Wallington, Surrey, southeast England, and Nathaniel Savory from the United States.

We know that several of the original settlers came from England. We know specifically that the influential islander Thomas

Webb was from Surrey, which lies in the area reported to have had this allophonic distribution in the nineteenth century.

This complementary distribution is also reported for New England at the time of the American Revolution in the late eighteenth century (Forgue 1977). This is the time when Nathaniel Savory (born 1794, Bradford, Essex County, Massachusetts) underwent acquisition of his mother tongue. In other words, this pronunciation could be the influence of Englishman Thomas Webb, but it is more likely that it was handed down from American (and most influential islander) Nathaniel Savory, the grandfather of Charles Washington.

We usually do not think of single individuals being able to influence the language of an entire generation, but in the case of the Bonins, this seems the only viable explanation. On the impact of individuals in small linguistically diverse communities such as this, Mühlhäusler (1998, 43) writes, "In the very small communities discussed here, there is ample scope for studying the influence of individuals on language structure and use." Ehrhart-Kneher (1996, 530), writing about the patriarch and sole native-English speaker among the original Palmerston Island settlers, says, "He obliged his children—and later on his grandchildren—to speak English all the time. However, the language of the [Cook Island Maori] mothers is likely to have produced interferences. According to witnesses, Marster's influence was greater than the Bible on what is known to be a religious island." She finds that the English of the island is a variety of English (rather than a creole), and one of the factors behind this seems to have been Marster himself. She writes, "For the first two generations, William Marster's linguistic norm was a law everyone tried to follow as much as possible" (Ehrhart-Kneher 1996, 530).

## 5.4. SUPRASEGMENTAL PHONOLOGY

5.4.1. WORD ACCENT. Accent in varieties of Bonin English is stress-based and closely resembles the stress accent patterns of U.S. English. In words where British and U.S. accents differ (such as *aluminum (foil)* and *laboratory*), U.S. accents are the norm.

5.4.2. INTONATION. As pointed out above, observations have been made by nonlinguists that Bonin English has a New England ring to it. The existence (persistence) of such an accent seemed to me highly unlikely considering the tiny percentage of New Englanders among the original settlers. However, audio recordings made of speakers born in the late nineteenth century verify this impression. This impression is due to certain segmental features (nonrhoticity, vowel quality), but also to sentence intonation patterns. There may be other explanations for this intonation. For example, it may be that the foreign-accented English spoken by the original Oceanic and European settlers combined to contribute to the development of intonation patterns which by pure coincidence sound this way. These sorts of possibilities will need to be considered, but it may simply be that the small number of New Englander settlers had such an influence on island-born generations that certain characteristics of their "New England accent" were handed down to the next generation.

## 5.5. LEXICON

The complexity of Uncle Charlie's vocabulary indicates that, while there are indications of language contact in his speech, the English variety spoken on the islands is best termed a creoloid. Nevertheless, the complexity of his vocabulary indicates that his English has also seen the reintroduction of mainstream English features (decreoloidization).

Uncle Charlie has interesting pronunciations of some individual words (as opposed to categorical phonological differences) such as *Russian* ['ɹuʃɒ]. His vocabulary reflects the many and varied influences upon Bonin English, particularly nautical terminology, as seen in *belaying-pin* ['bleːn pɪn] (trans. verb), *forecastle* ['foːsəl], *gudgeon* ['gʌdʒən], *kedge* ['kɛdʒ], *pitchpole*, *ratlin* ['rætlɪn], *scupper* ['skʌpəː], and *demi-john* (a large container for water). This nautical influence is also seen in his pronunciation of *northeast* [nɒːˈwɛst] and *southwest* [sɑʊˈwɛst]. Other interesting expressions include *skew-whiff* [skiːˈwɪf] (adjective meaning 'askew'), *tipping the elbow* 'drinking', *stash* (a person's name) 'to get rid of', *Bible leaf* 'to thinly slice', and *greener* 'rookie'. Saying that he has no secrets to hide, he uses the expression *nothing to stow away*, and when describing someone drinking heavily in a bar, he says *he was hoisting it up.*

Even today, Bonin Islanders typically refer to refrigerators as *reefers*. This term was, and still is, used to describe huge refrigerated compartments in a ship. Using it as the everyday word to describe a home kitchen appliance is a feature that makes Bonin English unique.

Uncle Charlie uses *yet* for 'still', a feature typical of many English dialects.

3.  a.  I was only a boy yet. He was only, had a half long shirt with no back on it. I'm telling you the truth! I was a boy yet.
    b.  He went aboard to the captain and said "This man is, belongs to the Emperor, yet."
    c.  Well he was, he was teenage yet when he came from South Island, Hahajima came here…was sick.

Interestingly, he shows a tendency to use *yet* and *still* in tandem as well. Bastimentos Creole English, spoken on a Panamanian Island in the Caribbean Sea, has constructions such as *im stilyet hav a haas* 'he still has a horse' (Michael Aceto, pers. comm., Nov. 10, 1999). Uncle Charlie's speech does not combine these into a single word, but rather uses them to frame the verb or entire clause, as seen in the following examples.

4.  a.  Three times I nearly lost my neck. Three times. But still I'm here yet.
    b.  Well, anyhow, I've been kicking around this world, and I'm still kicking yet!
    c.  She and others, they set fire to the island. It's still burning yet, I heard.

## 5.6. INTERFERENCE FROM JAPANESE

Uncle Charlie, we must keep in mind, was born, raised, and educated as a Japanese person. He was completely bilingual (although

he admits he had a low level of functional literacy in Japanese, saying that he did not know many kanji characters). Nonetheless, he
shows surprisingly few linguistic traits we can definitely say are the
effect of Japanese. In the interviews he speaks to interviewers who
understand no Japanese and generally avoids using the language.
Even so, he occasionally answers a question with *so, so* (meaning
'yes, yes'). This is one of the few signs of Japanese interference in
his English.

Another is his interesting use of the Japanese word *ria-kaa* 'a
cart with two large wheels pulled behind one'. Etymologically, this
word is a Japanese formation from the English words *rear* and *car*.
The object and the word are quite common in Japan (Japanese),
but the formation does not exist in English. As we see in (5), the
word confuses Charlie.

> 5. Poorest funeral I saw him last time in my life. Since I know myself. . . .
>    You know these "ria kaas," "real ackers" they got here? That's what
>    they put the coffin on. And a fella pulling it along, you know. And
>    what is this, Edith, you know, my daughter, and Edith and Arthur's
>    brother, the only two followed the coffin.

From this example, we can deduce the following. Uncle Charlie knows the word *ria-kaa* from Japanese. Moreover, he seems to
realize that it is an English word, since he uses it in an English sentence (and the mixing of Japanese words in an English sentence
is otherwise absent from his speech in these interviews). He even
attaches the plural marker -*s* to the end of the word. But even as he
is doing this, he realizes something is amiss and attempts a repro-
nunciation of the word, but his split-second attempt to find the
English etynom of the word fails, and he blurts out "real ackers."

## 5.7. TRACES OF THE NINETEENTH-CENTURY
## CREOLOID

Some nonstandard features of Uncle Charlie's speech indicate the
presence of an underlying creoloid. He uses both standard English
and zero forms in his plurals (e.g., "four daughters," "one of her
granddaughter," "they were short of womans here on the island").

At times, Uncle Charlie seems to switch into another more creoloid variety, as seen in (6). (The transcriptions are presented in standard orthography for easy readability and to highlight grammatical and lexical characteristics. Phonetic renderings are used only when phonological features are highlighted.)

6. Yeah, she was living over there all alone at first and one of her granddaughter came and they were living together and she pegged out.... I went over there to see her once or twice. I told her, "Alice" I says, "You've gone right down to nothing but skin and bone." I says, "Why don't you eat plenty?" Oh, she says, "Tabete imasu" ['(I) am eating']. She say she eating bellyful, but she was telling me a lie because I heard it from, from Kathy, my daughter, used to take little bit over for her, you know. Next time she go the same thing which she takes over there is all moldy. She never eat it. She starved herself to death.

The grammatical construction "she say she eating bellyful" seems indicative of a creoloid basilect. It differs from mainstream (noncontact) varieties of English ("she says she is eating a bellyful") in its lack of third-person single -s marking on the verb *says*, its lack of *be*-verb in the progressive aspect construction (*she eating*), and the lack of indefinite article *a*. *Belly* is also commonly used in contact varieties of English.

It is almost as if simply remembering that this conversation was with a fellow islander (one we would not be surprised to find Uncle Charlie using a basilect island variety with) has triggered a code-switch from acrolectal mainstream English to features with which he associates his fellow islanders.

Uncle Charlie's use of the term *plenty* is also intriguing. Nonstandard usages of *plenty* are found in most of the English-based contact languages of the Pacific (Clark 1979). Uncle Charlie does not use the word (in a nonstandard usage or otherwise) anywhere else in the two hours of taped interviews. The lack of someone's use of a word is weak evidence indeed, but it is interesting that he avoids answering with the word even when the interviewer uses it twice (in its standard usage). It is as if Uncle Charlie considers the word a part of the "broken English" that he is trying to avoid.

One construction that Uncle Charlie does use several times is *by'n'by*.

7. a. By'n'by he came after us again saying that he was short of men and one thing another, and wanted us to come along and help him out again.
   b. So, I waited. By'n'by he came.
   c. He'd served his time in the navy. And he fooled around here and by'n'by, this last war, you know. We left him home to work, to work with the government, or the navy boys here, you know?

These usages of *by'n'by* are indeed mainstream (and not pidgin or creole) English, but this phrase is the source of expressions such as *baimbai* throughout Pacific contact varieties of English (Clark 1979). It is interesting to speculate that the phrase *by'n'by* appears in Uncle Charlie's speech because it is similar to one in his basilect.

## 5.8. CREOLOID IN REPORTED SPEECH

When considering the question of whether Uncle Charlie spoke a more creoloid (basilectal) variety of English as well as a more standard-like (acrolectal) one, some comments from my 1999 interview with Irene Savory Lambert (mentioned in section 4.5) are enlightening. When she imitated the way he used to speak English, she affected a more creole-sounding speech style than he used on these tapes, indicating that he was indeed switching into a more formal lect for the benefit of his interviewer. She vividly remembered Uncle Charlie saying things like *bloody bastard* [blədɪ bɑːstɑːd] and [dɜːtɪ bɑgɑː]. She pronounced these with nonrhotic vowels (even though the English that she speaks now is rhotic). Because the pronunciation she remembered of the latter phrase was so different from her own phonology, she did not know the meaning of the phrase and was surprised when I told her this was *dirty bugger*. Other phrases she recalled also reinforce our hypothesis that the English spoken on the island had "creole-like features but [was] not a full creole" (to use Mark Sebba's [1997, 162] definition of a creoloid). She remembered Uncle Charlie often teasing and complimenting her simultaneously, saying, "Many a baby I see in my life but not one ugly like you. But now, look at you!" When Irene would tell Uncle Charlie she was scared of obake ('ghosts'), she recalled him always replying, "Obake? You no have to worry. You worry about two-legged obake." (In Japanese culture, *obake* float around with no legs; Charlie was warning his young teenage neighbor to be more careful around the lonely, young sailors stationed on the island.) Usage of *no* + verb as a prohibition is found in contact varieties of English.

Irene recalled her grandfather Samuel Savory (1897–1951) saying to her, "You be good girl [gɜːl]. I come back." These are only two tiny snippets of speech (and information remembered decades later), but they indicate lack of articles and a lack of future-tense distinction, both simplifications we would expect in nonna-tive influenced varieties of English. At the same time, there are features not typical of contact varieties, such as the two-word verb formation *come back*, and the use of first-person pronoun *I*; most English-based pidgins and creoles in the Pacific at the time were using *me* in all grammatical cases (Clark 1979). This information again is consistent with the view of a creoloid English being used on the islands.

This remembered information would, on its own, be of no aca-demic value. Neither would the snippets of linguistic information upon which we based some admittedly speculative hypotheses. But if we want to make any educated guesses about the speech of the islands in the late nineteenth century, this kind of "linguistic glean-ing" is one of our only choices. It is significant that all evidence points in the same direction: a contact variety of English existed on the nineteenth- and twentieth-century Bonin Islands and (in the case of at least some speakers) existed alongside a more main-stream variety of English in a diglossic situation.

## 5.9. MORPHOSYNTAX

In morphosyntactic features as in other aspects, Bonin English runs the gamut from those used in informal situations when interacting with fellow insiders to those used in formal situations when speaking with English-speaking nonislanders. The former way of speaking is known as the basilectal (language) variety, and retains features thought to derive from the nineteenth-century Bonin Creoloid English. The latter as the acrolectal variety has been influenced to varying degrees by standard American English.

We find some examples of obsolete morphological constructions that were largely obsolete in the twentieth century, at least in the major varieties of British and U.S. English, such *drogge* (past tense of *drag*). The U.S. influence is in the use of *why* as a discourse marker: "When there's a storm, why, they'd put a bar across."

The speech of Uncle Charlie and other islanders includes many morphosyntactic constructions which are nonstandard, but probably derive from British or U.S. dialect forms rather than an earlier Bonin pidgin. He displays variation between standard and nonstandard grammatical forms. For example, he has standard subject-verb agreement in "they were married," but not in "some of the old descendants was laying [in wait] for him." This feature, however, is a trait not only of contact varieties but of traditional dialects of English as well.

Other examples of nonstandard morphosyntactic features are discussed below with examples from the Uncle Charlie interviews.

5.9.1. DOUBLE MODALS. Uncle Charlie uses double modals, as in the examples of *might could* in (8).

> 8. a. Well, you've got many more days. I might could tell you more lies.
> b. I thought if he run came back he might couldn't make the harbor here inside, toward where the pier here, but he may be over Aki Beach, you know.

Although double modals are common in nonstandard dialects of English, they are associated with the southern United States, the north of England, and Scotland (Montgomery and Nagle 1993; Mishoe and Montgomery 1994), not with the regions where Bonin Islanders trace their ancestry. At present, we have no explanation for this feature's existence in Uncle Charlie's speech, but this enigma brings home the fact that we are not dealing with the simple transplantation of native dialects of English to the Bonin Islands, but rather with the complex reality of multiple language varieties coming into contact with one another and producing new varieties of Bonin English.

5.9.2. OTHER NONSTANDARD CONSTRUCTIONS. Uncle Charlie uses *we were* once ("Oh, yes, we were all evacuated") but uses *we was* 14 times. He uses both *they were* and *they was*. The following is the only instance of nonstandard concord in the second person.

> 9.  We stayed there till it got so cold, why, you was painting and looked somewheres else, the brush'd drop out of your hand.

In these recordings, Uncle Charlie uses several nonstandard past-tense verbs which are regularized forms of irregular standard English conjugations. These include the following three occurrences of *knowed* (10a), one of *drawed* (10b), and two of *beated* (10c).

> 10.  a.  And that's all I knowed about him till the last year I was in Dutch Harbor. Yeah talking to a captain which I knowed, Captain MacEmborough, an old whaler, too you know I knowed him down Ponape.
> b.  I always drawed my advance before I left.
> c.  Well anyhow, I beated the two Japs, I caught more than the two of them caught. And on our way coming home, you know, one of the boys said he'd been sealing here for four or five years he says he never was beated as badly as this, you know.

We cannot be certain if these forms are categorical (as opposed to variable, with standard forms) for Uncle Charlie, but we do find that he has zero occurrences of the standard English conjugations of these verbs on these recordings.

Uncle Charlie uses other nonstandard constructions as well, such as the contrastive expression in (11).

> 11.  I was more happier there, with all the boys, you know.

## 5.10. IN SUMMARY

In conclusion, we can summarize by saying that the speech of Charles "Uncle Charlie" Washington on these tapes gives us insights into the unique variety of English that developed on the Bonin Islands and was used as the language of everyday communication in the late nineteenth century.

As we have seen, his speech shows the influence of the non-native varieties of English that we assume were spoken by first-generations settlers for whom English was not a first language. It also retains some traits of unmistakably British and U.S. varieties of English. The combination of these influences came together to produce a variety of English unique to the Bonin Islands.

# PART III
# EARLY TWENTIETH CENTURY

# 6. SOCIOHISTORICAL OVERVIEW: ENGLISH IN THE EARLY TWENTIETH CENTURY

## 6.1. INCREASING BILINGUALISM AND DIGLOSSIA IN THE EARLY TWENTIETH CENTURY

In 1898, the American Philip Clayton Van Buskirk (introduced in section 4.5) stayed on the Bonins for 3 months, from February 3 to May 4. He had been to the islands previously, first in 1853 (Burg 1994), aboard the USS *Plymouth* as a member of Commodore Matthew Perry's crew, again in late June 1880 (we do not know for how long because brief portions of the diary for that year are missing), and finally from April 19 through mid-July 1881.

His interest in the islands stemmed from his visit there decades earlier. He kept a daily journal during his stay as he had for decades. At first, there appear to be no great linguistic revelations in his journal, but we can in fact glean several insights from its contents. He did not speak Japanese, a fact we know from many comments about people not understanding English or about others translating for him. He was in close and continuous (daily) contact with the Westerners, especially children to whom he took a particular liking. If they had been unable to understand English, this would have been impossible. His visit was over 20 years after the Japanese administration of the islands. The children he met and even the young adults of this era had grown up knowing no other government, no other citizenship than Japanese. Nonetheless, even the smallest children in the Westerner community still retained English as their mother tongue—or one of their mother tongues at least.

By the Taishō era (1911–25), the Western children had become bilingual. We know, for example, that islanders like Charles Washington, Jesse Webb, Jerry Savory (1914–93), Jeffrey Gilley (b. 1924), and Nicky Savory (b. 1920) are (or were) bilingual.

As mentioned in section 4.2, in the 1860s and 1870s, Japanese people served as translators. By the time of the early Shōwa era (1925–89), it was the Western islanders who had become the translators. A 1929 book states that Joseph Gonzales served as an officer of Tokyo Prefecture and functioned as a translator every time foreign ships came into port (*A Compendium of the Ogasawara Islands* 1929, app. 103).

According to the memoir of Masao Aono, the second-generation ethnic-Japanese islander quoted previously, the Western community (society) on the island had become diglossic.

The elderly (Western) islanders who had not received a school education almost never used Japanese, and those older than the youth didn't use it well. The children used Japanese at school or around town, but it seems it was usual for them to use English at home. [1978, 143]

From these facts, we can see that the Western islanders had become bilingual and their society was diglossic with the use of Japanese in public and English in private situations.

This diglossia lasted for several decades up to World War II. As the children (and probably younger adults) began to learn Japanese in the 1870s, they began to use it for various formal and out-group purposes. These "high" or H domains included school education, work for which they received pay (working in an office or shop, as opposed to farm work or fishing), speaking to ethnic-Japanese, serving in the military, and so on. On the other hand, Bonin English was used for informal or in-group communication ("low" or L domains), such as services at the Christian church on the island, conversations within the Westerner community, within the home, and so on. But English was also used for "super-high" functions such as when foreigners came to visit the island and even (perhaps the ultimate irony) when the emperor of Japan came to visit the island and Joseph Gonzales wrote a chapter—a chapter in English—in the hardcover book produced to commemorate the occasion (*A Compendium of the Ogasawara Islands* 1929, 103–5).

## 6.2. ISLANDERS WHO SERVED AS
## JAPANESE-ENGLISH INTERPRETERS

Following in the footsteps of Joseph Gonzales years earlier, many Westerners served—at various times, in varying capacities, and at the service of different authorities—as translators or interpreters. A twentieth-century namesake of the original settler, Nathaniel Savory (1908–88) translated for the Japanese army during World War II. Grover Gilley (1885–1957) used his skills in written English to translate documents for his fellow islanders during the U.S. Navy period.

Jerry Savory explains in a 1990 television documentary how he was ordered to translate English broadcasts into Japanese when he served in the Japanese army during World War II (NHK 1990). Furthermore, Head and Daws (1968) tell of a Westerner, Fred Savory (b. 1912), translating for U.S. Navy officers immediately following the war (figure 6.1).

American troops under Marine Colonel Presley M. Rixey arrived in October to begin the repatriation of Japanese soldiers, and in the tedious days that followed, victors and vanquished played baseball on the scarred small-plane airstrip. With Rixey came Fred Savory, great grandson of Nathaniel, to work as an interpreter. [1968, 73]

## 6.3. PEOPLE'S NAMES

It was during the early twentieth century that the Bonin Islanders took Japanese names, and as such this seems the most appropriate place to deal with the topic of people's names and the changes in them throughout different historical periods.

There is something of a misconception among Japanese—or at least among that minute percentage of the population that has any knowledge of the subject—that the Westerners of Ogasawara acquired Japanese family names when they were naturalized as Japanese citizens back in the early Meiji era. This is not true.[5]

When the original inhabitants of the islands began to be naturalized in 1877, only a few took Japanified names. Among these was the almost legendary German figure Frederick Rohlfs (1823–98), who settled on Hahajima and aided subsequent Japanese arrivals when they were on the verge of starvation. He was commonly called "Rose," probably because this is how his name sounded to Japanese listeners when pronounced by English speakers. His legal Japanese name was composed of five kanji (Sino-Japanese) characters chosen strictly for their pronunciation. Although they convey no coherent meaning, when combined the characters (pronounced as Rōsu Rarufu) sounded something like the two pronunciations of his family name. Rohlfs was in the minority, however; most of the Westerners (referred to as *kikajin* 'naturalized people' in those days) used katakana renderings of their own Western family names as the official names in their *koseki*, or Official Lineage Registries. These were not Japanese family names, nor Japanified versions of their Western names, but simply adaptations of them to the Japanese phonology and representations of them in the Japanese script (e.g., *Gilley* became Gērē, *Savory* became Sēborē, *Webb* became Uebu, *Washington* became Washinton, *Gonzales* became Gonzaresu).

The usage of katana names continued for a couple of generations. It was not until the Sōshi Kaimei (創氏改名 'Establishment of Family Names and Alteration in Given Names') law that people with non-Japanese surnames were forced to change them. This 1940 law is mainly known for its effect on the millions of colonized people in Korea, but it also affected the Bonin Islanders. Elderly islanders today recall choosing their own last names, often hurriedly and quite randomly.

In the following excerpt from the Shepardson recordings, Uncle Charlie tells of the random way in which his Japanese name was established.

12. UNCLE CHARLIE: I have a Japanese name now.
SHEPARDSON: Yes, what is it?
UNCLE CHARLIE: Kimura Saburō. Yeah Well, you see how I changed it Kimura Saburō. My, my son, what I was living with not long ago, he was in Japan and he took a wife up there you know, and I don't know how it happened, but he change up his name up there, you see? Stashed his name here, and so I was

thinking now what the dickens to do. "Ah hell," I said, "let it go." I changed, put mine to Kimura Saburō. But nobody calls me, nobody holler at me "Kimura Saburō." They call me Charlie.

We think of names as being passed from father to son, but this is an unusual case of a name being passed from son to father. Uncle Charlie's daughter Edith clarified this episode in a February 1999 interview with me (conducted in Japanese). Her brother telegrammed from the mainland to the island (in 1940 or 1941) asking his family to choose a surname for themselves, but he settled on Kimura before they could respond and his parents and siblings followed his lead.

Some of the islanders chose kanji characters that either sounded like their original names or expressed some significant meaning. The Savorys became Sebori (瀬堀), and the Ackermans, the Akaman (赤満) family. The Webbs chose characters that could be read as Uebu (上部) (though the name is pronounced Uwabe today). Other families decided on a name with some symbolic value. The Gilleys, proud of the "South Sea Islander" part of their roots, chose the name Minami (南 'lit. south'). Other families abandoned the idea of names in which either the sound or the meaning of the kanji held significance. In most cases, different family names were chosen by distant branches of the family tree, so that the Gonzales family descendants became either Ogasawara (小笠原) or Kishi (岸).

During the war years, Westerners gave their children Japanese names. Children born after World War II (during the U.S. Navy period) were given only English names, and they use these today—written in katakana—as their official Japanese names.

Following the reversion to Japan, Westerners adopted the practice of giving Japanese names—written in kanji—to their children, but even here, we find cases of islanders identifying with their cultural roots. One case of this is Nasa Sēborē (セーボレー那沙), born in the 1980s, whose name, although written in kanji, is an homage to his ancestor Nathaniel (pronounced "Nasanieru" in Japanese).

Some of the Westerners legally changed their surnames back (from Japanese ones forced upon them in 1941) to their older katakana names following the changes in the Japanese law in the 1980s.

In many cases, a single individual has possessed four legal names in the span of his or her life. A case in point is Able Savory. He was born Sēborē Ēburu (in katakana, セーボレーエーブル), was forced to changed his name to Sebori Eiichi (in kanji, 瀬堀栄一) at the start of the war, and used Able Savory (in the Roman alphabet) during the Navy Era. After the 1968 reversion, he reverted to his wartime kanji family name, but used the katakana "first name" given to him at birth, resulting in the name Sebori Ēburu. In the 1980s, when some of the Savory clan changed their surname back to the katakana Sēborē, he decided four names in one lifetime were enough and retained the kanji surname.

In Ogasawara today, one finds many interesting name-related phenomena. Nicknames—in both Japanese and English—are the norm. Then, most of the Westerners have two names; many have both Japanese and English surnames and given names, which means there often are at least five or six ways to refer to most Westerners.

As the quote from Uncle Charlie indicates, however, many of the Westerners seldom use their official Japanese names in daily life, either with fellow Westerners or with ethnic-Japanese friends and neighbors. Uncle Charlie's daughter Edith uses the Japanese name Kyōko Ōhira today, but people of her generation call her Edie.

One young islander today, Saburō Kimura is named for his great-grandfather, Charles Washington. Naming children after an ancestor is a typical naming practice in Western culture, but in this particular case, the name is confusing in Japanese. Uncle Charlie chose for himself the Japanese name Saburō (三郎), a name which includes the kanji for 'three' and indicates that the possessor of the name is the third-born son in the family. This is an appropriate name, since Uncle Charlie was indeed the third son. His namesake, however, is the firstborn son in the family, but his father (against the protests of his ethnic-Japanese friends and relations) bestowed upon the child the name of his great-grandfather. Thus, the custom (of naming children after an ancestor) is Western; the name itself, Saburo, is Japanese.

## 6.4. THE ENGLISH SPOKEN BY A JAPANESE
## ISLANDER OF THIS PERIOD

Contained in the Shepardson recordings is a short interview with an ethnic-Japanese female named Osute, who married into a Westerner family and acquired English well into adulthood. The inclusion of her data here warrants explanation.

It is important to realize the sometimes vague nature of the distinction between ethnic-Japanese and Westerners on the Bonins. By the beginning of the twentieth century, it was becoming less clear and dichotic due to intermarriages and close social contacts. Many self-identified Westerners were raised in households with one Westerner and one ethnic-Japanese parent. In some of these households, English was maintained as a home language, often along with Japanese. But even as most of the Westerners were becoming bilingual, so a few of the ethnic-Japanese were acquiring some degree of English. Many grew up with Westerners as their close friends and neighbors, and those who had the wherewithal enrolled in English classes attended by both ethnic Japanese and Westerner children alike.

Osute Kikuchi Webb (1881–1976) was born on Hahajima into a family of Hachijōjima settlers that are still prominent on the islands today. Although she was born in the same year as Charles Washington, I have included her in this chapter about the twentieth century, because (unlike Uncle Charlie, who learned English as his first language and thus can be regarded as a late nineteenth-century speaker) Osute acquired English later in life, in the early twentieth century. She did not attend the English classes Joseph Gonzales offered on Chichijima, but there were non-Japanese settlers on Hahajima (e.g., German, Chinese) and it is possible that she picked up some English (albeit a nonnative variety) in communicating with them. She married into one of the Westerner families but, following her husband's death at sea in 1903, moved to Saipan in the Northern Mariana Islands. Over the next few decades, she lived on Saipan on several occasions including the early 1920s, when Saipan had come under Japanese administration. These years spent in Saipan must have influenced her English. The comments below do not indicate that her English was incomprehensible to Bonin Islanders.

Let us examine the English of Osute. In the following passage, she is discussing a hardworking Westerner woman who helped her with child-rearing. (Transcriptions in standard English orthography are followed by pronunciations given in the International Phonetic Alphabet.)

13. OSUTE: Yeah, Kind old woman, ne? My husband die, my small young man live, and helpin' nursin', brought them up. Just like man. Work hard, catch stuff, go fishing too. Stoppin' at this—behind this island. Stony Beach. Stony Beach, been stop.

[jea kain old woman ne. mai hazban dai mai smoːl yaŋ mæn ɾiv æn halpɪn nasɪn boːt dem ap. ʤes ɾaik mæn. woːk haːd keʧ stuf, go ɸɪʃɪn tu. stapɪn ætuː dɪs bahain dɪs aiɾen. stona biːʧ. stona biːʧ bɪn stap]

SHEPARDSON: Stony beach?

OSUTE: Yes Stony, over there, just behind island. Ah, Stony Beach, Sandy Beach, Calef Beach. All American, our family been stay there before. Now, sealing time, sealin's gonna come, that's the way(??) All this island people, men go sealin', sealin'.

[jɛs, oba dea, ʤes bahaina ailen. stona biːʧ sana biːʧ kelef biːʧ. oːɾ əmeɾiken awa ɸamiɾi bɪn stei dea biɸoa. nau ʃiɾɪn taim, ʃiɾɪns gənə kəm æstəwei oːl dɪs alien mɛn go ʃiɾɪn ʃiɾɪn]

SHEPARDSON: Oh, sealing? Sealing.

OSUTE: All die, died. Lot capsize, uh?

[oːl dai daid, loto kæpsaid ə]

Her speech contains some interesting characteristics that are similar to those found in many other English-based Pacific contact languages. One is the use of the lexeme *stop* to mean 'live, stay, be in a place', which she uses repeatedly. This is a feature found in Palmerston and most contact varieties of English all across the Pacific (Clark 1979; Ehrhart-Kneher 1996). She also uses the term *stay* (with the same meaning) found in current use in Guamanian English (Middlebrooke 2001).

A second is the use of *been (a)* + verb to mark the past (often a continuing past action or state) as in "been stop," "been a stay," "been marry," and "been a die," although she also uses zero-marking ("my husband die"), standard English past tenses ("I forgot it" and "I met them"), and multiple markings ("been a married"). Past-tense constructions with *been* are common to almost all English-based contact languages in the Pacific region, including Pitcairn and Palmerston (Clark 1979; Laycock 1989; Ehrhart-Kneher 1996).

A third feature is the use of the lexeme *capsize*. In this context, Osute is discussing a fatal boat accident so *capsize* is entirely correct as standard English usage. Derivations of *capsize* are, however, found in Pacific contact languages with broadened or shifted semantic fields (e.g., Tok Pisin *kapsaitim* 'to tip, pour', Pitcairn *capsize* 'to fall, to upset anything', Norfolk *capsaez* 'to be overwhelmed by'). It seems more than coincidence here that a speaker with a limited English vocabulary such as Osute has chosen a comparatively difficult word like *capsize* over more basic terms such as *sink, drown, die,* and so on.

Phonologically, Osute's speech has features we associate with Pacific contact varieties in some cases and features of "Japanese English" in others. She has the stop [d] (rather than [z] or [ʤ]) for /ð/ in *this, there,* and *them*. She has no problem with closed syllables, as seen in her pronunciations of the final consonants [p, b, f, v, t, d, tʃ, k] in *stop, Webb, stuff, live, bought, died, catch,* and *like.* Conversely, in some other words, she drops final consonants, not only simplifying clusters in *just, island,* and *behind,* but categorically using the pronunciation [ɸai] for *five.* In Japanese English we would expect neither of these outcomes, but rather the insertion of vowels after the word-end consonants.

Even though she does pronounce labiodental consonants in *stuff* and *live,* most of her *f* sounds use the Japanese bilabial fricative heard in her pronunciations of *fishin', family,* and *before.* Moreover, although she produces a good [l] in the syllable-final or preconsonantal position (*old, small, helping*), it does not appear she makes a phoneme distinction between the two English liquids; in other positions she has the Japanese flap [ɾ] for both English /l/ and /r/.

The comments of Uncle Charlie in reference to Osute's English are informative:

14. SHEPARDSON: [an islander] told us to talk with Jesse Webb's mother, he said that she was an old lady and remembered plenty.

UNCLE CHARLIE: Yes. Well, she do. It's worthwhile listening to what she tell you.

SHEPARDSON: But now she is Japanese, isn't she?

UNCLE CHARLIE: She's pure Jap.

SHEPARDSON: But speaks English?

UNCLE CHARLIE: Well broken English, something like myself.

SHEPARDSON: If it's something—

UNCLE CHARLIE: No, she, she can't—you wouldn't understand her.

SHEPARDSON: I see, we'd have to have somebody interpret for us.

UNCLE CHARLIE: Yes, that's right. Oh, she knows a lot, but she wasn't born here. She was born on Hahajima, yes. She was married to one of the Webbs, old Webb's son. Fella name of Moses, eh?

[We should note that Uncle Charlie's use of the word *Jap* is colloquial and not derogatory.]

Now, we know Uncle Charlie himself was multilingual (speaking Japanese as well as varieties of English), and we know from interviews with his children that he spoke Japanese to them and to their Japanese mother. Indeed, everything we know about language use in the community in the twentieth century indicates that Uncle Charlie would have spoken Japanese to Osute, so the two of them probably did not use a contact variety of English to communicate. Nonetheless, the indication here is that Uncle Charlie (although no doubt being courteous to Osute) positions his own English not far from the "broken English." I am not implying that Uncle Charlie and Osute shared a common single variety of contact English, but rather I wish to highlight the likelihood that multiple varieties of contact English (creoloid, nonnative English of Japanese speakers, a Marianas Island English-based lingua franca) coexisted on the early twentieth-century Bonins. In addition to the homegrown Bonin Creoloid English of the Westerners and the nonnative English spoken by the Japanese residents, there were Pacific contact varieties brought in from other places, such as Osute's "broken English," due to the contact with Japanese-administered colonies like the Northern Marianas.

# 7. EARLY-TWENTIETH-CENTURY BONIN ENGLISH AND THE PREWAR OGASAWARA MIXED LANGUAGE

U͟P TO THIS POINT we have examined the nineteenth-century varieties of English used on the islands and some of the sociohistorical
background leading up to the twentieth century. In this chapter,
we will look at features of the English used in the twentieth century.
We will look at both Bonin English and the Ogasawara Mixed Language (OML), which has Bonin English as one of its components.

## 7.1. THE ENGLISH OF AN EARLY-TWENTIETH-CENTURY MALE

The Shepardson recordings include several short interviews with
islanders, most of whom were born in the later nineteenth or early
twentieth century. Some interviews are only a few minutes long,
but nevertheless provide valuable glimpses into the English used
on the islands almost a century ago when these speakers were
acquiring the language.

We will look at one such fragment of data next. The male
speaker in (15), Jesse Webb (1903–77), was born of a Westerner
father and a Japanese mother. Here is the entire transcription from
his interview with Shepardson. English orthography is followed by
his pronunciation in the International Phonetic Alphabet.

15. SHEPARDSON: . . . Jesse Webb, telling us about his fishing.
    JESSE: About fishing? Tomorrow, I intend to go out fishing, you
    see? If the water fine, but I don't know yet. But I sure I be
    going out tomorrow, you see? And try tow some wahoo. and
    'bout, all day tomorrow, I be back 'bout three o'clock. That's
    all I have to talk, okay?

133

[əbautˀ fɪʃiŋ. tumaɹə ai intend tu go autˀ fɪʃiŋ, ju si. ɪf ðə watə
fain, batˀ ai don noː yɛtˀ. batˀ ai ʃʊa ai biː goːn autˀ tumaɹə,
ju si. æn tɹai toː sam wahuː æn bautˀ ɔl deː tumaɹə ai biː bækˀ
bautˀ tɹiː əklak. ðæts ɔl ai hæv tu tɔːk, oŋe]

SHEPARDSON: That's fine. [break in recording] Now what kind of
a boat do you go fishing in?

JESSE: My boat is canoe. Canoe.

[mai boːdɪz kənuː. kənuː]

SHEPARDSON: You fish all by yourself?

JESSE: Yes I go fishing all by myself. More ... easier if – by yourself,
you know. Everybody go in a canoe fishing by theyself.

[jɛs ai go fɪʃin ɔl bai maiself. moː iziɚ ɪf bai jʊself, ju no. ɛvɹi
badi go ɪnə kənuː fɪʃin bai deself]

SHEPARDSON: And where do you go to fish?

JESSE: Go 'round the island 'ccording the wind, everything. Way
the wind—we go leeward to the wind, you know, and fishing.
Up east coast, west, south go around, many thing good for
fishing.

[go ɹaun di ailən kɔdɪn tu di wɪn ɛvɹiθiŋ. we ði wɪn. wi go lʊad
tu ðə win ju noː æn fɪʃiŋ. ap ɹːsu coːs wɛs saus go aɹaun mɛni
θiŋ gʊd foa fɪʃiŋ]

SHEPARDSON: Do you go far out from land?

JESSE: No, about half a mile, or quarter mile or so. Just 'round the
island you know.

[no əbautˀ haːf ə mail aː kotaː mail aː soː. ʤʊs ɹaun də ailən ju
no]

SHEPARDSON: You used to go fishing during the war time also,
didn't you?

JESSE: Yeah, I was fish'man from my small days, you know. And I
don't do nothing else but fishing, make my living fishing.

[jɛː ai wəz fɪʃəmən fɹʌm mai smal deːz ju no. æn ai don du
nəˀn ɛls batˀ fɪʃiŋ mek mai lɪviŋ fɪʃiŋ]

SHEPARDSON: Did you once live on another island where you
fished?

JESSE: Before we used to go—when the navy time, we go Hahajima and 'round Mukojima in a canoe and leave early in the
morning about three o'clock, come back about two in the
afternoon then we clean our fish and everything and put it
in a reefer ['refrigerator'].

[bifoɑ wi justu go wɛn də neːvi taim wi go hahaʤima æn ɾɑun
mukoʤima ɪn jə kənuː æn liːv ɑːliː ɪnnə moːnɪŋ bɑut tɹiː əklɑk
kəm bæk bɑut tu əklɑk ɪnnə ɑftɑnun ðɛn wi klin ɑwɑː fɪʃ æn
ɛvɹiθɪŋ æn pʊt ɪt ɪnnə ɹiːfɑ]

SHEPARDSON: Did you ever live on Mukojima?

JESSE: I been live there about three years
[ai bɪn lɪv ðɛɑ əbɑut θɹiː jiɑs]

SHEPARDSON: When you were young?

JESSE: When I about eighteen
[wɛn ɑi əbɑut eːtiːn]

SHEPARDSON: About eighteen. Did you ever go to school here?

JESSE: School only I been to four grades, you know. And we was
pretty hard and my mother pretty hard to s- that thing, have
the living and we used to go work, get out the school and go
work, you know.
[skul onli ai bɪn tu foː ɡɹeːdz ju noː. æn wi wɑz pɹɪti hɑːd mai
məðɑː pɹɪti hɑːd tu s– ðætˀ θɪŋ æn wi justu go woːk ɡɪt ɑut ðə
skul æn go woːk ju noː]

SHEPARDSON: This was after you father was lost at sea.

JESSE: We wasn't born when my father lost to the sea, and my
mother was carrying us yet. So my mother had hard time to
brought—bring us up, you know.
[wi wəsntˀ boːn wɛn mai fɑdə los tu də si æn mai məðə wɑz
kɛːɹɪn ʌs jɛt. so mai məðə hæd hɑːd taim tu bɹɑu bɹɪŋ ʌs ʌp, yu
no]

SHEPARDSON: That's you and your twin brother?

JESSE: Yeah. So we had hard time, them days, you know.
[jɑː. so wi hæd hɑːd taim ðɛm deiz yu no]

SHEPARDSON: Yes pretty hard. Okay that's fine.

Jesse's speech is an intriguing amalgam of features of native
English (standard and nonstandard varieties) on the one hand and
features common to contact varieties of English on the other. This
is in line with our characterization of the Bonin English of the late
nineteenth and early twentieth centuries as a creoloid.

Let us first examine some phonological traits. The overall
impression one gets from the tape is that Jesse is NOT speaking Japanese-influenced English. He speaks fluently and has no problems
in comprehension. He does not speak in "open syllables" (with all

syllables ending in vowels), as we would expect of a Japanese-native speaker, but has many "closed syllable" words. He not only has words ending in various consonants (/m, f, v, t, d, s, z, ʃ, ŋ, k, l/: *time, self, live, but, hard, yes, days, fish, bring, work,* and *mile*), but has many consonant clusters as well (e.g., *small, clock, pretty, that's*).

Jesse distinguishes clearly between /r/ and /l/ as Uncle Charlie did, although he often substitutes the Japanese flap [ɾ] for the approximant [ɹ] in initial posistion. This distinction is typically difficult for native-Japanese speakers and is often absent from English-derived contact varieties, even those like Tok Pisin and Solomon Islands Pijin where the official orthography makes a distinction (Lynch 1998, 226; Jourdan and Maebiru 2002, p. 20 of introduction).

His *th* sounds (both voiced and voiceless) are variable. He has mainstream English [θ] and [ð], but he also has the [t] and [d], which (in addition to being found in many nonstandard varieties of English) are the variants we would expect in a contact variety. He does not (at least in this short snippet of data) use the variants of *th* we would expect from Japanese speakers of English (i.e., [z] or [ʤ]).

He has variation between [n] and [ŋ] just as many native varieties of English do, seen in his use of both *fishin'* and *fishing* (see Hibiya 1995 on this phenomenon in the English of Japanese-Canadians).

Jesse is nonrhotic. (I have left one instance of [ɚ] in the transcriptions above because it sounds like a rhotic vowel, but I also realize that one must be careful about making such a judgment considering that the word is followed by a vowel: *easier if.*) He appears to have compensatory vowel lengthening for his "*r*-dropping," and I have indicated those vowels which impressionistically struck me as lengthened, but the question of whether this is phonemically significant will have to wait for future analysis on different data (considering that this speaker has long ago passed away).

Jesse's vowel system (figure 7.1) is far more similar to those of mainstream varieties than the five cardinal vowels that one would expect in contact varieties of English or in Japanese-influenced English. He has 10 (perhaps 11) vowel phonemes. The combina-

FIGURE 7.1
Jesse Webb's English Vowel System

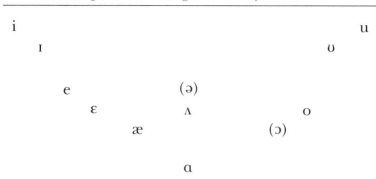

tion of the less than ideal sound quality of the recording, the small amount of linguistic data, and, alas, the present author's skills in English phonology make a detailed analysis difficult. (I have left the vowel symbol [ɔ] in the transcriptions because this is how I heard some vowels, but his [ɔ] and [o] are quite close phonetically and do not appear to be clearly distinguished phonemically. I am not counting [ə] and [ʌ] as separate phonemes. Also, for the record, this author has a clear CAUGHT/COT distinction, so this is not a factor in my transcriptions.) At any rate, what I can emphasize with confidence here is that Jesse does NOT have the five-vowel system that one would expect from a contact variety of English.

From the lexical standpoint, his English does not show any evidence of admixture (e.g., words from Hawaiian); if his everyday speech DOES contain high frequency of such words, this speaker has learned to avoid them when speaking to a nonislander. This lack of admixture does not come as a surprise, however. We see throughout this book that the lexemes of non-English (and non-Japanese) origin used on the Bonins are few in number and largely limited to names of plants and animals.

Grammatically, as with his phonology, Jesse's speech is creoloid, exhibiting more nonstandard features than Uncle Charlie's, but mixing mainstream English variants nonetheless. As seen in the passage, he uses the invariant *be* copula ("I be going out") or deletes the copula altogether ("if the water fine"). He also uses null subject ("Go 'round the island"), a feature found in many contact languages. Jesse's articles generally follow standard English usage, but not always ("My boat is canoe," "I was fisherman," "have the living," "get out the school and go work"). He uses *been* to mark the past tense ("I been live there"), a feature common in other Bonin speakers and indeed found throughout the Pacific.

Jesse uses *yet* for 'still' ("my mother was carrying me yet"), a feature that Uncle Charlie uses numerous times. This feature is common in contact varieties of English such as Bahamian (John Holm, pers. comm., Nov. 10 1999), Hawaiian Creole English (Sarah Juli-anne Roberts, pers. comm., Nov. 9 1999), and all three varieties of Melanesian Pidgin: Tok Pisin (Sankoff 1993); Bislama (Miriam Meyerhoff, pers. comm., Nov. 11 1999); Solomons Pijin (Geoff Smith, pers. comm., Nov. 10 1999). Of course, in noncontact varieties (including standard ones) *yet* and *still* are semantically close (cf. "it has not rained yet" and "it still has not rained").

Jesse uses *before* adverbially to mean 'some time ago' ("Before, we used to go"); a similar usage is found in Hawaiian and Melanesian pidgins (Carr 1972, 123).

## 7.2. THE PREWAR BEGINNINGS OF OML

Firsthand accounts (such as those of Van Buskirk mentioned in section 6.1) as well as the memories of elderly islanders today all indicate the same thing: English remained the first and dominant language of the Westerners for many decades even after the Japanese takeover of the islands. In the early twentieth century, this situation flip-flopped, with Japanese becoming the first and dominant language, especially in households with a Japanese mother. We cannot give a clear date for this change. Of course, many social factors influenced this, so the situation differs from one individual to the next. But English appears to be the first language of young-sters at the turn of the century, while Japanese is the first language of people born in the 1920s. So the shift occurred during the first couple of decades of the twentieth century. This is not to say all speakers of this generation became monolingual in Japanese. Although a few did, many others retained English as a subordinate language at varying levels of proficiency, especially those in households where both parents were Westerners. But another phenomenon, stranger than mere bilingualism, appears to have begun in this period, although it reached full fruition in the subsequent Navy Era. That is the complex intertwining of the two languages into a single language system with both grammatical and phonological features (as well as mere lexical ones) from both languages. This phenomenon too is more prominent in households where both parents were Westerners.

Here, we will examine data from one speaker, Able Savory (1929–2003), who was raised by a Westerner mother and Westerner father and is as typical a Westerner speaker of the prewar generation as we may expect to find. (The varied linguistic experiences of individual Westerners render the concept of a "typical speaker" somewhat meaningless.) The data from Able are from tape-recorded interviews and informal conversations that I conducted between 1997 and 2003. From these data we can gain insights into the language being used on the Bonin Islands during the first half of the twentieth century. The sound recordings and complete transcripts of these interviews have been published as a research report with accompanying CD-ROM (Long 2003).

Let us examine some characteristics of Able's speech. First, the language which could be regarded as his vernacular—that is, the language he uses with his spouse, children, intimate friends, and so on—is a mixture of Japanese and English. Moreover, this mixing is not random and haphazard. There are clearly patterns in the way the two languages are mixed. This indicates that he and other speakers in the community are not simply mixing the two languages but are using parts of the two original languages to construct a third language system—a new language, as it were—which I argue in chapter 10 shares features of other so-called "mixed languages."

Able spoke Japanese fluently—and by "Japanese" here, I mean the island variety of standard Japanese that does not mix with English. His Ogasawara Standard Japanese sounds similar to the

Japanese of Tokyo. He can hold long conversations in English—and by "English" here, I mean a variety which does not mix with Japanese. His English is not fluent, however, showing some signs of language attrition due to a prolonged lack of usage. (As he himself explains at the beginning of the interview, "I, little bit, forgot English, you know? I talk only Japanese everyday, see? I forgotten.") At the same time, his English is not what one would expect from a Japanese speaker who had learned English as a second or foreign language. He retains many words that would be considered "hard words" by many speakers of English in that they are somewhat technical or specialized terms used by a specific group, namely people of the sea, sailors, fisherfolk, and so on. Simply put, this is because this vocabulary is present in the English component of his vernacular, Ogasawara Mixed Language.

Here are some examples of this type of nautical terminology.

16. a. *rifa* or *riifaa* 'refrigerator' (from English *reefer* 'refrigerated train car or ship'). The long and short vowel distinction is phonemically significant in Japanese, but this distinction is vaguer in the speech of the Westerners, especially in words such as this which do not exist in standard Japanese.
    b. *strike* 'to lower a sail'
    c. *tack* 'to zigzag through the sea to make best use of winds even when they are not blowing in the direction one wishes to go'

There are also many lexemes found in modern day Bonin English and OML that are of neither English nor Japanese origin. One such term is *longusta* 'lobster' (SJ *ise ebi*) from Spanish. (Incidentally, the Chamorro language spoken in Saipan and Guam, to the south of the Bonins, was heavily influenced by Spanish, but this term is not used in Chamorro.) We will deal with more lexemes of neither Japanese nor English origin in section 8.5.

Perhaps the most striking lexical aspect of OML is not the technical, exotic, or complex vocabulary, but the fact that it typically incorporates extremely mundane everyday words—like *wind*, *fish*, *rope*, and *miss*—from English into the Japanese sentence matrix. Ironically, it is precisely because there is nothing special about these words that their usage is striking.

*Wind* is a good example of the incorporation of basic English vocabulary. It would be ludicrous to think that any of the Western-ers did not know the Japanese word for 'wind' (*kaze*), and yet pre-war OML (and postwar OML speakers, as we will see later) typically use *wind* instead. In the published transcription of a February 1999 interview with Able (Long 2002a), he discusses subjects such as windsurfing and trident (spear) fishing, so the topic of wind comes up often. He speaks of the concept of 'wind' in seven utterances; in two of these he uses the Japanese term *kaze*.

Two of his utterances containing *wind* are completely in English, in response to questions in English (posed by myself), so that accounts for his usage of the English word *wind* in (17). (Able's nonuse of *when* to mark what would clearly be a subordinate clause in standard English deserves note as well and cannot be attributed directly to interference, because in Japanese such a construction must be overtly marked.)

17.  a.  LONG: Do you still do that [windsurfing] sometimes?
           ABLE: Yeah, [when] it's a strong wind coming, eh, I go on the
                 beach and....
                 [jɛɑ ɪtsə strɔn wɪn kamiŋ ɛɑ ɑi go ɔn ðə bitʃ æn]
     b.  LONG: So it gets warmer in March?
           ABLE: Just this month is a very cold, every year, you know. The
                 wind is too cold, see? That north wind, eh?
                 [dʒɛs dʒɪs mɑnsɪzə vɛri koˑl ɛvˑɹi jiɚ jəno. ðə wɪnz ɪz tuˑ koˑl
                 siˑ. ðæt noˑs wɪn ə]

The three remaining usages of English *wind* are embedded in Japanese sentence structures (and in response to questions posed in Japanese). These usages come in spite of the fact that my Japa-nese colleague and I had emphasized to Able that this interview was for use in a Japanese radio documentary and that he needed to speak Japanese for that reason. I will give all examples of *wind* with the complete utterance to show the context and because the utter-ances contain many other examples of the intertwining of English vocabulary elements (e.g., *fishing, tide, sit down, line, strike, rope, slip, swing,* and *tack*) in OML.

18.  a.  Grandfather ga ne, zutto tsunagatte kita wake ne. De, ima mō
inai shima ni. boku dake nokotta no. Anō, mane suru hito
ha iru kedo, but, tsukinbō no fishing ha sono, kekkō taihen
na tokoro ga aru wake yo. Wind mo minakucha ikenai shi,
tide mo minakucha ikenai. Soshite, fune no nagashikata mo
keiken shinakereba wakaranai.
'My grandfather, eh, it continued all down from him. And,
now there's only me left. Uh, some people imitate it, but trident fishing is, well, there is a difficult side to it. You have to
watch the wind, have to watch the tide. And you have to experience how the boat drifts also.'

b.  Koko ni sit down suru desho? Suwatte. De, koko ga, asoko ni
dekkai ho ga tatsu kara. De, kono line de strike shitari ne.
Hippattari shite, de, koko de suwatte, rope ha sono rope ga kō
kite, kono shita de kō funderu wake, slip shinai yō ni, ne. De,
wind un to atatta toki ni sukoshi slip shite kō yurumeru ka ne.
Swing shite hashiru wake. Koko ni hikkakeru wake.
'You sit down here, right? Sit down. 'Cause, here, over there
is where a big sail stands. And, with this line you strike and
all, pulling and all. And here, you sit, and the rope goes like,
come like this, and under here, you press on it with your foot,
so it doesn't slip. And when the wind blows hard, you let it
slip and give it a little slack. It swings and you start to run. You
hook it here.'

c.  Jū jikan kakatta-ssu yo. Demo iki-kiranakatta. Dō shite to iu to,
about, you know, eh, wind, eh, chōdo mukai kaze ga so I tack
and tack, tack. Kō yatta desho? Sore de time ga kakatchatta.
So, boku no kangae de wa, six hour ne, six hour de iku tsumori de ita no. Asoko made go-ji-kkiro, eh? Hahajima made.
Sore de ichijikan de, anō, jikkiro, ne. Sō suru to, go jikan de
go-ji-kkiro deshō? Ato, one hour mite about roku-jū-kiro ni
shite roku jikan iku tsumori de keisan shita kedo, dame data.
'It took ten hours. Even then I couldn't make it all the way. The
reason why is, about, you know, the wind, huh? Just that time
there was a head wind, so I tacked and tacked [zigzagged],
like this, right? Because of that it took a lot of time. So, in my
way of thinking—about six hours, I intended to do it in six
hours. To there it is about 50 kilometers, huh? To Hahajima.
Then, for one hour, that's 10 kilos. In 5 hours, that's 50 kilos,
right? Then, give one hour, and for 60 kilos, it would take, I
calculated, 6 hours, but it didn't work.'

## 7.3. PHONOLOGY

In postwar OML, examined in chapter 10, words of English origin usually maintain their original phonological structure, but in the prewar OML of Able Savory and his generation, the pronunciation of English words is quite variable. Some original phonological elements not found in Japanese are maintained while others show the influence of the Japanese phonological structure; there is much variation even within a single speaker.

Many of the vowel distinctions made in English are maintained, but again this is variable, and the influence of Japanese can be seen in some speakers more than others. Nonetheless, while the number of distinct vowel phonemes differs among speakers, it is significant that English words are NOT pronounced as they would be by native Japanese speakers, that is, using only the five cardinal vowels of that language. Able has [ɪ] (not [i]) in words like *it* and *wind*; [ɛ] (not [e]) in words like *very*; [æ] (not [a]) in words like *tack*; [ɔ] (not [o]) in words like *strong* and *on*; [ə] in words like *the*. He pronounces *church* as [ʧɛːʧ], probably influenced by the [ʧɜːʧ] pronunciation of speakers like Uncle Charlie (section 5.3.1). This pronunciation is traceable back to New England English (Wells 1982, 520–21). On the other hand, we find Japanese substitutions in the vowels of *coming, month*, and *north*.

With the liquid consonants, English alveolar approximant [ɹ] and alveolar lateral approximant [l] are sometimes distinguished, but other times—even in English words—the Japanese flap [ɾ] is substituted for these sounds. In (17b) Able says the phrase "very cold, every year" [vɛɾi koˑl ɛvɹi jiɚ], substituting the Japanese flap for the /r/ in *very* but using the English phonemes in *cold* and *every*, and even pronouncing an American English-like rhotic vowel in year. He also has consonant clusters in words like *strong* (which are not allowed in Japanese phonology and would result in [sutorongu]).

We find reduction of final consonant clusters (e.g., *wind* and *just* in 17 and *grand* later in 31), but these are common in many dialects of English and do not seem to be the result of Japanese influences (Japanese deals with foreign consonant clusters by inserting vowels between them); it is much more logical to interpret this as a reflection of the phonological structure of the source language Bonin English itself. This interpretation is reinforced by the fact that so many other aspects of the phonological system of OML's English elements (e.g., phonemic distinction between liquids) have also at least variably resisted the influence of Japanese.

With the *th* sounds, we find Japanese-influenced variants, those of mainstream English, and (most significantly) variants that reveal the influence upon the OML of the nineteenth-century Bonin Creoloid English. We find examples of the Japanese influence in (17b), where *north* and *month* become [noːs] and [mɑns] and *this* becomes [d̠ɪs]. The examples in (17) also show the usage of English variants in *the* and *that*. We find the creoloid variants in [t] for /θ/ in words like [tri] for 'three' (ex. 21).

## 7.4. THE JAPANESE COMPONENT OF THE OGASAWARA MIXED LANGUAGE

Let us now take a brief look at some of the Japanese components of the OML used by Able. As mentioned briefly in section 2.7, various dialects brought by settlers from mainland Japan and Hachijō mixed to form Ogasawara Koiné Japanese. This koiné in turn forms the Japanese component of OML. In (19) I have listed a few nonstandard Japanese lexemes found in his interviews. As we see in the examples below, these are not found in any single mainland dialect of Japanese.

19. a. *bukkoru* (Jap *ochiru*) from *buchi*- 'emphatic verb prefix found in Eastern Japanese dialects' + *okoru* 'fall'. Found on Hachijōjima (Izu Islands). Similar forms, *buchi-ochiru*, etc. are used in Gifu, Aichi, Yamanashi, Shizuoka, and Ibaraki.

   b. *(mori) gotsu* '(harpoon) and all' (Jap *goto*). Used in the sense of "The sea turtle swam away harpoon and all." Found in Hachijōjima and its "daughter dialect" on Minami Daitō-jima.

   c. *hibo* 'rope' (Jap *himo*). Found in Aichi, Mie, Ōshima Island (Izu Islands), and Kagawa.

   d. *kirui* 'clothes' (Jap *kimono, irui*). Used on Aogashima in the Izu Island chain, but not reported for Hachijō.

e. *morokoshi* 'corn, maize' (Jap *tōmorokoshi*). Found in Iwate, Gumma, Saitama, Chiba, Tokyo, Izu Islands, Kanagawa, Yamanashi, Nagano, amd Shizuoka.

f. *muguru* 'to dive (into the ocean)' (Jap *moguru*). Also found in Aomori, Sado Island, Fukushima, Ibaraki, Chiba, Kanagawa, and Shizuoka.

g. *nomoru* 'to sink, to be swallowed by a wave' (Jap *shizumu, nami wo kaburu*). Found on Hachijōjima, and Minami Daitō-jima.

h. *shima no dōnatsu* 'deep fried sweet cakes' (like hush-puppies but made of flour and sweet). A Bonin invention and a local word.

## 7.5. FUNCTIONAL LEXEMES

The mixed language of the Bonin Islands can be seen in very rough terms as the linguistic intertwining of a Japanese grammatical system and Bonin English vocabulary. Moreover, much of this English contribution is found in lexical morphemes. The English lexical morphemes seen in the modest body of data gathered for the present research are varied. They do not indicate that functional or semantic aspects of lexical items are relevant in predicting their source languages. Nouns of English origin run the semantic gamut and include, for example, *spear, line, hook, paddle, club, fish, wind, weather, flood, face, head, name, grave, balance, jail, orphan, book, school, language, facility, education, history, passport,* and *alien* (some verbs and adjectives are listed in section 7.6). There are functional morphemes from English as well. Adverbs include modal expressions like *maybe*, temporal expressions like *sometime*, and locatives like *here*. Pronouns, counters, and conjunctions are functional morpheme classes in which English words dominate.

Let us examine a few sentences from OML in order to grasp the essence of it. Examples are shown in three lines. The first is the original utterance, the second is a morpheme-by-morpheme gloss, and the third is a loose English translation. In these examples, words of English origin are set in small capitals to distinguish them from Japanese-origin words. Explanations of the abbreviations for parts of speech are listed in the front matter of this book.

The first-person form *I* (ex. 20) is unusual among the data and may result from standard English influence. This use of first-person *I* is one of the major differences between the prewar OML found in speakers like Able and the postwar OML used among speakers of his children's generation (in which the English-derived *me* is used regardless of the grammatical case). We will examine this postwar variety of OML in chapter 10.

> 20. I  GO  CEMETERY  chotto.
>     I  go  cemetery  little
>     'I am going to the cemetery a while'

The Japanese language has a counter system that is semantically, phonologically, and syntactically complicated. To avoid this complexity, islanders' use of English counters has become common in OML. As seen in (21) and (22), both the numbers and the nouns they modify are realized in English.

> 21. Soko  de  ABOUT TWO WEEK  OR  TRI    WEEK  ita  ne
>     there  at  about two week        three  week  be   FP
>     'I was there about two or three weeks'
> 22. Mō   ato,  ALMOST ABOUT FIVE KILO  gurai,  go    kiro
>     More  left  almost about five kilo   about  five  kilo
>     gurai.  De,    SUNDOWN,  eh.
>     about  CONJ   sundown   FP
>     'With almost about five kilometers left—and then, sundown, you know.'

Temporal concepts are also usually words of English origin, as we see in Able's use of *sundown* in (22). Some of the temporal expressions, such as Able's use of *tea time* in (23), are no doubt used in their English forms because of their relationship to English-based culture.

> 23. Itsu mo TEA TIME ni kore wo taberu.
>     'Always, at tea time we eat these [island donuts]'

However, non–culturally bound examples of temporal expressions abound as well, as in Able's use of *winter time* and *everyday* in (24) and (25).

24. Ima, chōdo WINTER TIME de itsu mo, hora, ano, umi ga areteru kara dekinai kedo. . .
    'Just now, it's winter time, and usually—look, uh, the sea is rough so you can't do it, but. . .'
25. Nerima ni ite, EH? Tōkyō no ne. Soshite kondo wa EVERYDAY WAR, BOMBED, EH? Soshite nigeta wake yo, kōjō kara.
    'In Nerima, eh? In Tokyo, huh? And then, after that, everyday, the war, [being] bombed, eh? Then, I ran away from the factory.'

The use of temporal expressions of English origin may well be an extension of the use of English numbers. A look at the names of the months in Japanese helps to explain this relationship. For example, 'November' and 'April', in standard Japanese, would be *jūichigatsu* 'lit. eleven month' and *shi-gatsu* 'lit. four month'. The use of English numbers in OML stems from an avoidance of the complex systems of Japanese counters, including words like months of the year, which, although in English have nothing to do with numbers, are number-related words in Japanese. To get an idea of the complexity of Japanese number words (and these are just some temporal expressions, without getting into the different counter words for flat objects, long objects, fish, birds, people, etc.), we could list words like *jūik-ka getsu* 'eleven months', *yon-ka-getsu* 'four months', *ichi nichi* 'one day', *tsuitachi* 'first day (of April)', *ni-jū nichi* 'twenty days', *hatsuka* 'the twentieth', and *ni-jūyokka* 'the twenty-fourth'.

English conjunctions are also prevalent, although connective words seem to derive from both languages. It is difficult to determine whether this is an indication of inherent variability in the mixed language or the result of decades of influence from mainstream varieties of English or Japanese. In (26) and (27), we see the usage of both English *or* and Japanese *ka*.

26. Ēto, ABOUT FOUR TIME OR THREE TIME
    'Umm, about three or four times'
27. Ore  ne,  are,   HOW MANY YEAR  datta  ka  ne,  mō
    I    FP   umm  how many years   was    Q   FP   already
    sō   ne   SEVEN YEAR  ka  EIGHT YEAR  ni  naru     ka  ne,
    so   FP   seven year  Q   eight year  in  become   Q   FP
    bosuton  itta       no  yo.
    Boston   go-PAST   FP  FP

'I, you know, umm, how many years has it been, seven years or eight years maybe, I went to Boston.'

Example (28) contains Japanese *kara*, equivalent here to the English conjunction *because*. The same example contains the English *but*. Example (29) shows the usage of *sorede*, an expression corresponding to *and* but used when linking verbs or clauses (as opposed to nouns).

28. Tsuku   kara        FISH   ga      sukoshi   yowaru   yo.
    stick    because    fish   NOM    little     weaken   FP
    SOMETIMES   sugu    shinu,   BUT   SPEAR   suru   to        sugu
    sometimes    soon    die       but    spear   do     COND    soon
    shinu   no       mo    iru   shi...
    die      NOM    also   be     and
    'Because you spear them, the fish weaken a little. Sometimes they die soon, but if you spear them, some of them die, and...'

29. Sensei   ni    tsurete   ikerarete   sono   EMPEROR   no    ne
    teacher   by    escort    go-PASS    that    emperor   of    FP
    sono   PICTURE   ga       aru   yo.   Soko   ni    tsurete   ikerarete
    that    picture    NOM    be     FP     there   in    escort    go-PASS
    BUCKET   no   naka      ni    WATER   irete   sorede      ONE HOUR,
    bucket    of    interior   in    water     insert   and then   one hour
    ichi   jikan   gurai   tat-asa-reru          n     da yo
    one    hour    about   stand-CAUS-PASS   be    FP
    'We would get taken out by the teacher, and there was a, uh, picture of the, uh, emperor there, and they'd put water in a bucket and make us stand there (holding it) about an hour.'

It is difficult to estimate the proportions of Japanese-derived and English-derived lexemes, because the mixed language itself is not always seen as a coherent and independent system by its speakers, but often as simply the "mixing of English and Japanese." (See section 11.6 on language attitudes.) Moreover, there is a continuum ranging from this mixed language to standard Japanese in the one direction and to a nonmixed variety of English (more basilectal or acrolectal depending upon the individual speaker) in the other.

## 7.6. MORPHOLOGY

Words in OML basically undergo the same morphological changes that they did in the source languages. This being said, it should be pointed out that neither of the languages (Bonin English or Japanese) is morphologically complex in the first place. Japanese has, for example, no morphological alteration of verbs according to person or number, no singular/plural noun marking, and no gender classes. Thus, there is no subject-verb or adjective-noun agreement along any of these lines as there is in, say, European languages. On the other hand, Japanese does rely heavily on morphological alterations to express various other grammatical functions, and these features are seen in OML as well, including tense (ex. 27), negation (30), passives (29), and causatives (29). Aspect is another area in which morphosyntactic characteristics of Japanese have been carried over intact into OML, as seen in (30) in the forms *change sarete iru* 'has been changed' and *hashitte ita* 'was running'.

30. Ima   wa    mō,        CANOE  no  STYLE  ga        ne,  CHANGE
    now   TOP   already    canoe  of  style  NOM       FP   change
    sarete    i-ru        wake    desu  yo.  De,  dōshite-tte  yū
    do-PASS   be-PRES     NOM     COP   FP   and  why-QUOT     say
    to,  mukashi  wa      sail  de,  ho   de   hashitte  i-ta,
    if   past     TOP     sail  by   sail by   running   be-PAST
    PADDLE  de  koide   iku   desho. Demo,  ima  wa      ENGINE
    paddle  by  rowing  go    COP    but         now TOP engine
    ga      tsuite  iru   kara,    mō         sail  tsukawanai
    NOM     attach  be    because  anymore    sail  use-NEG
    kara     USE ENGINE EVERYTHING.
    because  use engine everything
    'Now, it's that the style of the canoe has been changed. What I mean is, they used to move by sail a long time ago, rowed by paddles, right? But now, because they have engines, they don't use sails anymore, they use engines for everything.'

Morphological inflections for English words are uncommon in OML, but this is probably not so much the influence of Japanese as it is of the other source language, Bonin Creoloid English, which, as we saw in the limited data of Jesse, had lost some of the mainstream English inflection. Singular and plural distinctions are not shown morphologically, as seen in (26) and (27).

English verbs used in prewar OML are simple words to describe high-frequency (in the lives of the islanders) actions, such as *sit down, shine, miss, slip, spear, lock, swing, cut*, and *change*. These are almost always used in their English unconjugated forms. English verbs are usually followed by the Japanese verb *suru* 'to do' conjugated according to mainstream Japanese grammar (e.g., *spear suru* in 28, *change sarete* in 30), although verbs are occasionally used without any overt tense and aspect marking, either from English or from Japanese.

English adjectives also run the gamut semantically, including such words as *barefoot, wrong, tough*, and *free*, but (unlike English verbs) are not made to adhere to Japanese grammatical rules. Those not found in predicate position tend to precede English nouns, as in *big typhoon, big book, good head, small boat, new language*, and *poor country*. As with the nouns seen above, the language of origin for verbs and adjectives does not seem related to any semantic categories. Though few in number, there are occurrences of English words modifying Japanese nouns using the structure employed with Japanese "nominal adjectives," as in *special na ki*. There are also cases of modifier + *no* + noun, as seen in (31).

31. Gran    no     papa    ga     ne…
    grand   GEN    father  NOM    FP
    'Grand father, you know…'

## 7.7. SYNTAX

Typologically, the two source languages could hardly have been more diverse. Japanese has basic SOV (subject-object-verb) word order, while Bonin English is SVO (subject-verb-object). Japanese has postpositions; Bonin English has prepositions. With other properties of the English component of OML that differ from mainstream English, it is difficult to determine if this divergence occurred during the formation of OML or if these divergent forms were already conventions of Bonin English. This is because we know so little about the exact linguistic nature of nineteenth-century Bonin English itself. For example, OML lacks a distinction between singular and plural noun marking and between definite and indefinite articles. Japanese also uses no number marking or articles, but this characteristic of OML seems not to result from Japanese interference, but rather to reflect the nature of Bonin English. Being a contact variety of English, it would come as no surprise that Bonin English itself lacked number marking and articles.

While we do see examples of plural -*s* and article usage in the OML and Bonin English data, their usage is highly variable and seemingly inconsistent. This is not to say that islanders cannot speak standard English—some can, and code-switching is common among standard Japanese, OML, standard English, and the twentieth-century incarnation of their local English.

In OML, free grammatical morphemes (such as particles) are basically from Japanese, although some English conjunctions are to be found in the data. English words are generally limited to lexical morphemes. We do not find grammatical categories being transferred, as revealed in the fact that English pronouns and verbs do not undergo modification (case changes, conjugation) as they would in mainstream varieties.

The issue of syntax, particularly the source language of word-order rules, is a critical one in the identification of a mixed language. OML is generally constructed around Japanese sentence structure. English word order is also frequently found at the phrase level, however, when English lexemes are used, as with expressions like *last Sunday*. Moreover, in (20), "I go cemetery chotto," English word order (SVOAdv) is used for the entire sentence. In Japanese, not only would the object procede the verb, but the adverb would most likely precede the predicate, and the subject would be omitted (at least in the unambiguous context in which this particular sentence was produced), yielding (S)AdvOV. Although this sentence stands out among the data here for its adherence to English word order (not only for the English morphemes, but for the Japanese adverb as well), we have no compelling reason to consider this sentence as unique and may well encounter other examples in further data collection.

The language components of OML are simplified in comparison to their source languages. First, we find that several of the many subsystems of Japanese are missing. In particular, we see that OML (1) lacks alteration in the formality levels of personal pronouns, (2) lacks formal verb endings (*teineigo*), and (3) lacks honorific (*keigo*) forms of verbs, adjectives, pronouns, or other words.

These differences from mainstream varieties of Japanese are more profound than speakers of a language such as English may appreciate, since English expresses politeness in subtler and less grammatically structured ways. Japanese has a personal pronoun system that is bound up in the honorifics and politeness systems. Whenever speakers choose a first-person pronoun, they are positioning themselves in relation to their listener, exhibiting distance or familiarity, arrogance or humility, and so on. There is no default "neutral" pronoun that allows speakers to avoid this social positioning, just as there is no "neutral" form to express number in English; nouns are either singular or they are plural. Similar statements could be made about the usage of informal/formal and nonhonorific/honorific verb forms. The fact that these grammatical components of style-shifting were not among the features of Japanese requisitioned for this mixed language may be related to the egalitarian mindset of the original Westerner speakers. It is also true that these markers of formality and respect were less important in the closed society in which OML has long been used. The usage of English pronouns in OML may also result from Westerner speakers' attempts to eschew this kind of social positioning altogether.

Second, the English components of the mixed language are also simplified compared to mainstream varieties of the language. This simplification is seen in (1) the simplification of verb tense and aspect forms, (2) lack of articles, (3) lack of subject-verb agreement, (4) lack of case marking in personal pronouns, and (5) lack of singular plural distinctions. However, these simplifications do not seem to have occurred as a result of the two component languages combining to form OML. Rather they reflect the nature of the English component itself.

We must not forget that OML is not the result of the intertwining of mainstream Japanese and mainstream English, but of

Ogasawara Koiné Japanese and Bonin Creoloid English. This is not to say that OML has not been influenced by mainstream varieties of English. It has, and the influence of standard (or at least mainstream varieties of) English is recurrent throughout the islands' 130 years of linguistic history. We saw evidence in chapter 5 of Uncle Charlie's code-switching between a basilectal island variety and an acrolectal mainstream variety. We will see some of the influences of standard English (or at least noncontact varieties of mainstream English) subsequently in chapter 10 on the postwar variety of OML (e.g., use of expressions like *chotto pissed off shiteiru* 'to be a little pissed off'). The influences of standard English on these varieties are comparable to the processes of decreolization.

# PART IV
# NAVY PERIOD

# 8. SOCIOHISTORICAL OVERVIEW: ENGLISH DURING THE U.S. NAVY PERIOD

In CHAPTER 7, WE EXAMINED the prewar situation of language intertwining. In chapter 9, we will see how this intertwining came into fruition during the Navy Era, but first we will examine the sociohistorical situation of English during that Navy period.

During the last days of the war, almost all of the civilian population of the islands was evacuated to the mainland. Following the war, the islands came under the jurisdiction of the U.S. Navy. The Westerners appealed to the U.S. military to allow them to return to the island. They had lived for decades without problems alongside their Japanese neighbors on the islands, but on the mainland, they had been the targets of ethnic hatred, and they wanted to return home.

In October 1946, only 135 islanders—Westerners and their ethnic-Japanese spouses—were allowed to return to the island. (This group was the bulk of the Westerners who had lived on the island prior to the war and their forced evacuation. Some Westerners chose to remain in mainland Japan, while a handful of others left Japan for Guam or the United States. It would be a quarter of a century before the ethnic-Japanese islanders would again be allowed to return to their homeland.) From 1946 to 1968, the entire chain of islands was a secret U.S. military installation, and no one (whether Japanese or U.S. citizen) save these "Western" islanders and the Navy personnel (and their families) assigned to oversee the area were allowed in or out of the region.

## 8.1. JAPANESE AND THE OGASAWARA MIXED LANGUAGE AS LOW LANGUAGES IN THE POSTWAR DIGLOSSIA (1945–68)

Ogasawara has a history of diglossia, but the high language used in formal contexts has changed several times in less than two centuries. With the postwar U.S. Navy occupation, the diglossic language situation on the islands saw a major turnover. In the early to mid-nineteenth century, the dominant language on the islands had been English, then had switched to Japanese for three-quarters of a century from 1870 to 1945. After the war, English again became the high language on the island. The population of the islands consisted of only 130 some-odd Westerners and (at most) a few dozen Navy personnel, their families, and a handful of American civilians they brought to the islands (the Japanese-American school teachers from Hawaii, a missionary, etc.). The one and only source of cash income on the island was the U.S. Navy, and those who desired such work (house cleaning for an officer or his family, asking the Navy to transport the fish one caught to Guam to sell for cash, etc.) had to be able to use English because the Navy personnel could not speak Japanese. English was also used in high (outgroup) domains, such as visiting the Navy doctor, church services (where Navy personnel mixed with islanders), school education, and so on.

## 8.2. ENGLISH LANGUAGE EDUCATION DURING THE NAVY ADMINISTRATION

A Navy report from the era (classified at the time but declassified since) contains some important facts about the sociolinguistic state of the island. Most of this information has been verified in my interviews with the islanders since 1997, so I have included several quotations here. Where the report includes misinformation, I make corrections.

[At the time of repatriation of the "Westerners" to the island in October 1946] Navy personnel marveled at the preservation of American traits in these people of American, British, Portuguese, Spanish, Polynesian and Japanese blood and the ability of the adults to speak English—a facility which had been cherished through the generations of Japanese rule. [Pesce 1958, 30]

Like the rebuilding of the island economy, education for the children at Chichijima got off to a slow start. In early 1947, Frank

Gonzales (1885–1987), younger brother of teacher and preacher Joseph, began teaching the 16 island children, aged 4 to 14 years. (Pesce erroneously states that they were father and son.) "The children first had to be taught English, as the use of that language had been forbidden since 1938" (Pesce 1958, 33). Another islander, Grover Gilley (1885–1957), also served as a volunteer teacher in this period. Children were discouraged from speaking Japanese at school but were not punished for it.

Frank Gonzales had attended a prestigious high school in Tokyo and, after graduation from Rikkyo University, had spent many years as a clerk with an English exporting firm in Tokyo.

He [Frank Gonzales] has an excellent command of the English language and was invaluable in getting the younger children, who spoke only Japanese, started in English. Following Mr. Gonzales' retirement, the wives of naval personnel and missionaries stationed on the island gallantly shouldered the educational load—without pay.... In 1955, a sum of $13,000.00 was included in the budget of the Naval Administration Unit on Saipan (SWON) for educational needs at Chichi Jima. This included the salaries of two young men recruited from Honolulu and school supplies. Robert Hashimoto and George Yokota, both graduates of the University of Hawaii arrived on 29 March 1956. Both young men were single, spoke Japanese and were born at Hilo, Hawaii. [Findley 1958, 74–75]

The report quotes from a semiannual report of the Military Government Representative:

The school system is staffed by two paid teachers and one volunteer (Mrs. Kell, wife of the Missionary) who conducts the kindergarten.
The school is organized into classes from grade 1 through grade 7 and closely follows the American school system curriculum and standards. The language barrier (Japanese spoken in some homes) has been completely broken down in school and is no longer a problem. Classes in agriculture are included in the curriculum. [Findley 1958, 75]

The Westerners formed a tight community and had no trouble communicating among themselves because they mixed the languages. Nonetheless, some speakers were more fluent than others in either (mainstream) Japanese or (mainstream) English or both.

Charles "Uncle Charlie" Washington tells of one of the Savorys who was summoned before the American army for questioning and asked Charlie to go along "to speak for him" (this occurred on mainland Japan after the war's end before the Western islanders were allowed to return). This could mean simply someone to collaborate his story or to come along for moral support, but the implication is that the Savory man did not feel as comfortable in English as Uncle Charlie seemed to be (Long 2001a, 80).

From the time that the U.S. Navy established a presence on the islands in 1952, the older Chichijima students began to go to American-controlled Pacific Islands to further their studies. The first were two girls who went to Saipan to study, but this was not successful and they returned home. In an April 1955 letter, Lt. Commander Clayton E. Frost, the ranking Naval officer on Chichijima, states that island boys become fishermen or farmers upon reaching the age of 14 and that the girls help with the housework (see Records Regarding the Bonin-Volcano Islands, U.S. Naval Historical Center Operational Archive, Washington, D.C., boxes 97–102). By the early 1960s, island children were going to Guam to attend junior high and high school (grades 7–12). In 1962, a seventh grade was established on Chichijima, and, as these students passed into higher grades, classes were extended through the ninth grade.

Upon completion of the ninth grade, island youngsters boarded a Navy plane to Guam (with brief stops in Iwojima and Saipan), where they lived with a Navy "sponsor" family and attended a local high school (George Washington High School and later John F. Kennedy High School). Sometimes there were two Chichijima teenagers to a household. Some of their classmates were the children of U.S. military personnel and some were local Chamorro. Classes were conducted completely in English.

Not all island teenagers went to school in Guam; a few went on to private English-language schools in Japan. Charles Savory and Hank Kokichi Washington, for example, attended St. Joseph's International School in Yokohama. Nobuo Webb attended International Christian University in Tokyo, a school which offers a bilingual Japanese and English education.

## 8.3. THE LANGUAGE ABILITIES OF WESTERNERS DURING THE NAVY PERIOD

There had been large individual differences in the levels of (standard) English proficiency among the Westerners raised during the prewar Japanese period. Postwar changes meant that some islanders had more trouble than others adjusting to this new life in which most daily affairs had to be conducted in English.

At the advice of the U.S. Navy, a five-member Island Council was established on Chichijima in 1946 and functioned until 1968. The *National Geographic* article written just before the reversion explains it as follows.

We attended a meeting of the island council, whose five members represent the Savorys, Gilleys, Robinsons, Webbs and other Chichi families. It reminded us of any small-town council in the States. [Sampson 1968, 130]

Meetings were reportedly conducted in English, but it seems that English may only have been used for the benefit of and in the presence of Navy overseers. In a Japanese article researched and written in the same period, one member of the Council complains that he (in spite of being a Westerner) cannot follow the English proceedings of the meetings.

Although the Council of Five position has been pushed off on me, I can't understand what's going on in the meeting at all. My wife who comes from Gumma [in mainland Japan] is even worse off than me. [Tamura 1968, 72; my translation]

It is important to remember that the man here is not saying that he cannot communicate in any language variety with his fellow councilmen—these are the people he was raised with and the prospect of him not being able to communicate with them is unthinkable—rather, he is saying that English is the language imposed as the medium of communication among islanders.

As mentioned previously, I telephoned Paul Sampson, author of the 1968 *National Geographic* article, on December 23, 1997, to ask him about his memories of his interviews. He said, "I had no communication problems with the people there. Some people didn't speak English at all, and I didn't have an interpreter, so I wasn't able to interview them."

As we have seen, there were differences among the linguistic abilities of the islanders. There are still age differences, namely that those raised and educated prior to and after the U.S. occupation are (in general, but not always) more adept at standard Japanese than at standard English. In addition, many anecdotal references indicate that, among those who had already reached adulthood at the beginning of the Navy occupation, the men were more adept at English than the women. This is primarily because the majority of the adult men living on the island during the U.S. occupation were ethnic-Westerners married to ethnic-Japanese women. Their wives had been allowed by the Navy to return to the island only because they were spouses of Westerners. In addition, all of the men were employed by the Navy either directly (as laborers) or indirectly (as fishermen selling their catch through the Navy). Most of the adult women did not work outside the home, thus limiting their opportunities for verbal interaction with the Americans.

## 8.4. THE LINGUISTIC REPERTOIRES OF INDIVIDUAL SPEAKERS

The English varieties spoken by the islanders varied widely along a continuum. In the case of the Bonins, however, this is not simply a continuum between a standard English acrolect at one end and a basilectal contact variety of English at the other, the postcreole continuum familiar to us in many creole situations. On the Bonins, we have not one but two acrolects (standard English and standard Japanese) and the Ogasawara Mixed Language (OML), a contact variety that contains features of both of them.

There are large individual differences among speakers. For example, as mentioned in section 4.6, Jerry Savory attended a private English mission school in Yokohama at the beginning of the twentieth century, while his cousin Able Savory (15 years his junior) attended public Japanese schools on Chichijima. Able maintained that his elder cousin's English was better than his own and credited the differences in their education as the reason (pers. comm., Sept. 24, 1997).

In figure 8.1, we provide a model of the linguistic repertories of individual speakers. Here, individuals have the basilectal OML as their first language. Speaker 1 represents the older and younger generations, those raised during Japanese rule prior to World War II or following the U.S. occupation; speaker 2 represents the middle generation speakers, those raised during the U.S. occupation. We could also posit a speaker 3, who has OML as his native tongue but has acquired proficiency in both of the acrolectal languages.

The horizontal width of the bars represents the likelihood of hearing these varieties on the Bonins. It can be interpreted as being the proficiency of an individual speaker or of a number of people on the island with this ability. Either of these interpretations gives us an equally appropriate (though rough) idea of the language situation. In other words, the fact that the bars get narrower and narrower as they proceed toward the acrolects means that we could expect the average speaker to have relatively decreasing proficiency, the closer one gets to the standard variety; at the same time, the number of people with such proficiency on the islands is only a portion of those who speak OML.

FIGURE 8.1
Usage of Island and Mainstream Language Varieties

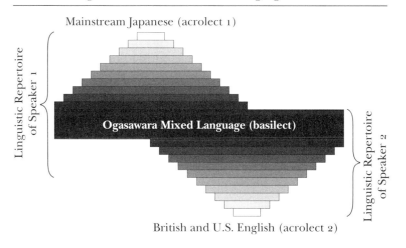

This acrolectal-basilectal situation is vastly different from that on other island communities, such as Norfolk Island. On Norfolk some speakers have a basilectal variety as their native tongue and switch into standard English; in these people's case, they have only one acrolectal variety, namely standard English, to negotiate. On Ogasawara, there are two standard languages to master and use: English and Japanese.

Within the code-switching practices of this society, OML is largely limited to more informal or private situations; in other words, it is the basilectal variety. The acrolectal varieties are those used in formal or public situations. In between these are infinite levels of mesolects. These related language varieties form something comparable to the typical postcreole continuum. In most postcreole continua, there is only one acrolect or high variety, but as the model here indicates, members of this community have both mainstream English and mainstream Japanese as acrolectal varieties into which they shift (or attempt to shift) when situational factors such as formality (or the language repertoire of the listener) require it.

The type of code-switching implied by the model in figure 8.1 is referred to in the discussion among Navy-generation islanders in (32). It is an excerpt from transcriptions of a discussion held on the tenth anniversary of the island's return to Japan, in which Westerners who were students at the time talk frankly about their language usage and abilities (Ogasawara Elementary School 1979). The translations are mine.

> 32. INTERVIEWER: By the way, at home, you were speaking Japanese, weren't you?
> A: At home it was Japanese. But it was not like the Japanese we are speaking now.
> B: To give the simplest example, we used Japanese like "omae" ['you'] and "mii" [Eng. 'me'] from the time we were children.
> INTERVIEWER: You can all speak English and Japanese as well. That's great.
> A: Our teacher K used to tell us, "You guys are pitiable because can't really speak English or Japanese." And it's true.

c: Our English grammar isn't right, so we can't write properly.

d: In that sense, we are the most "half-assed" [chūtohampa].

e: Now, at present, our Japanese and English comprehension is about half and half. With F and them, their English is a bit better than their Japanese. Because they had a longer time in English education than we did.

f: From the viewpoint of my generation, we are envious of E and those students who had more Japanese language education.

e: Those people older than F understand English perfectly.

f: But the tradeoff is that their Japanese is weak.

b: We received enough Japanese education to be able to read a newspaper. But the paperwork in everyday life, for example tax returns and things, whether or not we can effortlessly manage those, or expeditiously take care of paperwork that comes in at work or not, that's doubtful. Our generation may not be able to do that, but our children have been raised in a Japanese language society, so they don't have the problem of being half-baked. In all things, we just didn't have any leeway. This was different from [the situation in] Okinawa.

## 8.5. PACIFIC ISLAND INFLUENCES DURING THE NAVY YEARS

Contacts (linguistic and otherwise) with the nearby Pacific Islands did not cease with the end of Japanese rule but continued all throughout the U.S. Navy occupation because, like the Bonins, the other "South Sea Islands" of the Japanese Empire (Saipan, Ponape, Yap, Truk, Palau, etc.) also passed to U.S. rule. Several adults went to Guam or Saipan for short periods to work or receive training in various vocations, and children of high school age attended school there. In their time on Guam or Saipan, Bonin Islanders had not only superficial contact with Austronesian languages, but, unlike some members of the prewar generation who had learned a little Chamorro during their stays on Saipan, Chichijimans of this generation learned only a few phrases of the language. More important was their contact with Micronesian varieties of English, because people from various Pacific islands (Palau, the Federated

States of Micronesia, the Phillipines) lived on these islands (as they do today).

As mentioned earlier (in sections 3.7 and 3.8), most of today's Bonin Islands words not of Japanese nor English derivation originated in Oceanic languages. Those of Hawaiian origin appear in written sources from the nineteenth century; those of Chamorro origin do not. (For English sources see, for example, Hawks 1856, Robertson 1876, Van Buskirk 1898; for more thorough listings see Nobushima 1998.) This is despite the fact that the Bonins had extensive contact with both Saipan and Guam in the era before the Japanese; European and American settlers made trips back and forth to these islands, and influential settlers (such as Nathaniel Savory's wife Maria delos Santos) were themselves Chamorro. Chamorro words apparently entered the island either before the war, when Saipan and the Bonins were both part of the Japanese empire and both people and products moved between the two islands, or after the war, when islanders traveled to Guam or Saipan for education, training, and work.

Some examples of Chamorro words thought to have entered Ogasawara speech during the twentieth century are listed in table 8.1.

TABLE 8.1
Oceanic Words Thought to Have Entered Ogasawara Speech
in the Twentieth Century

| Bonin Word | Meaning on the Bonins | Proposed Etymology (original meaning when different) |
| --- | --- | --- |
| guiri | 'gray chub, *Kyphosus bigibbus*' | Chamorro *guili* 'species of chub' |
| kankon | 'water spinach, *Ipomoea aquatica*' | Chamorro *kankong* |
| shiikamba | 'yam bean, *Pachyrhizus erosus*' | Chamorro *hikamas* |
| tagantagan | 'white popinac, *Leucaeana leucocephala*' | Chamorro *tangantangan* |

# 9. "NAVY GENERATION" BONIN ENGLISH

## 9.1. REPORTS OF SPOKEN ENGLISH IN THE 1960S

Throughout the U.S. Navy occupation, the islands were isolated, greatly limiting linguistic contact with the outside. Records at the Navy Historical Archives in Washington, D.C., indicate that at least one American journalist and a researcher from the University of Hawaii applied for permission to go to the island and were refused.

Even if linguists had been aware of the island's unique situation and applied to the U.S. Navy for permission to do a linguistic survey in this era, they undoubtedly would have been turned down. At any rate, there is little linguistic data from this period.

The first (and to my knowledge the only) outside journalists allowed on the islands between the end of World War II and the reversion were the *National Geographic* staff writer Paul Sampson (mentioned previously) and his partner, photographer Joe Munroe of *Life* magazine. This was in December 1967 and January 1968, when the islands were on the verge of being returned to Japanese control.

Sampson's article contains a statement concerning the islanders' English that is confusing in light of other firsthand accounts we have seen about the early nineteenth century. Note the following, for example, from Nat Savory born in 1908.

The Yankees who grew up on Chichi before the war attended Japanese schools, but learned English in their homes, "I had to speak English to my father or he would beat me," recalled Nat Savory, a great-grandson of the original Nathaniel. [Sampson 1968, 130]

The father mentioned here was raised by parents who were both Westerners. Nat's mother had also been raised by a Westerner father (albeit with a Japanese mother). On the one hand, his statement shows that speakers of his generation (born three decades into the Japanese era) still grew up speaking English. On the other hand, it shows that there was a tendency for them to use Japanese as well—to the extent that they had to be disciplined to prevent them from doing so.

Sampson's statement here reinforces what we have seen about diglossia. However, Nat's account of being beaten for not speaking English to his father implies that the diglossic situation was in a state of flux at this time and that the social domains in which Japanese was used (school, workplace, church) were expanding to include the home.

Here, Nat explains that he was forced to use English in the home in the prewar period of Japanese occupation when he was a youngster and indicates what we have already seen about Japanese as the language used at school and at other public situations. Ironically, this situation seems to have done an about-face, however, during the Navy occupation. For, it is recorded that the Navy-employed schoolteachers had to prohibit the island children's usage of Japanese within the school and, in fact, punished offenders. We can hardly imagine a need for the Navy to prohibit the use of Japanese if children had not shown an inclination to use Japanese—and this, during a period when the islanders had been almost completely isolated from outside Japanese contact for over two decades.

Let us now turn to some other references regarding the speech of today's elderly islanders who were raised before World War II. A Japanese journalist who visited the islands just after their return to Japan, a time when ordinary Japanese private citizens were still not allowed on the island, talked to the head of the fisherman's cooperative (a Westerner), who reported that his children corrected his English, chiding him for his pronunciation of *two* /tu/ comes out like [tsu] (Tamura 1968, 72). Incidentally, the Japanese language has [tsu] but not [tu] phonemically, and this comment may be interpreted to mean that the then middle-aged man, although a Westerner, pronounces English *two* as [tsu] as a result of interference from his first language (Japanese). This man was born and raised in the pre–World War II era and was educated entirely at Japanese-run schools on the island, like any Japanese child. His children, while most certainly able to speak the same koiné Japanese as he spoke, indeed probably having it as their first language, were educated in postwar U.S. Navy–administered schools and thus had more exposure to, and presumably a better command of, a standard-like English acrolect than their father.

The actual structure of older and middle-aged speakers' English was probably influenced very little by the Navy personnel, although they may have picked up new English expressions and actually used the language more often in daily life. However, because of their young age, we would expect the influence of the Navy on younger speakers to be much greater.

## 9.2. EXAMPLES OF WRITTEN ENGLISH FROM THE LATE 1960S

Here I would like to consider the question of how well young island-ers during the Navy Era could speak mainstream (standard-like) English. As children grew into teenagers and adults, they had more exposure to standard varieties of language (standard English, stan-dard Japanese) through education, travel to Guam, increased con-tact with U.S. Navy personnel, and so on, but younger children's speech—before they experienced these external influences—should reveal more about the children's first language and in turn about the community vernacular.

Regrettably, there are no sound recordings of the children speaking during the Navy Era. We can interview these same speak-ers today (and indeed data from speakers of this generation—now middle-aged—are included in this book), but it would be informa-tive to know what their speech sounded like before they had under-gone several years of English education and subsequent decades of speaking English (intermittently in the case of those who remained on the island, daily in the case of those who moved to the United States).

One of the only glimpses we have into the English of children during the Navy time is in the form of some sentences written as class assignments. The sentences in (33) are taken from handwrit-ten compositions that third- and fourth-grade elementary school children wrote immediately after the education system switched to

Japanese in the summer of 1968. Some of the children did not do the assignment, turning in pages with only their names written. Most compositions consisted of only two or three sentences. All seven of the children below had Western fathers and Japanese mothers.

33.  a.  I think that I will ball / Im going to play witt [English-speaking father and Japanese mother]
     b.  I am W my sisters name is X an my Brothers name is Y an my Father's names is Z. [Japanese-speaking Westerner father and Japanese mother]
     c.  I have 1 sister and 1 Brother. and my sister name is X and my Brother names is Y. [English-speaking father and Japanese mother]
     d.  I felt lonely when I came to this new Japanese school because the teacher was new. I felt lonely when my Navy friend were gone. One of my classmade are gone to state. [semi-English-speaking father and Japanese mother]
     e.  I felt lonely. When navy was gonE. When I came to the new Japanese school becuase the teacher was new. I felt lonely When my navy friend were gone. one day I felt very lonely [English-speaking father and Japanese mother]
     f.  I was play with toy one day houes with X. [English-speaking father and Japanese mother]
     g.  Read It quietly. Dear Teacher, I feel like I am alone Today So I am going fishing Today and If I caught 7 Fish I will bring It to Teacher. you could fry the fish and eat It. All my family feels fine and Good. yesterday I went swimming with my sister. [English-speaking father and Japanese mother]

These compositions may be seen in two opposing manners. One is that the children make "mistakes" in English that native children would not, in the (lack of) distinction between plural and singular, for example.

On the other hand, the sentences seem remarkably close to mainstream English to have been written by children who acquired English only after entering school; these children's English is certainly more naturally constructed than that of Japanese students even at the college level. The sentences also—while containing deviations from standard English—are not what we would expect from children whose mother tongue is a true creole (as opposed to creoloid) variety of English. For example, we find "complex sentences" using relative clauses and subordinate conjunctions: "I think that I will…"; "I felt lonely when…"; "I feel like I am…."

I contend that these children were able to learn to write natural-sounding English after only a short period of schooling because they were not starting from scratch but had knowledge of English words and phrase-level grammatical structures from their ability to speak the Ogasawara Mixed Language (OML).

Before pursuing this line of thinking, however, let us analyze, in more detail, the ways in which the children's linguistic ability differs from mainstream English.

The writer of (33b) uses the possessive -*s* in "sisters name," "Brothers name," and "Father's name." Of course, there are discrepancies in his use of accepted punctuation practices, but these are insignificant to the argument at hand. On the other hand, writer (33c) does not use the possessive -*s* at all ("sister name," "Brother name").

There may indeed be interpersonal variation in plural -*s* as well, but in the data of three individuals here, plural -*s* does not appear. Writer (33f), "I was play with toy," would have plural -*s* in standard English. Writers (33d) and (33e) both use the same sentence "my Navy friend were gone," and (33d) also uses "one of my classmade are gone to state."[6] Here, *state* signifies 'the (United) States' and would be plural in standard English. This sentence differs from standard English in complex ways. The grammatical subject of the sentence is *one*, so the standard verb would be *is*. However, in this construction, *classmate* would be plural. If the student had written *one of my classmates are*, the sentence (although incorrect as standard English) would at least have been an easy "error" to analyze because of the *classmates are* agreement. But, rather we find that the writer (in spite of using the singular *classmate*) has used the plural form of the verb *are*.

There are places where definite articles are missing. In (33e) we find "When navy was gonE," which would of course be *the navy* in standard English. What is more, writer (33d)'s "one of my classmade are gone to state" would be *the states* in standard English. On the other hand, not all of the definite articles are missing. Writers (33d) and (33e) both use the same sentence (possibly one was copied from the other) containing *the teacher*. This shows that the students sometimes used (correctly) the definite article but not consistently.

There are usages of nouns and pronouns that differ from standard English. Writer (33g) writes "If I caught 7 Fish I will bring It to Teacher. you could fry the fish and eat it." The *Teacher* here obviously refers to the child's own teacher, the intended reader of the classwork composition. Standard English would simply use the pronoun *you* here (which interestingly the student does in the following sentence); the use of *Teacher* is ungrammatical in English. In Japanese, however, using a pronoun for a person in a higher position (as from a student to a teacher) is improper. It appears that this is a case of a transfer or of interference between the two competing acrolects (standard English and standard Japanese). Possessive pronoun usage is also different from standard English. Writer (33f)'s "I was play with toy" would probably be *with my toys* in English.

There are differences from standard English in verb tense and modality. With "If I caught 7 Fish I will bring It to Teacher," writer (33g) is talking about an uncompleted (future) action in the subordinate clause; in standard English the nonpast form *If I catch*. In the main clause as well, the subjunctive voice would be used in standard varieties of English, yielding *I would bring it*. Writer (33f)'s sentence "I was play with toy one day" describes an action in the past and would be simply the past-tense *played* or (depending upon the exact meaning) the past-progressive *was playing* in standard English.

The above deviations from mainstream English notwithstanding, one is left with the impression that these third- and fourth-grade children had more than merely classroom exposure to English. All of these particular child writers had fathers from either completely or at least partially "Western" backgrounds. All had ethnically Japanese mothers and most of those from mainland upbringings.

Regarding the home language used in these days, we find different reports. Interviews with islanders (given in more detail in section 10.2.4) reveal that some households "mixed" Japanese and English, while others report using Japanese. It is important that we not forget the role of older children in the linguistic development of younger children, however, and interviews also reveal that children were using OML from the early days of the U.S. Navy administration. It is also important to remember that OML incorporates not only English at the individual word level, but entire phrases as well—and in doing so, incorporates phrase-level grammar as well.

For contrast, let us examine a longer composition by a junior high student, written in roughly the same period (Sept. 1968) as the examples in (33) from the younger children. We see enormous differences in the English usage in the two sets of data. If we ignore a few orthographic quirks (e.g., misspelling of "aboard," all capitals in "ZOO"), the writing is mainstream English.

34. School Excursion, Eighth Grade

> The ride on the monorail to Haneda Airport was exciting and The airport was very big and beautiful. I was very glad that I was able to go abord the huge ship at I. H. I. [Ishikawajima-Harima Heavy Industries] The N. H. K. Broadcasting Center was one of the most beautiful places I have seen. The Tokyo Metropolitan Children's House was a very happy place. I had a good time playing with the children. The three schools we visited were the places I like the best during the excursion. The students were all nice and kind to us and I am very thankful.
>
> Kodama was very fast and very comfortable. Atami and Hakone were both unforgettable places.
>
> I felt like I was at home when I was at Ueno ZOO because everyone looked happy and the place was noisy.
>
> Mitsukoshi was a very big store but I like shopping at smaller department stores and putting more time on my shopping. The place where we stayed during the excursion was a good place. The Kuroshio rocks too much and I don't like it. [Someya and Toshiyuki 1972, 164–65]

In general, we find that young islanders' English grows more similar to mainstream English as they progress through their education (as one would expect). Nonetheless, differences among individual speakers cannot be trivialized. In June 1969, one year after the reversion to Japanese authority, Ogasawara High School gave students a questionnaire regarding their plans following graduation. They were asked to write whether they wanted to seek employment on mainland Japan or on the island and the reasons for their choice.

35. a. The reason is that I like by myself away from my parents so that I can stand on my two feet. And also I like to work among lots of people and make a living myself. [checked "employment on mainland"]

    b. It will be much easier for me, for I doesn't understand Japanese too well. [11th grade; circled "employment on island"]

    c. I'll go to the mainland for room and board at the relative's, to work by night and to attend a night school by night for another try at an entrance exam. [circled "mainland"]

    d. Because of the language barrier. [circled "island"]

    e. Working on the Japanese mainland means working in a new environment, which means having difficulties and troubles. Nope, I rather work on this island. [circled "island"]

Although this is precious little data, it is all the written English from young people of this era that we found, and more importantly, it points in the same direction: island children DID learn English as a second language, but they did NOT learn it as a completely foreign language because of the English component of OML, which they had acquired naturally before entering school.

Aside from the English used in these short compositions, we should briefly note the content as well. We see that the young islanders had an uneasiness about the prospect of living and working or studying in mainland Japan. While not specifying language as a problem, the writer of (35e) mentions "difficulties and troubles." Others are more overt about the source of their prospective difficulties, as when writer (35b) says, "I doesn't understand Japanese too well," and writer (35d) remarks that he prefers the prospect of staying on the island "because of the language barrier."

Thus far I have contended that mainstream English was (while not totally alien) a second language to island children of the Navy

Era. One could challenge my claim that OML was the children's first language, and ask whether island children were not simply native speakers of Japanese learning L2 English the same as millions of mainland Japanese children. But there is much evidence to support that NEITHER English NOR Japanese were native tongues of this generation, but rather languages learned later.

We find evidence in the comments of the high schoolers above, who write of not being able to understand (mainstream) Japanese well enough to get along in mainland Japan. In published sources as well, we find references to contradict the idea that young islanders were proficient in mainstream Japanese. In the 1968 *National Geographic* article written on the eve of the turnover of administrative power from the U.S. Navy to the Japanese government, the author writes, "Isaac Gonzales … teaches children Japanese to prepare them for the return to Japan's sovereignty" (Sampson 1968, 130).

While it is true that some of Gonzales's job was instruction in reading and writing, interviews with islanders (including Isaac himself) confirm that these classes also involved spoken Japanese. An analysis of the Japanese language proficiency of this generation is beyond the scope of the present volume, but I have examined essays written in Japanese by young islanders just after the return to Japan in 1968 (Long 1998a). The conclusion from analyzing these compositions was that they exhibited numerous features of nonnative Japanese. As we will see in more detail in chapter 10, the children raised during the Navy Era acquired a mixed language first and learned mainstream Japanese and mainstream English later (if ever).

## 9.3. LANGUAGE VARIETIES INFLUENCING THE BONIN ENGLISH OF THE NAVY GENERATION

The English spoken by the Navy generation is an interesting mix. Language varieties that contributed to its formation or influenced it include the following:

NINETEENTH-CENTURY BONIN CREOLOID ENGLISH: This was the first language of most of the Navy generation's grandparents, and so they have at least passive abilities in this variety.

PREWAR VARIETY OF THE MIXED LANGUAGE: This was the first language of many of the Navy generation's parents, and the language most of the Navy generation themselves give as their home language when they were growing up.

POSTWAR VARIETY OF THE MIXED LANGUAGE: This is the first language of most (if not all) of the Navy generation themselves. It should be reiterated here, however, that most prewar and postwar OML speakers see themselves not so much as speaking a mixed language, but as "mixing Japanese and English." (For significant exceptions to this, i.e., views that they were speaking a unique mixed language, see chapter 10.)

HAWAIIAN ENGLISH: This was the variety spoken by the civilian schoolteachers brought from Hawaii by the Navy. These people had a great influence on the English of the Navy-era children.

VARIETIES OF U.S. ENGLISH: Navy personnel, their wives, and their children would have brought the dialects of their various home regions to the Bonins and thus exposed the islanders to a range of U.S. dialects. These people were the principle outside sources of English for adult Bonin Islanders during this period as well.

GUAMANIAN ENGLISH: Most of the postwar generation of Bonin Islanders went to Guam to attend high school (a few went to Saipan). There they were in contact with U.S. Navy teenagers as well as locals.

VARIETIES OF JAPANESE: Several of the mothers and a few of the fathers of the Navy generation were ethnic-Japanese people who came from a variety of dialect regions in mainland Japan including Niigata, Tochigi, and Okinawa. Not all of the ethnic-Japanese brides and grooms brought from the mainland during the Navy period were mainlanders. There were also ethnic-Japanese who

had been born on the island before the war and who returned during the Navy period to wed Westerner spouses. These spouses of
Westerners were the only ethnic-Japanese who lived on the islands
for the quarter century from 1946 to 1968.

## 9.4. FEATURES OF THE BONIN ENGLISH
## OF THE NAVY GENERATION

Talking with the Navy-generation Bonin Islanders today, one can
hear traces of the language varieties that influenced their postwar
Bonin English. Consider some consonantal features. The Navy generation speakers make a phonological distinction between /l/ and
/r/, something that older AND younger speakers cannot do. Speakers raised in the prewar period (as this generation's own parents
usually are) often lack a distinction between /l/ and /r/ because they
are (even when bilingual) linguistically Japanese-dominant. Speakers raised postreversion (as Navy generation speakers' younger siblings or children often are) often lack this distinction for the same
reason.

Now it is true that the Navy generation's grandparents, like
Uncle Charlie, had an /l/-/r/ distinction, but the question is: did
the Navy generation simply reach back in time and resurrect the
Bonin Creoloid English of their grandparents' generation? The
answer is no. The English (and here I mean the English-only code,
as opposed to the English component of OML) spoken by the Navy
generation is NOT simply the results of them teasing back apart the
English and Japanese components that had become intertwined
in the early twentieth century. We can see phonologically, for
example, that they commonly have *th*-stopping when they speak
OML, but only rarely when they speak the English-only code. Furthermore, Navy generation speakers are rhotic when they speak
English, pronouncing /r/ after vowels as in *park* and *over*. This distinguishes them from their parents and younger siblings, who had
more Japanese influence, but also from their grandparents' generation, whose speech still retained the nonrhoticity of the original
settlers.

In general, Navy-generation speakers have /v/ distinct from /w/, but one does hear the influence of nineteenth-century Bonin English in their occasional use of [β] for /v/ in words like *reversion* [ɹiβɚ·ʒən] and *Virginia* [βɚ·dʒɪniə] (section 10.3.1).

Navy generation speakers have mainstream U.S. English vowel distinctions, including the CAUGHT/COT distinction (which is being lost in some varieties of U.S. English). Unlike mainstream U.S. English, however, they have long vowels rather than diphthongs in pronunciations like [se:] rather than [sei] for *say* and [bo:t] rather than [bout] for *boat*—a trait which they share with Uncle Charlie. They do have diphthongs for [ai] as in *bike* [baik].

Lexically, twentieth-century Bonin English shares much with U.S. English, such as *mad* 'angry' and automobile vocabulary, which entered via the U.S. Navy. Perhaps the most striking feature of twentieth-century Bonin English is the vocabulary not found in other varieties of English, such as *moe-moe* 'fornication', *arahii* 'species of fish', *biide-biide* 'species of tree', *nuku mome* 'a species of fish', *piimaka* 'raw fish cured in vinegar' (table 3.5); *jumpa* 'hermit crab' (table 4.1); *reefer* 'refrigerator' (section 5.5); *kiikii* 'species of bird' (probably onomatopoeic in origin), *wilowilo* 'species of bird' (etymology unknown), and *dongara* 'to miss a target' (from a Japanese whaling term).

Grammatically, when Navy-generation speakers use OML, they do not distinguish clearly between definite and indefinite articles or between the singular and plural, but in their "English-only" code, these distinctions are grammatically close to standard English (with, understandably, some interference from their first language, OML).

So historically it is correct to say that English was declining in usage during the 1920s and 1930s, but it received a shot in the arm from U.S. Navy personel postwar and made a comeback. That being said, postwar English on the Bonins was NOT simply nineteenth-century Bonin Creoloid English resurrected. Rather, postwar Bonin English should be seen as having several sources: Bonin Creoloid English and varieties of U.S. English (particularly Hawaiian English, but also Guamanian English and many various U.S. mainland varieties).

# 10. POSTWAR OGASAWARA
# MIXED LANGUAGE

## 10.1. THE POSTWAR OGASAWARA MIXED LANGUAGE

Up to this point, we have examined the original English dialects brought to the island, how they "mixed" with the many other languages brought in by first-generation settlers, and finally how this mixture resulted in a creoloid variety of Bonin English, that is, a variety not exhibiting the drastic grammatical restructuring seen when pidgins nativize into creoles but nonetheless showing various non-native (i.e., contact-based) features. Furthermore, we saw (chapter 4) how, with the arrival of Japanese in the latter nineteenth century, the original islanders began to become bilingual.

I examine this language intertwining and the subsequent language system that grew out of it from the standpoint of what Bakker and Mous (1994) call "mixed language." This phenomenon has been given other names (section 10.5), but here I will retain their original term.

First, I examine the historical context of multilayered language contact which gave rise to the Ogasawara Mixed Language (OML). Next, we observe structure with examples from the lexicon, morphology, syntax, and phonology. Then, factors relating to the genesis of the mixed language are also examined, including bilingualism, first-language acquisition, the active role of children, code mixing, and language death. I analyze social and interactional factors such as intelligibility, the attitudes held both by and toward users of OML, and also the identities of the speakers. Finally, I speculate on the future of OML.

## 10.2. GENESIS OF OML

We begin by contemplating possible factors associated with the formation of OML. Research by scholars such as Bakker and Mous has identified several possible explanations for the genesis of mixed languages, and to facilitate comparison between Ogasawara and similar mixed languages, I will deal with these possibilities individually.

First, we examine OML in relation to processes in language death. Second, we consider the role of second-language acquisition and bilingualism in the genesis of the OML. Third, we examine the possibility that OML originated in the mixed Japanese-Westerner households of the early or mid-twentieth century, as the children in these families acquired the mixed language as their first language. Fourth, we look at the possibility that the children of the mid-twentieth century created the language as some kind of group code used among themselves. Fifth, we examine the development of OML in a larger historical context, considering the possibility that it developed in the increasing bilingualism of late-nineteenth-century speakers, drawing upon Myers-Scotton's Matrix Language Turnover hypothesis. In the sixth section, I claim that (while code-switching was one of the processes involved in the initial genesis of OML) in its mid-twentieth-century form, OML is distinguishable from code-switching and code-mixing.

10.2.1. LANGUAGE DEATH. Language death processes have been identified as playing a role in the development of some mixed languages (Bakker and Mous 1994). Of course, neither Japanese nor English has ever been in danger of dying out on a global level, but to the members of the tiny community of Westerners, both languages have come under siege on several occasions. These pressures have had, at different times in their history, various and dramatic effects on language use.

The first language crisis came with the massive incursion of Japanese settlers who arrived in the 1870s and almost immediately vastly outnumbered the multiethnic band of islanders. The Japanese government, nevertheless, made surprising concessions to the naturalized islanders, and English was used for many years alongside Japanese as a medium of education. Many Japanese settlers even took advantage of their unique environment and encouraged their children to learn English. At any rate, English (in its Bonin form) was also maintained as the language of daily communication among the band of Westerners. The English language came under a more fierce and concerted attack in the years of increased militarization leading up to the Pacific War (World War II), when its use, even in private, was forbidden.

After the war ended and the Westerners alone were allowed to return to the island, the Japanese language became the target of contempt and suspicion by the occupying U.S. Navy. Almost all contact with mainland Japan was cut off, and U.S. English became the language of work (the Navy was the sole source of employment). Before the war, Japanese officials who heard language mixing had deemed it "English" because of its English components. Now after the war, Americans who heard OML considered it Japanese for the same reason. In the schools, children were punished for using Japanese. These various attempts from forces outside the spunky, resilient, and independent Westerner community to mandate its language usage may actually have fueled islanders' desire for their own unique way of speaking.

10.2.2. SECOND-LANGUAGE ACQUISITION. It is conceivable that OML originated in processes of second-language acquisition, as the generation of Westerners who naturalized in the 1870s struggled to acquire some rudimentary Japanese skills. However, this explanation would not account for the continued use of OML in subsequent generations. Moreover, although a possibility, no evidence at present indicates that second-language acquisition was responsible or relevant for the genesis of OML.

The home language of Westerners in the late nineteenth century remained Bonin English for several decades after the arrival of Japanese in the 1870s. Nonetheless, almost all Western children attended the bilingual schools established by the Japanese, and the islanders needed a knowledge of Japanese to work and maintain an active life on the islands. Thus, from the educational and social situation on the islands at the time, we know that younger Westerners were acquiring a high level of proficiency in Japanese as a second language (at least at the spoken level). These speakers were raised in an environment conducive to bilingualism, and the individuals about whom we have specific information were indeed bilingual.

OML may thus have been the result of these speakers beginning to mix the two languages.

This hypothesis nonetheless raises various questions. Why did the islanders not simply switch back and forth between the two languages? What purpose or benefit could the intertwining of the languages have served? What factors would have facilitated it? If English was decreasing in its importance in the community, then why did it not simply begin to disappear? The answers to these questions are tied up with the need for Westerners to retain their unique identity and will be dealt with later in this chapter. There is an even more confounding problem, however. OML has never been a contact language between the ethnic-Japanese and the Westerners. The language is used only among the Westerners, not by the ethnic-Japanese, and it has always been this way.[7] A paradox occurs here when we consider that OML is essentially a Japanese substrate language that is spoken by a non-Japanese group. Thus, when considering the genesis of the mixed language, we are faced with the question of why and how ethnic-Westerners could have "borrowed" grammar. In cases of language contact, it is generally the lexicon that is borrowed by a group that unilaterally creates a contact language, but in the case here, Westerners in effect borrowed Japanese word order, syntax, and grammatical morphemes. A possible explanation for this situation relies on the processes of syntactic convergence and Myers-Scotton's (1993) concept of the Matrix Language Turnover (MLT) model, especially as elaborated by Fuller (1996). The application of the MLT hypothesis to the situation of the Bonins will be examined in section 10.2.5.

10.2.3. FIRST-LANGUAGE ACQUISITION. In the literature on mixed languages, there are many cases of the new language being created by children or adolescents whose fathers and mothers speak different languages. Most significantly, it seems to be common for the mother's language to supply the syntax and the father's the lexicon (Bakker and Mous 1994). On Ogasawara as well, this seems to have been the case. After the incursion of Japanese settlers in the latter half of the nineteenth century, an increasing number of Westerners began to marry Japanese. Although this was true of both

Westerner men and women alike, the Westerner women often left the island when they married, whereas the men tended to remain on the island, whether their brides were raised on the island, in mainland Japan, or (in a few cases) in other countries. Because of this, households with an ethnic-Japanese mother and an ethnic-Westerner father became the rule rather than the exception by the early twentieth century. This situation continued throughout the mid-twentieth century. Even in the postwar era, male islanders sometimes journeyed to Japan (with U.S. Navy permission) to find wives, and indeed many children on the island during these days also were raised by a Westerner father and an ethnic-Japanese mother.

10.2.4. CHILDREN'S ROLE IN THE CREATION OF OML. An alternative to this theory, and one embraced by "Navy generation" informants, is that OML was developed by the children in these mixed households during the postwar U.S. occupation. Speakers who were elementary school children during the Navy era often speak of how they created the language.

Irene Savory Lambert (b. 1948) and Gail Savory Cruz (b. 1951), two Westerner women born and raised on the island during the Navy occupation, spoke (in English) to an American interviewer in the 1990s about their language use as children. (Plans to use these interviews as part of a larger project about the islanders never materialized, but the two interviewees provided me with their copies of the tapes to use in my research.) In the transcribed conversation below, they express the commonly heard belief here that it was the children of the Navy generation who are responsible for creating the mixed language.

36. INTERVIEWER: Did you speak both Japanese and English at home?

ISL: Uh-uh. (negative response)

GSC: Uh, no. Japanese was at home. English was at school. And when we played, it was all in Japanese, but some words were a mixture...

ISL: ...mixture of Japanese

> GSC: It was made up. It was just the words that island people
> would know, so that other Japanese wouldn't know what we
> were talking about. It came in handy, didn't it?
> ISL: Island lingo, which is a mixed, made-up word. We literally
> translated Japanese into English, but it's not found anywhere
> else.

This same conviction, that OML was created by the children, is seen in the comments of Stanley Gilley (b. 1948), a male contemporary of the women quoted in (36), who I interviewed on February 15, 1999. The interview was conducted in Japanese, albeit with a good mixture of English (translation is mine).

> 37. SG: There is a language that we made ourselves, us kids, among
> ourselves. Not the language that our parents spoke, not Japa-
> nese, and not English; our unique language that we made
> as kids when we talked among ourselves. I spoke it too. But
> then the reversion came and we forgot it. People who went
> off to America before the reversion still remember it and
> use it there among themselves to communicate. When they
> come back here and use it to me, I don't understand.
> INTERVIEWER: Because you forgot it?
> SG: Yeah. It's like Ainu talk, not understandable. I don't know
> what they're saying. And they say, "Don't be silly! It's the lan-
> guage you used as a child, isn't it?"
> INTERVIEWER: But doesn't it come back to you after 2 or 3 days?
> SG: Well, sometimes when my mind goes back to that situation.
> But I've practically been brainwashed [to speak proper Japa-
> nese].

Interestingly, language contact expert Sarah Thomason (2001), in an examination of the sociolinguistic circumstances under which mixed languages throughout the world have come into and remained in existence, promotes the theory that they are all conscious creations. She writes, "It seems that deliberate deci-sion … plays a prominent role in genesis of all bilingual mixed languages" (204)

Many of the postwar speakers who see their generation as the originators of OML do acknowledge that their parents used a mix-ture of English and Japanese in the home. (Some prewar speak-ers report their home language was Japanese, others English. Still others, however, have stated that their home language was "a mixture of English and Japanese" [Able Savory, pers. comm., Sept. 24, 1997]). Nonetheless, these postwar speakers contend that the mixture they used differed from that of their prewar-born parents. The existence of categorical or quantitative differences between these two codes remains to be seen. It is, however, clear that Westerners used some sort of mixture of the two languages even before World War II, and some speakers of this generation alive today still use a mixed language among themselves. In fact, the data presented in this chapter come from speakers of both the prewar and the Navy generation.

These facts notwithstanding, we cannot completely ignore the impressions of many (perhaps most) of the Navy generation that they themselves created the language as children. The explanation to this apparent paradox must be that the mixed language was in use long before World War II, but that during the Navy era it underwent a metamorphosis sufficient to make islanders see it as a different language variety. Nonlinguists' perceptions of speech variation have long been a topic of my research and I have learned that even minor differences in regional or intergenerational variation can be of major significance to the speakers themselves, even when they are of minor consequence to the linguist.

In many language communities, speakers of different generations perceive differences between their own speech and that of other age groups, even when linguists find these differences minute and insignificant. In the case of Ogasawara, it does indeed seem that there were changes in the language during the mid-twentieth century that came to have symbolic value for speakers on both sides of the generational divide. One such difference is the usage of the first-person English pronoun *me*, which is the most salient feature of the postwar incarnation of the language and inevitably the first characteristic mentioned, but which seems to be absent from the speech of prewar speakers. This was the case in Ogasawara as well: the mixed language existed before the war (probably from the turn of the century), but postwar speakers, who inherited OML from their parents' and grandparents' generation, made their own contributions to its form and structure.

10.2.5. MYERS-SCOTTON'S MLT MODEL. The model most beneficial in explaining the probable processes involved in the genesis
of OML is the MLT model designed by Carol Myers-Scotton. One
article that helpfully clarifies Myers-Scotton's theoretical stance is
Fuller (1996). I will outline the MLT model below, relying heavily
on Fuller's interpretation and application of it. I will show that it
is the most appropriate model of the sociolinguistic processes that
occurred in the Bonins.

Two crucial distinctions that Myers-Scotton makes in the MLT
model are those between System Morphemes and Content Morphemes and between the functions of the Matrix Language and
the Embedded Language. I will maintain these distinctions below.
The MLT model is for historical or temporal change in a language
system. We will follow it in chronological order.

1. There are three social environment factors conducive to convergence. These are found in the late-nineteenth- and early-twentieth-
   century Bonins.
   a. A minority language exists in a milieu dominated by another
      language. In the Bonins, English existed in a milieu dominated
      by Japanese. From the 1870s the Japanese population outnum-
      bered the Westerners, who became Japanese citizens. From
      1872, English was taught by Joseph Gonzales, first in school
      and later in private classes held in the church, but the fact that
      it had to be taught in this way demonstrates its auxiliary nature
      in the community.
   b. The minority language is an index of primary social identity of
      its speakers. English was an index of primary social identity of
      its speakers. Even non-British/American islanders used English,
      and they adopted a common identity which was expressed in
      and based on the usage of English. Reports in the pre-Japanese
      era unanimously state that the islanders were indifferent to reli-
      gion, but in the Japanese era, the church became central to the
      original islanders' lives. It was the one institution where they
      could use English.
   c. A minority language's speakers are geographically and socially
      distant from a standard, or at least more stable, variety of that
      language. English speakers were geographically and socially dis-
      tant from a standard or more stable variety of that language. It

is true that there was some contact with the English-speaking community in Hawaii in the mid-1800s. There was communication in English with Guam during these days in spite of the fact that it did not become a U.S. possession until 1898. There was contact later with English-speaking communities, individuals, and institutions in Kobe and Yokohama (Cholmondeley 1915). Nonetheless, it was several days' journey by ship to reach these places.

2. There is code-switching by bilinguals. We do not have detailed records of people code-switching in this era, but we do know that people were bilingual from the fact that many served as interpreters. This means they would have code-switched into Japanese when speaking to monolingual Japanese people and at school (at first in the non-English classes and later in all classes as English was phased out). We also have evidence of code-switching in the statements of islanders like fourth-generation speaker Nat Savory, who said his father would beat him if he did not speak English; this is a type of coerced code-switching.

3. There is borrowing (i.e., the use of dominant-language words even by monolinguals). This step predicts the use of Japanese words even by those who can speak only English, that is, cannot speak Japanese. This step is commonsense enough that it may not require much evidence, but we do have anecdotal evidence of this in comments like "Uncle Benjamin [Savory] couldn't speak much Japanese" (section 4.5).

4. Speakers of the minority language become bilingual in the dominant language without having complete social assimilation. ("Developments leading toward a turnover in the ML [Matrix Language] may begin when the speakers of a minority language become bilingual in the socially dominant variety, but do not assimilate to the culture associated with that variety" [Fuller 1996, 494].) Speakers of English became bilingual in Japanese without being completely socially assimilated into Japanese culture. They maintained their separate Westerner identity in spite of intermarriages with ethnic-Japanese. Westerner names were maintained in informal usage in spite of their officially adopting Japanese names. In the cases of several specific individuals, we know that they were bilingual because of extant tape recordings, interviews, reports from their children, the fact that they served as translators, etc.

5. When code-switching increases to the point that it is intrasentential, one language (called the Matrix Language [ML]) sets the morphosyntactic frame for language production. (The other language
supplies lexemes, and later phrases, and is termed to Embedded
Language [EL].) In the Bonins, the ML in this early stage would
have been English, because the intertwining would have begun
by incorporating Japanese words and phrases in English. Next, a
three-phase change occurs in the selection of the language used
for the ML, so that eventually Japanese is the ML.

a. There is intrasentential code-switching, but system morphemes
are still from the ML (i.e., English).

   i. Early borrowings are motivated by perceived lexical gaps.
Japanese lexemes were used within English sentences for
things like food items for which English words were not
available. Such lexemes (*geta* 'footware', *tako no ki* 'Pandanus
tree', *saki-shop* 'pub', *sen* 'currency', *jinrikisha* 'rickshaw') are
even found in the writings of a visitor like Van Buskirk, so we
may guess that islanders would have used even more of these
than a temporary resident.

   ii. Later, core borrowings from the dominant language (Japanese) increase.

b. Before completion of the turnover, there is the intermediate
stage of a composite ML. We know this was in existence by
the 1920s because speakers who grew up in this era, like Able
Savory and Jeffrey Gilley, used a composite ML when they spoke
to each other.

   i. Certain system morphemes enter from the dominant language. An example is the preponderance in modern-day
OML of the Japanese conjuctive particle *to* 'and', even when
joining English nouns.

   ii. There is violation of congruence requirements, resulting in
lexical-conceptual features and morphological realization
patterns from both ML and EL.

   iii. If the ML contains several structures in variation (e.g., word
order possibilities), structure most similar to EL constructions will be preferred. For example, the thought 'I don't
know what I should do' can also be expressed in English as
*What I should do, I don't know,* and the latter would be preferred since it is closer to the Japanese word order: *nani wo
shitara ii ka wakaranai.*

c. We find system morphemes from the new ML (the dominant language, Japanese) occurring with content morphemes from the former ML (the minority language, English) constituting a turnover in the ML. This is in essence what we find in OML today.

6. "The mechanism which accounts for convergence is the turnover of the ML in codeswitching" (Fuller 1996, 494). There was a complete turnover in ML, so that Japanese became the ML, and English supplied many of the content morphemes. We still find system morphemes (many conjunctions, pronouns, etc.) from English in the OML today, and these appear to be leftovers of the pre-turnover stage of OML.

7. The result we are left with is "convergence." "Convergence is defined here as the adoption of lexical and structural features from one language to another; thus, it includes, but is more than, lexical borrowing" (Fuller 1996, 494). Today the Westerners of Ogasawara speak a language variety that seems to have, in effect, "borrowed" its structural components from Japanese (at least this is how the situation appears when we consider that the language of the early settlers was a type of English).

Speakers of the Navy generation report that they spoke Japanese at home with both their parents and their siblings. Those interviewed recall (in numerous independent interviews) OML as something used only by their generation of Navy school children and not by their parents. Speakers who report this tend to be from homes in which one parent was a Westerner and the other was ethnic-Japanese. This seems to indicate that OML did gel and coalesce during the Navy years in the hands of the elementary-school-aged islander children. But we also find that some speakers of the prewar generation use a language which shows extensive mixing of lexical morphemes in essentially Japanese sentences. Intriguingly, these older speakers seem to be those married to other Westerners (such as Able Savory and Jeffrey Gilley), rather than to ethnic-Japanese.

We can thus hypothesize the following scenario. Prewar, the children of Westerner-Westerner households grew up hearing the language mixing of their parents and acquired this mixed language. Postwar, when other Western children who had grown up in monolingual Japanese-dominant environments entered the

Navy school and encountered English usage there, they had no aversion to mixing the two languages. Why the tendency for these speakers to mix rather than separate the two languages and code-switch? These children had playmates raised in Western-Western households where the languages were already being mixed. Thus, OML probably became more homogeneous and formalized in the hands of the Navy generation children, but the precedent for the extensive intertwining of the languages had already been set by the prewar generation of Westerners.

10.2.6. OML, CODE-MIXING, AND CODE-SWITCHING. Although code-switching and code-mixing are thought to have played a role in the initial creation of OML, the language as it has been spoken from the mid-twentieth century to today should not be viewed as simple code-switching or code-mixing.

OML differs in many significant ways from normal code-mixing or code-switching between English and Japanese. When Japanese code-mix, for example, they generally do NOT: (a) ignore honorifics (*keigo*), (b) ignore polite forms (*teineigo*), (c) use English pronouns, (d) incorporate English whole phrase structure, (e) use English phonology, or (f) use English counters. These are all significant features of OML.

With the use of English pronouns (c), we should point out that Japanese has certain expressions using English pronouns such as *mai kaa* 'my car' and *mai hōmu* 'my home', but these clearly differ from the productive and unmarked usage of some English pronouns in OML. Similarly, with the use of English counters (f), we find set counter expressions like *wan rūmu* 'one room' and *tsū doa* 'two door' in Japanese, but these clearly differ from the productive usage of English counters in OML.

Speakers of OML are not simply mixing English and Japanese together for the benefit of outsiders. Much of the data from Able Savory analyzed in this book was collected by a pair of researchers working together, a bilingual native-English speaker (Long) and a monolingual native-Japanese speaker. Knowing this, readers may be left with the impression that the mixing of words heard in the data do not reveal a coherent mixed language system at all, but rather haphazard attempts by speakers to make themselves more easily understood to a monolingual, outsider listener. The reality of the situation, however, is just the opposite, and several factors underlie my contention that the language intertwining seen here is NOT being performed for the benefit of the outsider listeners.

See, for instance, example (38) (first introduced in section 7.5 as example 22):

38. Mō    ato,    almost about five kilo    gurai,    go    kiro    gurai.
    More    left    almost about five kilo    about    five    kilo    about
    De,    sundown,    eh.
    CONJ    sundown    FP
    'With almost about five kilometers left—and then, sundown, you know.'

Here the speaker (despite the fact that the Matrix Language, i.e., language supplying the sentence structure, is Japanese) first uses the English *five kilo*, then translates this to *go kiro*. Throughout this interview, Able repeatedly performed this kind of "self-translation." In almost all cases of this, we find: Japanese sentence structure, English lexeme, followed by its Japanese equivalent. In other words, the initial English word is, for this speaker of OML, the naturally occurring form. The order of the two languages tells us that the inclusion of the Japanese equivalent is an afterthought. Thus, while the supplying of Japanese translations in these interviews is most definitely for the benefit of the monolingual Japanese listener, the intertwining of the languages (i.e., the use of the mixed language) itself is not.

A more significant and more striking factor here, though, is that outsiders usually do not get to hear this type of self-translation at all. The Westerners use "pure" Japanese when speaking to Japanese listeners and "pure" English (not necessarily standard, but without Japanese expressions interspersed) when speaking to English speakers. In fact, they pride themselves on their ability to do this and tease those of their group who are not good at code-switching from OML into Japanese or into English. Most are embarrassed about using OML; it is used mainly among themselves. Indeed, in the Able Savory interviews, the speaker started out speaking in "pure" Japanese, and only began to switch into the mixed language after he had had considerable time to warm up to the outsider interviewers. This is typical of my seven years of experience conducting linguistic interviews with the islanders, sometimes alone, but often bringing in graduate students and academic colleagues.

Finally, it is often when speakers become emotionally wrapped up in their topic that they begin to drift from Japanese or English into OML. In other words, these speakers tend to use OML under conditions similar to those identified by Labov and his colleagues for the use of the "vernacular"—among people one feels comfortable with or when one is paying the least attention to speaking "properly" (Labov 1972).

Let us look at the following bit of text from a conversation I had with Irene Savory Lambert (born 1948), Flora Webb (1947), and Rance Washington (1950). Irene is talking about the aftermath of the disastrous 1960 Chile Tsunami on Chichijima, when she was a kid and everyone was too busy with cleanup to play with her. This reminds Flora of a later disaster that affected her as a student on Guam.

> 39. IRENE: SONO TOKI ME SAD DATTA YO, ASOBENAKU NATCHATTA MONO, MINNA ISOGASHII KARA. ['I was sad at that time, not being able to play anymore, because everyone was busy']
> FLORA: NDE, GUAM DE TYPHOON KAREN. ['Then, Typhoon Karen in Guam']
> IRENE: Oh yeah, and then we got hit by Typhoon Karen.
> FLORA: *Iya Kowai!* ['Oh, how scary!']
> IRENE: That was 1960 and we went to Guam '62. The very first year. Was it? WE WENT IN AUGUST NO OWARI. ['We went at the end of August']
> FLORA: *Denki mo nani mo nai.* ['Without electricity or anything']
> IRENE: NOVEMBER NI. ['in November'] Ah, typhoon Karen. It was the worst typhoon Guam had had up until that point.
> INTERVIEWER: And you were there during the time?
> FLORA: Yeah. *Sō.* ['Right']
> RANCE: Couple of years ago, Guam got hit by a big one.

Let me clarify that I do not contend that there is no code-switching in the text above. On the contrary, I believe there is code-switch-

ing going on, and it is common for users of OML to code-switch
into English or into Japanese (especially in the case of speakers
such as Rance or Irene, who lived in the United States for many
years). But the code-switching going on here is not merely between
Japanese and English, but code-switching among three languages:
Japanese (italic), English (plain), and OML (small capitals). In the
case of single-word utterances ("Yeah. Sō."), the question of which
language is being used is an unproductive one to pursue, but the
longer utterances make my point.

It is also important to reiterate that the lines I have drawn
between OML and the other language varieties of the Bonins are
theoretical divisions drawn for linguists. In actual usage, these are
simply points along a continuum (or perhaps a couple of continua, one standard-nonstandard continuum with Ogasawara Koiné
Japanese and Ogasawara Standard Japanese as its poles, and one a
"mixed to nonmixed" continuum with OML positioned between
English and Japanese). Speakers do not see themselves as switching
between distinct linguistic codes, but rather as making adjustments
in their speech.

## 10.3. FEATURES OF THE POSTWAR OGASAWARA MIXED LANGUAGE

In this section we will examine some features of the postwar variety of OML. The data are taken from the following interviews:
Irene Savory Lambert, Flora Webb, and Rance Washington (Mar.
13, 2001); Stanley Gilley (Feb. 15, 1999); and Ethel Savory Pack,
Minnie Savory Heiney, and Irene Savory Lambert (May 4, 2004).
Although there are differences among individual speakers, I have
not found any clear differences among the different "families" on
the island, four of which are represented in these data. Although
such "family" distinctions are occasionally alluded to by the islanders themselves, such linguistic differences do not seem to exist; not
only did the islanders of any given generation grow up acquiring
language from all those around them (and not just their father
and mother), but many families consisted of, for example, a Savory

father and Washington mother or a Webb father and a Gonzales mother.

10.3.1. TWO PHONOLOGICAL SYSTEMS IN POSTWAR OGASAWARA MIXED LANGUAGE. The postwar OML makes a much clearer distinction between the phonological systems of the two source languages. By and large, elements of Japanese origin are pronounced according to that language's phonological rules and the same applies for English. For example, a three-way phonemic distinction is maintained among the English alveolar approximant [ɹ], the alveolar lateral approximant [l], and the Japanese alveolar flap [r]. There are, of course, a number of words that derive from Polynesian and other Pacific Island languages, and these words often have widely varying pronunciations. For example, the word *marane* 'lascivious, horny' (whose origin is a mystery) is heard as both [marane] with the Japanese flap and as [maɹane] with the English approximant. *Ufu* 'parrotfish' derives from the Hawaiian word *uhu*, and while is occasionally heard with an [h], the Japanese bilabial approximate [ɸ] is the more common pronunciation. The word for 'hermit crab' *fumpa* (probably derived from the Ponapean term *mpwa*) is heard with both [h] and [ɸ]. (The spellings I have used here are simply based on common usage on the island, which is not always easy to determine.)

There are some pronunciations in the OML that reveal the influence of nineteenth-century Bonin Creoloid English. An example is the pronunciation of /θ/ as [t], as we find on Chichi-jima in pronunciations such as [tri] 'three', [tætʃ] 'thatch (roof)', and [teːnk yuː] 'thank you'. The nonlabiodental pronunciation of /v/ that we saw in the speech of Uncle Charlie, born in the late nineteenth century, can still be heard today in the speech of Navy-generation speakers born more than a half century later. The mainstream variant [v] is overwhelmingly predominant in this generation, but nonetheless, I have specific examples of Flora Webb's pronunciation of *Virginia* as [βɚʤɪniə] and Johnson Washington's (b. 1948) pronunciation of *reversion* as [ɹɪβɚʤən].

We saw previously (sections 7.1 and 7.3) that islanders born prewar retained many more vowel distinctions than one would have expected from speakers influenced by an earlier contact variety of English or by Japanese (or both). But compared to the prewar generation, Navy generation speakers' vowel systems are much more similar to that of U.S. English. There is a clear and distinct [ɔ] vowel and thus nothing like the U.S. CAUGHT/COT merger. In the examples of OML below, I have opted not to give phonetic transcriptions. This is partly because the emphasis is on the intertwining of the two languages and the examples' glosses and translations are already complicated enough. But it is also because the phonology of OML is largely predictable and variants are relatively rare. I will, nonetheless, briefly outline the vowel system of the English component of OML, with words from the examples from following sections.

In addition to the five cardinal vowels that we find in the expected places, we find the following.

[ɪ]    *simple* (ex. 44), *Christmas* (48)
[ɪ]    (not [ɛ]) prenasally; *remember, twentieth* (47)
[ɪ]    (not [ə]) in some unstressed syllables; *twentieth* [twɪntiiθ] (47) and *luckily* [lʌkɪli] (not [twɪntiəθ] and [lʌkəli])
[ɛ]    *pregnant* (47), *decorations* (48)
[æ]    *glass* (40), *spam* (46)
[ɔ]    *long* (57)
[ʌ]    *just* (52), *but* (57)
[ɚ]    *sponsor, water* (40)
[ʊ]    *book* (54), *good*
[ɪɚ]   *here* (47), *years* (57)
[oɚ]   *door* (40), *forty* (57)
[e:]   (not [ei]) *taste* (44), *day* (49)
[u:]   *you* (43)
[o:]   (not [ou]) *no, clothes* (43)
[ɑ]    *lots* (43)

10.3.2. PERSONAL PRONOUNS. In the prewar OML, we saw limited usage of English personal pronouns (ex. 20), but postwar OML abounds with them, especially the first-person pronoun *me*. In fact, the use of this pronoun is the single most salient feature of OML. It is the feature that nonusers of OML (e.g., visiting tourists, the children of OML users) find most striking, and it is the feature most mentioned by both prewar and postwar islanders when the subject of OML is raised. Example (41) shows this use of *me*. The English paradigm of cases and "persons" (*I, me, my, mine, we, us, our, ours,* etc.) is not used; only *me*. Grammatical information about case is supplied as it would be in Japanese, by postpostional case particles as shown in (40) and (41). (The context of example 41 is given in example 58 in section 11.6.1.)

> 40. Me no sponsor no, anō, nan to yū no? Sono French door, anō glass door ga warete, water ga up to the knee datta.
> 'My sponsor's—that, what do you call it? Their French door, that glass door broke and water was up to the knee.'
> 41. Me wa chanto shinai to.
> 'Me, I have to do it properly.'

Plural meanings are shown by adding a Japanese "plural" suffix *ra* (and in rare occasions *tachi*) to *me*, as seen in the conversation on linguistic differences in (42). Japanese does not have a plural suffix that obligatorily attaches to all nouns, as in the case of European languages, but the form *ra* attaches to a few nouns and to most pronouns.

> 42. ETHEL: Me ra tabako suu to yuu ja. Nihon wa chigau. Tabako nomuto yuu darou. ['We say "inhale tobacco" right? Japan is different. They say, "drink tobacco."']
> IRENE: Nomu? No kidding? ['Drink? No kidding?!']

The second-person pronoun in postwar OML is either the English-derived *you* (as in 43) or the Japanese-derived *omai*.

> 43. Uchi no Mama wa no leg man mo mita-tsutta zo. Anoo, heitai no clothes kite. You no ojiisan too, he had lots of stories. 'My mama said she was even saw a one-legged man, uh, wearing army clothes. Your grandpa too, he had lots of stories.'

Third-person pronouns (in the English sense of the word) are uncommon in Japanese itself, with the person's name or expressions like *ano hito* 'that person' being used instead. In OML, we find these types of third-person expressions used rather than English pronouns such as *he, she, it,* or *they*.

A fascinating, and as yet unexplained, similarity exists with the Japanese used by Japanese-Canadians in Toronto. Hibiya (1995) reports that, like Ogasawarans, speakers in Toronto use first-person *me*, second-person *you*, but not third-person *he* or *she*. Another striking resemblance is in their formation of plurals using an English singular pronoun and a Japanese plural suffix (as in *me-ra* in 42) rather than the usage of English plural pronouns such as *we*.

10.3.3. NUMBERS AND CLASSIFIERS. Prewar OML showed a tendency for numbers and the classifiers (counter words) which accompany them to be of English origin; in postwar OML, this trend is almost categorical (as in 22 and 23).

44. Doushite me ga sukidatta no ne. Simple taste ga suki de, anmari amakunai shi. Tree ka four gurai no ingredients ga haitte nakatta. 'The reason I liked it was, I liked the simple taste, and not too sweet. There were only three or four ingredients'

45. IRENE: Are wa itsu taberu tabemono? Corned beef. ['When is it you eat that, corned beef?']
RANCE: It's Irish, is it?
IRENE: Yeah, yeah. Oh, it's, it's ano, are. ['It's, uh, what-you-may-call-it.']
FLORA: Fifteenth.
IRENE: Fourteenth to fifteen yeah, yeah.
FLORA: St. Patrick's Day.

Interestingly, English is used for the numbers themselves and the counter words but usually not for structural words such as conjunctions. This is seen in (44) "tree ka four gurai no ingredients" and (45) "fourteenth to fifteen" using the conjugations *ka* 'or' and *to* 'and'.

Even counter words that are culturally associated with Japan are realized in English (24). During the Navy years, the islanders used U.S. dollars (when they used cash at all), so to speakers of this generation, the use of yen currency is a postreversion phenomenon; even more so for the speaker in (46), who moved to the United States before the reversion and has experienced the use of yen only on occasional visits back home to the island.

46. Takai  ja,    spam.   Six-hundred yen   to     ka  nanto ka suru   ja.
    high   FP   spam   six-hundred yen  and  or  something      FP
    'It's expensive, spam. It costs six-hundred yen or something like
    that'

10.3.4. TEMPORAL EXPRESSIONS. Another lexicosemantic area in which English-origin words dominate in both prewar and postwar OML is temporal concepts. Look at the conversation in (47) about the time that catastrophic Chile Tsunami ravaged Chichijima in May 1960.

47. IRENE: I remember I was only about twelve da kedo. Kinky tachi saa, Kinky to ka aretachi, Guam kara kaette kita ja, sugu. sou darou? May, May no twentieth da to omou n da yo ne. May twentieth ka May twenty-fourth gurai da to omou. ['I remember I was only about twelve, but Kinky and them, um, Kinky and all of them had come back from Guam, you know. About May twentieth or May twenty-fourth, I think.']

FLORA: Aa, sore gurai. Uchi no mama, Joann de pregnant datta kara. Joann was born in November dakara, sore gurai da ne. A, sore de graduation to butsukatte, soto de yatta darou. [name] to [name] tachi no graduation. ['That's about right. Because my mama was pregnant with Joann. Because Joann was born in November, so that's about right. Oh, and it fell on the same day as graduation and they had graduation outdoors, X and Y's graduation.']

IRENE: Sou shitara, kondo June ni kita, minna, sono toki ni, Seabees, they sent Seabees out here. Soshite, minna kawaii Seabees de. ['And then, after that, they came in June, everybody, at that time. Seabees, they sent Seabees out here. And all of them were cute, the Seabees.']

Here, the months *May, November,* and *June* all appear in their English forms, a tendency that is nearly categorical in OML. There is a tendency for other temporal expressions to derive from English as well. Some of these, like *Christmas* and *Fourth of July*, are culturally bound, but more general usages, like *every year* and *all day* in (48) and (49), are common as well.

48.  FLORA: Anmari Christmas oboete nai yo, uchi de wa. ['I don't remember Christmas very much, not at our house.']

IRENE: Every year. Mada aru yo, decorations, sukoshi. Twelve years old gurai no toki, chotto Christmas tree kazari hazimete. ['Every year—I still have them, the decorations, a few. When I was about twelve years old, we started Christmas tree decorating a bit.']

49.  Fourth of July wa, all day asobete— ['On the Fourth of July, we could play all day']

10.3.5. PORTMANTEAU STRUCTURES. We occasionally (though not often) find portmanteau constructions as in (50), where a portion of the same information is expressed in both languages. This works smoothly in the OML because Japanese and English have opposite word orders in many cases. In English the modifying word *about* comes before the number and in Japanese *gurai* follows the number. These complementary word orders facilitate portmanteau structures like "about three time gurai."

50.  It's about three times   gurai   yatta     ne.
     It's about three times   about   do-past   FP.
     'It did it about three times, huh?'

Miwa Nishimura, in her study of Japanese-English code-switching, found a number of portmanteau sentences; 15 (2.9%) of the 517 sentences in her data set were portmanteau. Her data, for example, has utterances like that in (51).

51.  We bought about two pounds   gurai   katte      kita   no.
     we  bought about two pounds   about   buy-PAST   come   FP

Nishimura (1997, 140) states:

In [51], "We bought about two pounds gurai katte kita no," the phrase "two pounds" joins the two equivalent sentences: "We bought about two pounds" and "Two pounds gurai katte kita no." Functionally, the portmanteau sentences in (4) seem to be Sean's attempt to reach out to the two types of listeners at the same time—the Niseis [Canadian-born] and native Japanese.

In other words, if one imagines that the native Japanese speaker can comprehend the phrase *two pounds*, then we are left with an utterance that would sound complete to a monolingual speaker of either language. In Ogasawara, portmanteau constructions are relatively rare in occurrence. In the conversation among Irene, Flora, and Rance, for example, only 2 (0.4%) of the sentences could be considered even partially portmanteau out of a total of 475 utterances. These two examples do not contain all the necessary information in both languages; they have only partial redundancy. This is true in (50) above as well as (52), in which only the words *just* and *dake* are redundant.

> 52.  sono uchi, sore de just the wife dake de atsumatte, soremo dan-dan nakunatta.
> 'After a while, so, just the wives only got together, then even that went away.'

Nishimura does not claim, as I do, that her data represents a mixed language; she only examines it as code-switching. So this is the major factor for the difference in the use of portmanteau constructions in the two communities. Another factor is that Nishimura points out the portmanteau sentences function to bridge the gap between the English-dominant and Japanese-dominant listeners. The OML is generally not used either with, or even in the presence of, outsiders. It is basically used among the Navy generation islanders themselves, so there is little chance that listeners would not understand the utterance without the speaker accommodating to them by using portmanteau constructions. Nor does the speaker need to bridge any kind of gaps among speakers, because the language is used among people who have a shared identity.

10.3.6. BASIC, CULTURALLY BOUND, AND COMPLEX VOCABULARY. The OML (prewar and postwar) is basically a Japanese grammatical structure with English incorporated at the word, phrase, and even clause level. I will look at three types of vocabulary here: basic vocabulary, culturally bound vocabulary, and complex vocabulary. Throughout our corpus of postwar OML data, as exemplified in (45) and (48) above, we find the incorporation of English words such as *corned beef and cabbage, graduation, Christmas tree, decorations, pillow case, baseball team, Red Cross,* and *church* into the Japanese sentence structure (and I reiterate that the English-derived words almost always retain their original phonology). The use of these terms in their English forms can be easily explained because they are concepts that themselves relate to the Navy Era or otherwise to a non-Japanese lifestyle. (For example, pillows in Japan were typically much smaller than Western ones and covered by wrapping them in towels rather than putting them into large bag-like cases.)

We also find many examples of "hard words" being used in their English rather than Japanese forms, such as *connotation, decapitated, transformer, louvers,* and *catered.* These concrete or abstract "nouns" (in the phrase *decapitated ni naru* 'to become decapitated', the word is used as the head of a noun phrase) were no doubt acquired through the English-medium school educations that speakers of this generation received.

One of the most surprising things in OML is the basic vocabulary concepts that are typically (in some cases, categorically) realized in their English-derived forms. In (53), the speaker (Stanley Gilley) uses the English words *face* and *name* joined, as is normal for OML, by a Japanese conjunctive particle.

53.  Dakara     face   to    name   ga    chigau     kara.
     therefore  face   and   name   NOM   different   because
     'It's because the face and name don't match up.'

*Wind* is another typical example of basic English vocabulary being incorporated in the Japanese sentence matrix. Just as we saw with Able Savory's usage of *wind* in the prewar OML, so this word (and other similarly mundane everyday conversational vocabulary) is common in postwar OML.

Let us look briefly at the semantic and grammatical properties of English-origin verbs. In postwar OML, English verbs are grammatically used in a similar way to what we saw in the prewar variety. That is, they are generally followed by the Japanese verb *suru* 'to do', conjugated according to mainstream Japanese grammar. These English verbs are usually in their unconjugated English forms, but there are exceptions to this in set expressions such as *pissed off,* an adjectival expression rather than a verb per se, which probably entered OML via twentieth-century American servicemen.

As we saw with nouns above, postwar OML retains the semantically simple English verbs found in prewar OML, such as *fix, mix, boil, steam, gather, fry,* and *invite,* while also incorporating verbs representing more complex semantic ideas, such as *survive, bomb, retire, revise, communicate, brainwash,* and *beg.* This is probably as a result of this generation being educated in English.

10.3.7. NOT ONLY INDIVIDUAL WORDS, BUT ENGLISH PHRASE STRUCTURES. As with prewar OML, postwar OML embeds not only individual English words but entire English phrases in the Japanese sentence matrix. Noun phrases, unlike individual words, contain grammatical information—that is, there is a right way (grammatical) and a wrong way (ungrammatical) to group words together in a phrase.

We see English nouns being used, usually just as individual lexemes (e.g., *education, book,* and *history*), but we also see small chunks of grammar—nominal phrases such like *poor country* (54) and *winter time* (24).

54. datte   sō    iu       education  shika  ukenakatta        wake
    but     that  kind     education  only   receive-NEG-PAST  NML
    da.     amerika  no    are   book  wa    minna   nihon  no
    COP     America  POS   FIL   book  TOP   all     Japan  POS
    history  wa    sore  shika  oshienai.   china  to    nihon
    history  SUB   that  only   teach-NEG   China  and   Japan
    yōsuru ni         poor country  de    ne
    in other words    poor country  COP   FP
    'Hey, but you see, we didn't get any education but that. All the
    American, um, books taught nothing but that about Japanese history, about China and Japan, in other words, poor countries, you
    know?'

In example (40) above, we find within the clause "water ga up to the knee datta" the embedding of an entire English clause, formed according to standard English grammatical rules, complete with compound preposition and definite article.

In Flora's response in (55), the English words dominate in number in a sentence that nonetheless can be seen as having a Japanese matrix. English has been embedded here not at the word or phrase level, but at the clause level.

55. IRENE: Flora, tsunami no toki, Flora nani shiteta? ['Flora, at the
time of the tsunami, what were you doing?']
FLORA: Aa, tsunami no     toki?   Me to     mama   wa
ah  tsunami GEN  time   me  CONJ mama  NOM
last one to get out of there,  yama     ni    nobotte.
last one to get out of there   mountain  LOC  climb
'The time of the tsunami? Me and Mama were the last ones
to get out of there, climbing up the hill'

10.3.8. LANGUAGE TRANSFER FEATURES. There are features of OML
that cannot be explained by mere intertwining of the two source
languages. In (56), note the form of the word *miru*, a verb of Japanese origin, but its semantics derive from English, not from Japanese (see table 10.1).

56. Mata   miru   yo.
again  see    PART
'See you again!'

The greeting *mata miru yo* does not exist in mainstream Japanese, in which the equivalent of *see you again* would use a form of
the verb *au* 'meet', not *miru* 'see'. In Japanese, the verb *miru* is
restricted to 'visual' meanings as in 'I saw a rare bird' (see table
10.1). This expression is the result of transference from English.
Furthermore, the transference here is not only of lexical information, but of grammatical information as well. In Japanese, the
equivalent of 'see you again' would be *mata aō yo*, using not the
present tense for *au*, but the hortative form. We cannot ignore
the influence of English in the use of the present-tense form *miru*
rather than the hortative *miyō* in OML.

TABLE 10.1
Semantic Correspondence between Japanese and English Verbs

| Sense | English | Japanese | OML |
|---|---|---|---|
| I met an old friend for coffee. | meet | au | au |
| I saw an old teacher today. | see | au | miru |
| I saw a rare bird. | see | miru | miru |

Example (57) uses both the verbs *au* (in its past-tense form *atta*) and *miru* (in its negative form *minai*).

57. But it's been so long. But, classmates? Atta! [Really?] Yeah, from Long Beach, forty years minai de.
'. . . But classmates? I ran into one! Yeah, from Long Beach, that I hadn't seen for forty years.'

Examples of transfer phenomena such as this are not rare in OML. The expression *imi shinai* is used in the sense of 'it doesn't mean anything', but such a construction is ungrammatical in mainstream Japanese, in which one must say *imi ga nai* 'lit. there is no meaning'.

Another lexicosemantic example is the word *kemuri* 'smoke'. In mainland varieties of Japanese, kemuri is something that one sees more than smells. Where an English speaker would say *I smell smoke*, a Japanese speaker would say *moete iru nioi ga suru* 'I smell something burning' or *kogekusai nioi* 'a burnt odor'. But in OML, one hears the expression *kemuri no nioi ga shita* 'I smelled something burning', a semantic transfer from the English *smoke*.

## 10.4. RESEARCH INTO MIXED LANGUAGES

Let us diverge again from the topic of the Bonins and discuss the importance of research into mixed languages. Until a few years ago, the concept of mixed languages did not exist. On the contrary, the kind of phenomenon that is now called mixed language was thought to be an impossibility.

Research has shown a number of language systems in the world that mix significant parts of two different languages into one coherent language system. This is a very different phenomenon from pidgins or creoles. In both pidgins and creoles, grammatical structures of the original donor languages are broken down and significantly reorganized. In mixed languages, the languages "intertwine" (Bakker and Mous 1994) but the parts which are brought from each language are brought in whole, not broken down.

The phenomenon of mixed language was first reported in the case of Michif, a language used by American Indians living in Manitoba, Saskatchewan, North Dakota, and Montana. In the Aleutian Islands, one is found called Mednyj-Aleut. Mixed languages have also been reported in Indonesia in the form of Javindo and Petjo (Bakker and Mous 1994).

Intriguingly, in most of these languages, there is a typical pattern between the genders of the parents and how the languages mix. The mixed language takes grammar from the mothers' language and vocabulary from the fathers'. In Michif, which has a verbal grammar from Cree and noun phrase from French, the original mothers were American Indian and the fathers were French. In Mednyj-Aleut, as well, where the fathers were Russian and the mothers Aleutian, we find the mothers' language contributing the verb phrase grammar. Javindo, which grew out of families with Dutch fathers and Javanese mothers, has Dutch vocabulary within a Javanese grammatical framework. The Batavian language of Petjo, which originated in similarly ethnically mixed families, is reported to have Malay syntax and morphology with vocabulary from Dutch. In Ogasawara as well, where many Western men married Japanese women, we find that it is the mothers' language that contributes the grammatical framework and the fathers' language that makes vocabulary contributions.

This relationship could just be a coincidence, but it is more likely a sociolinguistic tendency that tells us something about the relationship between the societal gender roles each parent plays and the way in which these roles affect how each donor language contributes to the newly evolving language.

## 10.5. MIXED LANGUAGES AS DUAL-SOURCE CONTACT LANGUAGES

The phenomenon that Bakker and Mous label "mixed language" has been called by other names, and analyzed in different ways. Carol Myers-Scotton has used the term "split languages" and discusses other possible terms as well. She writes:

Because of the negative connotations of 'mixed', especially in a volume that emphasizes systematicity, I propose a new name for such languages and will refer to them as split languages. Dimmendaal (1998, 105), following the lead of Hill and Hill (1986) regarding languages showing much borrowing, suggests the term 'syncretic languages'. I prefer 'split languages' as more transparent and hope others will use it too. Another possible choice is 'merged languages'. [2002, 246]

Rather than conceptualizing mixed languages like Michif as phenomena completely unrelated to pidgins and creoles, Trudgill (1996) proposes creating a new paradigm parallel to the time-tested pidgin-creole paradigm. He proposes the term "Dual Source Contact Languages" to distinguish these varieties from typical pidgins and creoles. (Sarah Thomason 2001, 197, uses the term "Bilingual Mixed Languages" for the same reason.) Trudgill refers to pidgins and creoles as "single-source varieties," apparently because they rely on one dominant superstrate language. I prefer to think of the these as "three-source varieties" because they typically have one superstratum and two or more substrata (hence the concept of "tertiary hybridization," Holm 1988, 5; Sebba 1997, 103).

In proposing this parallel paradigm, Trudgill opens up the entire paradigm developed over the past century or so by pidgin-creole scholars (prepidgin, early pidgin, stable pidgin, extended pidgin, pidginization, creolization, abrupt creolization, post creole continuum, decreolization, etc.) to scholars who work on language varieties of the Michif breed. Ostensibly, we can think of "Dual Source Contact Language" parallels to all these phenomena. The only concept of the "three-source contact language paradigm" that does NOT appear to have a parallel is "creoloid." Holm characterizes creoloids as partially restructured language varieties and notes, "Partially intertwined languages have never, to my knowledge, been reported" (Holm 2004, xiii).

Using Trudgill's idea for a parallel paradigm, then, we can say the following. With the prewar generation, some people spoke Ogasawara Koiné Japanese as their first language, while others spoke Bonin Creoloid English as their first language; many had a native (or near native) fluency in both languages. These people "mixed" the languages, but they had Bonin Creoloid English or Ogasawara Koiné Japanese as their first language(s), the language(s) in which they could think and conceptualize things. This prewar mixed language is in some ways analogous to a pidgin in that it was not the first language of its speakers, but an auxiliary form of communication.

Just as a pidgin is creolized when youngsters grow up around it and acquire it as their first language, so the OML became the first language of the postwar generation and progressed from simply being the "mixing of Japanese and English" to being a unified language system. The postwar OML is thus analogous to a creole; its genesis parallels "abrupt creolization." Unlike classic creolization, however, where the superstratum is not available to the language acquirers (contact linguists speak in terms of children in the community where a pidgin is spoken "not having access to" a standard variety and in terms of a lack of "normal transmission" from parent to child of the same native language; Thomason and Kaufman 1988; Sebba 1997, 135), in the case of Ogasawara, children had some access to both Japanese and English in addition to the OML of their parents and peers.

Comparing postwar OML to a creole brings certain points to the forefront. First, the postwar OML is the language in which the Navy generation thinks and conceptualizes. Second, postwar OML is the language in which these speakers are most comfortable and can express themselves the most accurately and eloquently; many of this generation say they feel they cannot express themselves as well when they are limited to the use of "only Japanese" or "only English." It is interesting to note that when I have done "fly on the wall" interviews letting Navy generation speakers talk freely among themselves, the code of choice drifts back and forth among (only) Japanese, (only) English, and OML, but when the speakers remember incidents like the Chile Tsunami on May 23, 1960, or Typhoon Karen on November 12, 1962, near-death experiences in the Labovian sense of the word, the speakers use OML.

Third, many speakers from this generation are able to speak "only Japanese" or "only English" in addition to OML, their mother tongue, but we must be careful not to misunderstand this situation and assume that these speakers have the innate ability to "separate" the languages. On the contrary, these language skills were acquired after first-language acquisition and through more formal education, not through natural language-acquisition processes. English was acquired at Radford School (the Navy school on Chichijima) and later in Guam. Japanese was sometimes acquired from a Japanese parent or from a Westerner parent who had a native fluency in Japanese. Note, however, that when both parents were Westerners, the tendency was for English and Japanese to be mixed at home.

## 10.6. THE FUTURE OF THE OGASAWARA MIXED LANGUAGE

Since the reversion of the islands to Japan in 1968 and the subsequent incursion of ethnic-Japanese (now outnumbering the Westerners ten fold), OML has fallen deeper and deeper into disuse. For elderly (those raised before the war) and middle-aged (raised in the Navy Era) Westerners, the decreasing usage of OML seems to correspond to a decreasing desire to distinguish themselves from their new and returned ethnic-Japanese neighbors. Even when they do wish to assert their uniqueness, there is less need to rely on language to accomplish that. The Westerners had many things in common with the Navy personnel, but they relied on OML (or on Japanese) to distinguish themselves from the Americans. These days, when it comes to differentiating themselves from the ethnic-Japanese, they have many nonlinguistic aspects which they can employ. These include their non-Japanese given and family names, their participation in the Christian church, their non-Asian physical appearances, and their common heritage and shared experiences.

Many younger Westerners have left the island behind for the Japanese mainland, Guam, or the United States. Even those who remain on the island today report they do not or cannot use OML. It appears, however, that there is another factor at work with this age group. It is difficult to find Westerners born and raised since the reversion who embrace their unique identity; most are content to meld into general Japanese society. These individuals find it not only unnecessary to use the mixed language to maintain their identity, but unnecessary to embrace a unique identity at all. There is little reason to be optimistic about the survival of the Ogasawara Mixed Language after speakers born in the mid-twentieth century are gone.

# PART V
# POST REVERSION

# 11. COMPARING SOCIOLINGUISTIC ASPECTS OF BONIN ENGLISH WITH OTHER ISOLATED LANGUAGE-VARIETY COMMUNITIES

## 11.1. SIMILAR LANGUAGE CONTACT SITUATIONS

In recent years, an increasing amount of attention has been focused on isolated dialects, or "dialect enclaves," particularly in work by Walt Wolfram, Peter Trudgill, and their associates. Trudgill (1997) has identified links between isolation and linguistic structure, namely morphological and phonological features. In this chapter, I shift the emphasis from linguistic structures to sociolinguistic aspects of the communities in which the isolated language varieties are used in an attempt to construct a framework for contrastive studies.

My analysis compares the Bonin (or Ogasawara) Islands in the northern Pacific with the island communities of Pitcairn-Norfolk and Palmerston in the South Pacific, Tristan da Cunha and the Falklands in the South Atlantic, and Ocracoke off the coast of North Carolina.

I have chosen these language communities because they share the following traits: (1) The language varieties are spoken by groups of speakers who have been isolated geographically. As we see below, the language varieties of the Bonins, Pitcairn-Norfolk, and Palmerston originally developed within language contact situations, but their speakers were isolated from the outside world. (2) All are recently established island communities: Bonins (1830), Pitcairn (1790), Palmerston (1862), Tristan da Cunha (1817), Falklands (1833), and Ocracoke (1770). (3) Unlike many tiny, isolated languages, these are varieties of a major language—English (and in the case of the Bonin Islands, Japanese as well). (4) Although their geographical isolation has tended to insulate them from the influence of other language varieties, including mainstream ones such as the standard, the fact that they are used only by a small number of speakers contributes to their instability. (5) In some cases, larger numbers of outsiders (speaking mainstream varieties of the language) live alongside the speakers of the traditional variety, further complicating the situation. (6) The local language varieties have low status (albeit to varying degrees), and the mainstream varieties serve as an acrolect for the speakers. (7) Finally, these communities are the subjects of current research, a fact which I hope will facilitate a "real time" discussion with the researchers involved.

Because of the large differences among the isolated language varieties discussed and the communities in which they are used, some of the comparisons made are tenuous.

There are cases similar to the Bonins in which Western men took small numbers of Pacific Islanders and settled theretofore uninhabited islands. English-based pidgins often developed as the common means of communication between the groups, as on Pitcairn Island, and these sometimes became the native language from the island-born second generation onward, as in the case of Palmerston Island (Ehrhart-Kneher 1996).

One reason that the English-based Bonin contact language is significant within the context of Pacific language contact relates to its early and largely independent development. South Seas Jargon is thought to have been still in its early stages of development and diffusion in 1830, and the interrelated varieties of Pacific pidgins and creoles that derived from it did not reach their peak until decades later. Pitcairn's unique position within the framework of Pacific contact languages owes much to the early date of its development (late eighteenth and early nineteenth century) and to its relative isolation during important periods in its development (Clark 1979).

A comparison of the language systems and sociolinguistic circumstances of Bonin English, Pitcairn-Norfolk, Palmerston English, and even Ngatikese Pidgin (Tryon 2000) will no doubt prove a beneficial (albeit arduous) task at some point in the not-too-distant future. In the meantime, I will only make some observations regarding language use and identity.

The Bonins and Pitcairn began with similar sociolinguistic situations (i.e., uninhabited island, isolated, Polynesian mothers and European fathers raising children), but they gave rise to a quite different set of language attitudes. The Westerners of the Bonin Islands have never used Ogasawara Mixed Language (OML) to reinforce their sense of identity as speakers of Pitcairn-Norfolk have. Källgård (1993, 91) reports that "Pitcairners consider their language inferior, funny and even ridiculous," but quickly adds, "it seems to be a general opinion on the island that Pitcairnese is important, and that it is, as one of the islanders put it, 'part of our heritage.'"

The greatest difference between this and the Bonins situation is that while Pitcairners see the unique language they speak as "low-status," Bonin Islanders in general are not conscious that the language they speak is a unique variety at all. The fact that the former is called "Pitcairnese," while the latter is referred to as "mixing English and Japanese," is quite indicative of the difference in linguistic consciousness. (Källgård [1993, 77] quotes a 1903 visitor to Pitcairn who wrote, "When questioned, they replied they were talking their 'own language.'")

The Pitcairn language has served throughout much of its history to define Pitcairners as a group and to contrast them with *strienjas* 'strangers' (i.e., nonislanders, whether white or Polynesian) (Maude 1964; Laycock 1989). In contrast, the Westerners of Ogasawara have, as their appellation suggests, contrasted themselves with their ethnic-Japanese island-mates and have sought to downplay, rather than accentuate, the differences between their variety of English and those used in the rest of the world. These sociolinguistic factors will undoubtedly be crucial to any further comparisons between Bonin English and other varieties.

For most of the cases dealt with in this chapter, the relationship between the language variety and community is unproblematic and self-explanatory. For example, we know that Palmerston uses a nonstandard variety of English, so it is clear that "code-switching" refers to the local basilectal variety and an acrolectal variety of (standard) English. However, the linguistic situation of the Bonin Islands is more complex and requires explanation.

As explained in chapter 2, there are several interrelated language varieties to consider when discussing the Bonin Islands. These include: (1) Bonin Standard English, (2) Bonin Creoloid English: (3) Ogasawara Mixed Language (4) Ogasawara Koiné Japanese, and (5) Ogasawara Standard Japanese. It is OML to which I generally refer in this chapter. OML may be compared to the other five language varieties because of its large English component, the bilingual English abilities of most of its users, and the fact that it functions as a basilect for the standard English acrolect. Also, unlike some of the other varieties of Ogasawara's nineteenth-century past, OML is spoken by people of today.

## 11.2. LINGUISTIC FACTORS

11.2.1. GENETIC CLASSIFICATION. Our language varieties differ in their genetic classifications, but we may think of them (in rough terms) as located along a kind of "contact continuum" depending upon the degree to which language contact played a role in their evolution. Most extreme among these is OML. The classification of the Pitcairn-Norfolk language variety is controversial, but it seems safe to say that, although functionally it may indeed be classifiable as an ingroup language "cant" (as Laycock 1989 contends), the role of language contact in its development is undisputed, as is the fact that it has many creole characteristics. Very little linguistic research has been conducted upon Palmerston English, but it is clear that it too developed out of a language contact situation, although there may be less restructuring than with Pitcairn-Norfolk, rendering the variety closer to mainstream English (Ehrhart-Kneher 1996). The three Atlantic varieties fit more neatly into the traditional dialect category, although Schreier (2003, 200) has pointed out that non-English-speaking settlers may have played a role in the formation of Tristan English, and Wolfram and his associates have pointed out the importance of dialect contact in the development of the Ocracoke variety (Wolfram and Schilling-Estes 1997, 7–15).

11.2.2. LINGUISTIC PROXIMITY TO MAINSTREAN VARIETIES IN TERMS OF INTELLIGIBILITY. Let us consider here the linguistic proximity between the island language varieties under examination and mainstream language varieties in terms of intelligibility. OML is to a degree "recognizable" to monolingual speakers of English or Japanese, but it is not intelligible to either group. Japanese speakers generally recognize the sentence structure, but often without being able to discern "what" has done "what action" to "what object" (because these elements are often manifested as English-origin words). For English speakers, the situation is just the opposite. The following utterance was glossed and translated as example (28) in section 7.5, but I give it here in original OML form to illustrate my point.

> 28. Tsuku kara fish ga sukoshi yowaru yo. Sometimes sugu shinu, but spear suru to sugu shinu no mo iru shi…

Monolingual English listeners would understand that the utterance had something to do with fish and a spear but would have no idea about the grammatical aspects of the sentence—whether it was interrogative or declarative, negative or affirmative, transitive or intransitive, and so on. It should be stressed here that comprehension of these English-origin lexemes is possible because words in OML generally retain their source language phonology. (For examples of exceptions to this general rule, however, see sections 6.1 and 7.5.) This stands in contrast to the borrowing of English lexemes into mainstream Japanese where the words are always adapted to Japanese phonology. This means OML maintains "recognizability" with its two source languages without possessing the level of intelligibility necessary for monolingual speakers of either language to interact (either through active usage or passive comprehension) with OML speakers. Such interaction is possible only when OML speakers accommodate (as they usually do) to their monolingual listeners by code-switching into English or Japanese.

The other island varieties have varying degrees of mutual intelligibility with mainstream varieties of English as a result of the opposing factors of contact and isolation. A visitor in 1903 comments that "all the inhabitants of Pitcairn speak perfect English, but when speaking among themselves they cannot easily be understood by a stranger" (quoted in Källgård 1993, 77). This seems an appropriate summation of the situation on both this island and Norfolk today.

Reports regarding the intelligibility of Palmerston English (to speakers of mainstream English) indicate that it is unique but not unintelligible. A report from 1954 maintains, "Their talk is quite easy to follow." Another referring to roughly the same period states, "When I was a child growing up with some Palmerston Islanders, it was barely intelligible.... In Palmerston now [1975] however, I could understand the people with little difficulty" (Ehrhart-Kneher 1996). Compared to the Pacific language varieties, the three Atlantic varieties exhibit a much higher degree of intelligibility with mainstream English.

## 11.3. GEOPOLITICAL FACTORS

11.3.1. GEOGRAPHICAL ISOLATION. As we saw at the beginning of this book, the Bonin Islands lie 1,000 km from mainland Japan and about the same distance from the Northern Marianas. It is because of this geographic isolation that they were not actively claimed by any nation until 1872, when they became part of Japan. Ironically, becoming part of Japan (in addition to bringing Japanese settlers) created ties between the original population and English-speaking communities in Yokohama, Tokyo, and Kobe, as well as close ties with the native populations in the Japanese possessions to the south of them (Palau, Saipan, and Yap). During the U.S. Navy administration (1945–68), they continued their relationships with these southern islands and had a close relationship with Guam as well. Since their reversion to Japan in 1968, they have been closely related to Tokyo.

Pitcairn is an overseas territory of the United Kingdom, located in the southeastern Pacific, over 2,400 km east of Tahiti. It was chosen by the *Bounty* mutineers precisely because of its seclusion; it was not correctly located on any navigational charts of the day. It remained so isolated that at one point its inhabitants were moved all the way across the Pacific to Norfolk Island. Today, Pitcairn has no airfield and can be reached only by infrequent freighter ship. Norfolk is currently an external territory of Australia, located 1,100 km northwest of Auckland and 1,400 km east of Brisbane. It has an airfield with frequent commercial flights to both Australia and New Zealand.

Palmerston is currently part of the Cook Islands. It lies, however, over 200 miles from the nearest island of Aitutaki and has been isolated from the rest of the country. Because of their heritage, the islanders are said to have felt closer to the United Kingdom than Rarotonga. Today the island is reachable only by sea, and ship service is unscheduled and infrequent.

Tristan da Cunha is often called the most isolated island in the world. It is an overseas territory of the United Kingdom, but it is located in the South Atlantic 2,778 km west of Cape Town, South Africa, and 2,334 km south of St. Helena Island, its nearest neighbor. There is no air transportation, nor even an airfield. There are no regularly scheduled passenger ships, but freighters from Johannesburg call on the island two or three times a year.

The Falklands lie in the South Atlantic over 700 km northeast from Cape Horn in South America. They are an overseas territory of the United Kingdom, but maintained close ties, until the 1982 Falklands war, with nearby Argentina. There is an airfield with frequent commercial flights to South America.

Ocracoke is located only a few kilometers from the coast of the United States, but it has been relatively isolated from mainland North Carolina because of continually shifting, but generally unfavorable, topographic conditions as well as by sociopolitical differences (aligning themselves with the North during the Civil War).

11.3.2. MINUTE POPULATIONS. In addition to geographical distance, the small number of speakers of the language varieties is a factor in their continuation. The descendants of the original Bonin Islands settlers number only a couple of hundred people and are outnumbered by the ethnic-Japanese islanders eight to one. Norfolk Island is in a similar situation in that only about half of the permanent residents (less than 1,600) in the 2001 census identified themselves as Pitcairn descendants. Pitcairn itself has a population of about 70, but almost all residents are descendants of the original islanders. The same is true of Palmerston's 49 inhabitants, and Tristan's population of about 300. The Falklands have a large U.K. military presence, but they do not mix much with the local population of about 2,200. In Ocracoke, the descendants of the original settlers number about 375, but they live alongside relative newcomers about their equal in number.

## 11.4. DOMAIN FACTORS

The domains in which a language variety is used are of particular concern because languages often shrink as they are replaced by other varieties in successively informal domains. Conversely, it is possible for low-status language varieties to expand and increase their legitimacy by replacing higher-status language varieties in increasingly formal domains.

11.4.1. USE AS A WRITTEN MEDIUM. The existence of an orthography facilitates the use of a language variety as a written medium. Pitcairn-Norfolk stands alone among the language varieties discussed here in that attempts have been made at developing spelling conventions. Källgård (1993) includes some examples of written Pitcairn from letters and schoolchildren's compositions. Nonetheless, Norfolk has competing orthographic conventions, and spelling of the local language is a controversial issue tied up with issues of local identity and self-expression (Hayward 2006). Pitcairn-Norfolk also differs from the other language varieties in that attempts (albeit limited ones) have been made to publish in the language. Portions of the Bible, for example, have been translated into the Norfolk variety.

OML basically retains the phonological traits of its two source languages and could be written satisfactorily simply by mixing Japanese and English standard orthographic practices. Its users are literate in English or Japanese or both and tend to use one language or the other when writing.

11.4.2. ROLE IN MASS COMMUNICATION. Language usage in the domains of publishing and other types of mass communication needs to be examined. On the one hand, the sheer smallness of the communities examined in this chapter limits their possibilities for mass communication. (Most could not support their own television station, for example.) By the same token, the small community size, high percentage of speakers, and easily definable community boundaries (all are islands) could facilitate media in the local language varieties such as radio broadcasts or weekly newspapers.

On the Bonins, there is a locally published monthly newspaper. Television viewing of any sort was impossible until 1976, at which time Ogasawara CATV was established, and cables were run to 233 out of the 720 households on Chichijima and Hahajima. Mainland Japan television broadcasts were recorded on videotapes brought to the island several times a month by ship. Local events (Village Assembly meetings, school graduations, athletic meets, local festivals) were videotaped, edited, and broadcasted from the cable television stations on each island. In 1984, with the advent of satellite television broadcasting, the all-volunteer cable stations were disbanded (Kino 2000).

11.4.3. PLACE IN SCHOOL CURRICULUM. Another area of comparison is the existence of pedagogical or reference materials for the language varieties. Have vocabulary lists been compiled? Does a grammar exist? Is there a textbook for outsiders trying to learn the language? Several written materials geared toward learning Pitcairn-Norfolk exist, including three dictionaries of Norfolk English (one combined with a language textbook), but virtually none exist for the other five language varieties (Palmer 1992; Buffett 1999; Eira, Magdalena, and Mühlhäusler 2002).

Are these materials being employed in local schools to teach the young indigenous islanders or their newcomer classmates? In none of the communities discussed here is the local language variety the medium of education, but it is noteworthy that the inclusion of Pitcairn-Norfolk has been proposed and considered on Pitcairn (Källgård 1993, 94–95). The local language was introduced into the school curriculum on Norfolk Island in 2002 (Mühlhäusler 2002).

On Ocracoke, special units focusing on language variation were designed by Wolfram's team and implemented in the junior high school (Wolfram, Schilling-Estes, and Hazen 1998). In the Bonins, there is no special school curriculum regarding the local language situation, but local teachers have prepared thorough textbooks with color illustrations for both junior and senior high schools detailing the unique history of the islands.

## 11.5. USAGE FACTORS

### 11.5.1. LINGUISTIC REPERTORIES OF SPEAKERS AND CODE-SWITCHING TOWARD OUTSIDERS. One important question when assessing the extent of a minor language variety's usage is whether or not the speakers use it when dealing with outsiders. This factor is related not only to the ability of the speakers to code-switch and use a more prestigious variety, but also to their propensity to do so.

Users of OML are bi- or trilingual, able to also speak standard Japanese or standard English or both, and they ordinarily code-switch into one of these standard languages when speaking to outsiders. OML is an in-group language. As we saw in section 10.2.4, islanders say, "It was just the words that island people would know, so that other Japanese wouldn't know what we were talking about. It came in handy." It is difficult for outsiders to hear it spoken because of this. This in-group function seems to have played a role in the language's development (although perhaps not in its initial genesis) and in its continued usage.

Laycock (1989) convincingly demonstrates from 200 years of firsthand reports that Pitcairn Islanders have always possessed a more or less mainstream variety of English alongside their local language, and the situation has been similar on Norfolk. Accordingly, as we have seen, records indicate that Pitcairn-Norfolk speakers have, for a couple of centuries, consciously code-switched between "their own language" when talking among themselves and mainstream English when conversing with outsiders. This conscious and clear-cut code-switching is consistent with Pitcairn-Norfolk speakers' conceptualization of their variety as a separate language.

The few extant reports concerning Palmerston English do not indicate the kind of code-switching so widespread on Pitcairn and Norfolk (Ehrhart-Kneher 1996). Palmerston English seems to be closer to mainstream English than Pitcairn-Norfolk. If this is true, then code-switching may be less common because it is less necessary for communication with outsiders. It is also likely that the comparative lack of contact with outsiders has been a large contributor to this single-variety usage (mono-varietalism?). Similarly, the close resemblance to mainstream English of the Ocracoke, Tristan, and Falklands varieties means there is greater mutual intelligibility, making bidialectalism and code-switching less critical and less common than in Pitcairn-Norfolk.

11.5.2. ACQUISITION BY OUTSIDERS. Some of the language varieties (Pitcairn, Palmerston, and Tristan) are spoken almost entirely by the original populations only, with outsiders arriving only in the form of individual teachers, clergy, the occasional linguistic fieldworker, or military personnel, large in number but having limited contact with the locals (as in the Falklands). In other cases (Bonins, Ocracoke, and Norfolk), numbers of recently transplanted outsiders outnumber the indigenous populations.

In the case of the Bonins, the question of transmission to non-group members is not a simple one. Outsiders do not ordinarily acquire OML, and it is a language of intragroup and not intergroup communication. On the other hand, there are several cases on the Bonins in which ethnic-Japanese became acculturated into the Westerner community, mainly upon marrying into it. They frequently acquire a Westerner identity and some of the speech patterns associated with it, whether this be Bonin Creoloid English, OML, or a working knowledge of standard English for communicating with the Navy.

There is anecdotal evidence of outsiders learning and using Pitcairn-Norfolk, not on Pitcairn Island itself where there are few people in general and almost no outlanders, but on Norfolk.

11.5.3. TRANSMISSION TO YOUNG SPEAKERS. Transmission of the language variety to younger generations is the most critical language factor of all, because in its absence the language variety is moribund, that is, bound for extinction. Nontransmission means that younger generations are acquiring or using an alternate variety, and in the case of the Bonins today, this alternate language variety is Ogasawara Standard Japanese. The middle-aged parents of today's Westerner children grew up with a strong influence from U.S. English (being taught by American teachers, attending high school in Guam while boarding with a Navy family). Accordingly, they are all able to speak fluent and natural English, Bonin Standard English. Middle-aged speakers today still use OML, but only when talking among themselves or to certain older islanders. To their children, Navy-generation speakers use Japanese almost exclusively. These Westerner children are in the minority among their peers today; their classmates are either shintōmin or kyūtōmin (section 2.11). At any rate, the children of today do not use the OML. The nontransmission of the language variety is, of course, tantamount to its becoming moribund, and all language varieties on the Bonins (chapter 2) except for standard Japanese seem headed for extinction.

As happens with many minority languages, the very parents who are not passing the language along to their children nonetheless lament their language's looming extinction, and with it the end (they fear) of the unique identity that it symbolizes. It should be pointed out here that, while the younger islanders are not picking up English as their native language, there are increasing opportunities for them to learn English. The Westerners have close relatives overseas (mostly in the United States) whom they frequently travel to see or with whom they stay in close contact through letters, phone calls, and (increasingly) e-mail.

In the Atlantic varieties of the Falklands and Tristan, the geographical distance from the speakers of other varieties of English (such as standard varieties) greatly retards islanders' acquisition of them. In other words, the isolation of the local language varieties facilitates (to a degree) their survival. Nonetheless, the twentieth-century developments in transportation and communication that have shrunk the rest of the world have touched the lives of the speakers in these communities, albeit not to the same extent (Britain and Sudbury 2000; Sudbury 2001).

There are also community-specific factors that have affected the amount of contact these peoples have had with the outside world, and thus the extent to which mainstream English has influenced them. In 1961, speakers of the Tristan language variety were evacuated to England because of volcanic activity on their island and were thus exposed to other varieties of English during their nearly two-year stay. Falklanders have experienced a limited injection of mainstream English due to an increased U.K. military presence after the 1982 war. This military presence has not been, however, as long or as deeply penetrating as that of the Bonins.

Wolfram and his associates show that younger speakers do not use as many features (such as local lexical items, Wolfram and Schilling-Estes 1997), in as many situations (122–24), and with the same degree of frequency and as older speakers do (Wolfram, Hazen, and Schilling-Estes 1999, 66–73, 132–41; but see exceptions, 86–100). They also report that many of the older islanders are disturbed by the prospect of the traditional island dialect disappearing.

Ironically, it may be that areas such as Ocracoke and the Falklands, which seem to have relatively less "linguistic capital" invested in their language variety, will sustain them the longest. On Pitcairn, the large linguistic differences between the local variety and mainstream English have been a factor in the strong feelings its speakers have toward it and the importance they place on its usage and its preservation, but these great differences also make the language variety unintelligible to outsiders, thus reducing the language's utility and inhibiting its sustained usage. People enjoy using Pitcairn because outsiders cannot understand it and it is something uniquely theirs, but this same uniqueness limits Pitcairn-Norfolk's desirability as well.

## 11.6. SOCIOPSYCHOLOGICAL FACTORS

On Ogasawara, one key factor in the transmission or nontransmission of English (either as an independent linguistic code or as a component of OML) to the new generations of islanders is identity. From the beginning of Japanese rule over a century ago, the Westerners have retained a separate identity, and this has contributed significantly to the maintenance of English. One of the reasons English is no longer being used by the younger generation is that the concept of Western identity is changing. If you ask people of the Navy generation about their ethnicity, they reply, "I am a Westerner"; if you ask the postreversion generation, they reply, "My ancestors were Westerners." There is a decreased desire (or need) on the part of the original Bonin Islanders to maintain a separate "personal identity" (as opposed to a "genealogical identity"), and this is leading to the nontransmission of its use to the younger generation.

Sociopsychological factors relating to language usage include (1) conceptualization of a language variety, (2) attitudes toward the local language variety, (3) attitudes toward the standard variety (varieties), and (4) speakers' identities of themselves collectively and as members of those collectives.

Linguistic abilities and language usage play a large role in the formation of the Bonin Islander identity, and in turn this sense of a unique identity reinforces language usage. I will examine the complex relationship between language usage and identity in both an historical and a contemporary context.

11.6.1. ATTITUDES TOWARD STANDARD LANGUAGE VARIETIES. Many nonstandard speaking communities suffer from what Japanese sociolinguist Takesi Sibata (1999) calls a "dialect inferiority complex" and Labov (1972) has termed "linguistic insecurity." The isolation of the communities discussed here has not shielded them from this affliction; if anything, it has exacerbated the situation. Speakers in these communities are reported as having positive opinions of standard English, although their ideas of standard English differ depending upon their political affiliations and other factors. The Bonin Islanders had U.S. English presented as the standard to follow during the Navy Era, and their English today reflects that.

On Ocracoke, some of the disappearing island features are being replaced by Northern variants, as opposed to Southern ones from the North Carolina mainland (Wolfram, Hazen, and Schilling-Estes 1999, 49–50), suggesting their shifts are not necessarily toward a Southern U.S. standard.

The dialogue in (58), transcribed from a recording between islanders Ethel Savory Pack (b. 1949) and Irene Savory Lambert (May 4, 2004), condenses mountains of information regarding language attitudes and identity into a few short sentences. To be consistent with the other examples in this book, I have used italics to differentiate the two source languages being mixed together.

> 58. ESP: I refuse to learn the *teinei* ['polite'] way. I refuse. I'm gonna stay Chichijima way.
>
> ISL: Me *wa chanto shinai to.* ['Me, I have to do it properly']
>
> ESP: They laugh at me, but that's okay.
>
> ISL: *Ii n da,* both *dekireba. Watashi wa chanto no nihongo mo hanaseru shi, kono Chichijima no nihongo mo yatteiru yo!* ['It's okay, if you can do both. I can speak proper Japanese, but I speak the Chichijima Japanese as well!']

As mentioned in section 7.7, one of the most salient aspects of OML (and of Westerners' usage of Ogasawara Koiné Japanese which is one of the source languages of OML) is its absence of honorifics or even "polite forms." Here, Ethel is overtly expressing her refusal to accommodate to these standard Japanese norms, adding that ridicule does not phase her. Irene counters that she has to use standard Japanese (sometimes), but adding that it is not a question of giving up one's roots or "correcting" your island speech, but of using two codes (to put things in linguists' terms). In this short dialogue, we see specific examples of the contradictory attitudes toward standard Japanese and the local variety. One speaker voices the realization that the local speech is stigmatized while demonstrating a stubborn alligiance to it. The other takes a "bilingual" view that recognizes the appropriateness of both varieties.

Although my main reason for presenting these data was to focus on the content, I should say a word here about the way the two languages are mixed in these utterances. The reader will notice that in the initial utterance here, Japanese and English are NOT intertwined in the manner usual for OML. The OML typically has Japanese as the matrix language and English as the embedded language (usually at the word or phrase level). The sentence "I refuse to learn the teinei way" is the opposite of this. The speaker has employed English sentence structure with a Japanese word inserted. This type of code-mixing is rare on the Bonins; it is mostly encountered among islanders who have lived in the United States for many years (as is the case with this speaker), although we do find an example of this type used by a speaker born prewar in section 7.5. Presenting this data may seem confusing to the reader and counterproductive to my argument that OML is a language system with its own rules and not simple code-mixing. I have chosen to risk this possible weakening of my theory because (1) although different from the OML and rare, this type of code-mixing does exist, (2) it shows the complexity of the linguistic milieu in which the OML exists, and (3) the content of the dialogue makes it too important to ignore.

11.6.2. CONCEPTUALIZATION OF THE LOCAL LANGUAGE VARIETY. Conceptualizations of a language variety include questions such as the following: Do speakers see differences between their speech and other varieties? Do they regard their speech as a unique dialect or simply as "the way we talk"? Is the variety known by a specific name?

Of all the language varieties under consideration here, only Pitcairn-Norfolk has been referred to as a "language," although this conceptualization is by no means held unanimously. Källgård (1993) relates an incident dating back a century (1903) in which an outsider has been unable to understand the islanders when they talk among themselves. The islander informs him that they were talking their "own language." In the 1930s several nonlinguist writers referred to the language variety as "Pitcairnese" (see specifics in Källgård 1993). Ross and Moverly's 1964 book *The Pitcairnese Language* both reflected perceptions of the variety as a "language" and in turn perpetuated them among specialists and nonspecialists alike. Other twentieth-century writers have referred to Pitcairn-Norfolk as a "dialect," but this conceptualization is still more generous than the characterizations as simply "bad English" typical of similar nonlinguists' writings regarding many nonstandard language varieties, particularly contact ones.

There are varying characterizations of OML, but it is not generally even viewed as a dialect, much less a language. Many people, both local speakers and outsiders alike, view it as simply "mixing the two languages together." I had an interesting discussion with a member of the Navy generation who at first felt this way. Johnson Washington is a fish researcher who by nature approaches issues methodically. He asked me, "What is it you are trying to find out about language on the island?" I answered that I wanted to know the patterns and rules by which his generation mixed the two languages. He countered, "There are no patterns; we just mix them up, that's all." At this time, I had been conducting fieldwork and analysis for a few years and knew this was not random mixing, so I strung some English and Japanese words together into a sentence, but ignored the rules I had found in OML. I asked him, "So, you mix them like this as well?" A surprised look came over his face as he realized that there was a hidden complexity behind the "mixing" that he had always done without thinking.

Significantly, however, a few islanders do view OML as a unique language. In section 10.2.4, I quoted two Westerners raised during the Navy occupation saying that OML is an entity unto itself, an "Island lingo, which is a mixed, made-up word. We literally translated Japanese into English, but it's not found anywhere else." This shows that they think of OML as something unique from both Japanese and English.

This same conviction was seen in the comments of a male islander, who said, "There is a language that we made ourselves, us kids, among ourselves. Not the language that our parents spoke, not Japanese, and not English; our unique language that we made as kids when we talked among ourselves."

11.6.3. ATTITUDES OF SPEAKERS TOWARD THEIR OWN VARIETY. Attitudes toward isolated language varieties are a key factor in understanding both synchronic aspects of their usage and diachronic changes over time. Many of the varieties discussed here are viewed negatively by their speakers, but there is a great range in this negativity. Källgård calls Pitcairn-Norfolk a "low-status language," but the attitudes held by the speakers themselves, as well as those views expressed by outsiders, seem surprisingly positive compared to those of speakers of other language varieties. As we saw above, a Pitcairn-Norfolk speaker is quoted in 1903 as saying that he has been speaking his "own language" (Källgård 1993). Today, as well, the expanding domains of Pitcairn-Norfolk reveal comparatively positive attitudes.

Attitudes of Bonin Islanders toward OML exhibit a love-hate dilemma that will be familiar to sociolinguists of nonstandard dialects. We saw some rather positive attitudes in the quotes in the previous section, but negative attitudes abound in the transcriptions of a group discussion from 1979 that we saw in section 8.3. These young adult speakers were attending the elementary school at the time of the reversion to Japan in 1968. Thus, they experienced education both in English under the Navy and in Japanese under teachers newly arrived from Tokyo. In contrast to the positive attitudes toward OML as something unique and special, the former classmates in this discussion concentrated on what they saw as deficiencies in both their English and their Japanese.

The negative attitudes displayed there are strikingly different from the relative pride expressed in the comments of Pitcairn Islanders and more intriguingly from the opinions expressed by other Bonin Islanders of the same generation.

It is unclear how natives of Palmerston conceive of their language variety or what their attitudes regarding it are, but with the evidence that does exist and in light of the standardization reported to be under way there, we have no reason to assume they are positive.

The three Atlantic varieties are generally conceived of as regional dialects or as simply "not talking right." Wolfram and his associates report that many Ocracokers, even the younger and more mobile ones, have a strong sense of pride in their local identity, but that these attitudes do not necessarily translate into a positive attitude toward the traditional local dialect (Wolfram and Schilling-Estes 1997, 23–24).

11.6.4. ATTITUDES OF OUTSIDERS TOWARD THE LOCAL VARIETY. The attitudes of outsiders toward the Bonin Islanders' language variety have been overwhelmingly negative. During the Navy administration of the island, OML was largely criticized as the failure on the part of its speakers to properly separate Japanese and English when they spoke. The use of OML, along with the monolingual use of Japanese, was discouraged by American teachers brought in by the Navy. When Japanese mainlanders came to the island as administrators, teachers, journalists, and so on, after the reversion in 1968, most showed strongly negative attitudes toward OML. They viewed it as a failure to separate the languages and use proper Japanese.

Outsiders' attitudes toward Pitcairn-Norfolk are generally more favorable than those exhibited toward the other language varieties. Some writers describe the local language variety as "a kind of gibberish" (1856), but this type of comment is matched or outnumbered by less negative terms such as "an extraordinary patois" (1905). A visitor in 1901 expresses the somewhat negative view that the language of Pitcairn is "at best a species of pidjin [*sic*] English," but the same writer terms this "a language of their own" (all quoted in Källgård 1993).

We have little information about the way outsiders perceive the speech of Palmerston, but the information we do have about the variety and its social situation do not give cause for optimism in this regard.

The attitudes of outsiders toward the dialects of Tristan and the Falklands have yet to be explored (but are reportedly not negative), but the number of outsiders who interact with the islanders is much smaller than in the Bonins or Ocracoke, and thus their feelings may be of less consequence.

Wolfram and his colleagues have shown that mainlanders view the dialect of Ocracoke either with a disdain typical of American's attitudes toward nonstandard (and "substandard") dialects or as an object of curiosity (Wolfram and Schilling-Estes 1997, 131–33).

11.6.5. IDENTITY. The necessity to maintain one's identity has played a key role in the development and usage of nonstandard language varieties on the Bonin Islands. Simple genealogy is only one of the factors that determines an islander's identity (as a Westerner or not). Before the arrival of the Japanese in the 1870s, the

Bonin Islanders were ethnically quite diverse. Throughout their history, the identity of the non-Japanese islanders has been defined more by what they are NOT (i.e., not Japanese, not American) than by what they are. There are no indications they saw themselves as a single group until the incursion of huge numbers of Japanese settlers in the late nineteenth century. From this time, they developed a unique identity in order to distinguish themselves from the Japanese by whom they were surrounded from 1875 to 1945.

Ironically, the arrival of U.S. troops in the post–World War II era gave the islanders an "other" on the opposite side of the ethnic spectrum, further defining what did and did not constitute a Bonin Islander. Young islanders also maintained an identity separate from the various groups they encountered in high school on Guam (children of mainland U.S. military personnel, local Chamorros, etc.). Although some Westerners see themselves as somewhat more American than Japanese, their unique identity served them well during the quarter century they lived with the U.S. military families. Many islanders of the Navy generation share the attitude of Stanley Gilley (aka Minami Stanley), who, when asked by me in a 1999 interview whether he felt more Japanese or more American, replied, "It's not a question of whether I am Japanese or American—I am a Bonin Islander."

The use of a separate language is perhaps the single most important symbol of this identity. It is likely that this separate identity was a crucial factor in the genesis and the maintenance of OML.

Since the reversion to Japanese authority in 1968, the importance that islanders place on maintaining a separate and unique identity seems to have waned drastically, a factor that has contributed to a sharp decline in the use of OML (and the use of English in any form, for that matter).

The importance of having a unique identity has played a key role in the history of Pitcairn-Norfolk as well, and speakers are reported (particularly at key points in the history of the language) to have viewed themselves as different from both other English speakers and from Tahitians (Laycock 1989). Wolfram and Schilling-Estes (1997, 23–25) report that for the island community of Ocracoke off the eastern coast of the United States, middle-aged males may be fortifying their local dialects in the face of increasing in-migration by mainlanders.

Thus far we have talked about identity as a single concept, but the sociopsychological reality of identity is multifaceted. Next I will examine some of the various factors which have been related to the formation and maintenance of a group identity for the Bonin Islanders.

1. HISTORICAL. They share a common heritage in that they can cite ancestors who arrived in the early to mid-nineteenth century.

2. GENEALOGICAL. They belong to clans that are traceable back to a small number of common ancestors. They retain Western family names (and use Western given names).

3. RACIAL. They have non-Asian physical characteristics.

4. RELIGIOUS. Although not all Westerners are religious, the church plays a central role in their community and has since the Japanese arrived in the nineteenth century.

5. POLITICAL. The Westerners were, in the late nineteenth century, called *kikajin* 'naturalized people' and had legal rights different from the ethnic-Japanese. Today they do not account for a large enough percentage of the population to elect their own village assemblymen, but they are seen by politicians as a political entity (bloc) whose votes have to be courted as such

6. EXPERIENTIAL. They have a sense of shared experiences: prejudicial treatment during the Pacific War, life under the U.S. Navy, schooling in Guam, etc.

7. CULTURAL. They have a shared and unique amalgamation of songs and dances, canoes and fishing methods, and ceremonial icons (floral funeral wreaths constructed according to a specific design handed down), cooking ("we don't put sugar in our turtle stew like the Japanese do"), and so on.

8. LINGUISTIC. English (both as a separate language and as a component of OML) ranks high on the list of sociolinguistic factors salient to islanders and outsider visitors. Islanders themselves and others see the Westerners as a definable group largely because of their use of English. This relationship is cyclical: language is a key factor in constructing identity, and espousing a common identity aids language maintenance.

We can find specific examples to illustrate the complexity of Westerner identity and the fact that genealogy is not the sole determining factor. When islanders are asked who is now the oldest of the Westerners, many answer "Gorohei Savory," even though he is an ethnic-Japanese born and raised on the mainland who became a Savory by marriage. Ethnic-Japanese are often "Westernized" when they marry into this community. Another case of this was seen in Osute Webb (section 6.4), the ethnic-Japanese wife of a Westerner who spoke of them in the first person: "All American, our family been a stay there before." With these people identity factors 6, 7, and 8 are present. Factor 2 can also be said to exist because of marriage, and even factor 1 by association. (Consider the fact that an ethnic-Japanese parent may have children who are part of this lineage even if he or she is not.)

The youngest generation today (those born after the return to Japan) have quite a different identity from that of their grandparents (prewar generation) or their parents (Navy generation). The older generations have a sense that they themselves are unique; with the younger generation—even those interested in their heritage—it is more accurate to say that they see themselves as having a unique ancestry. There is a difference between the two.

Today, the Westerner identity seems to be fading away, and all signs point to the rapid decline in the usage of English as a community language here. With its demise may or may not go the consciousness of a unique ethnic and cultural identity.

# 12. ENGLISH, JAPANESE, AND OGASAWARA MIXED LANGUAGE IN THE POSTREVERSION PERIOD

## 12.1. THE RETURN OF JAPANESE AS A HIGH LANGUAGE AFTER THE REVERSION

With the reversion to Japanese administration in 1968, Japanese once again became the dominant language on the islands. In the course of less than two centuries, the islands have gone from being a society dominated by English to Japanese, then back to English and back to Japanese yet again. At present English is still spoken by the Navy generation who learned it and used it in school. English is found in the speech they use among themselves, but it is not standard English, but the Ogasawara Mixed Language (OML), which includes English (as well as Japanese and to a minor extent other) elements. This generation of speakers often uses Japanese or OML when speaking to their parents (who are usually of the prewar generation). To their own children (usually raised after the reversion to Japan) they use Japanese, and these children are usually monolingual in Japanese. In this way, it can be seen that Bonin English, as well as OML, are moribund. That is, it is only a matter of time until no one in the community can speak or understand them. In fact, other than Ogasawara Standard Japanese, all of the language varieties that have been used on the islands in the past are either dead or moribund. This includes, of course, all the various languages of the original settlers (see chapter 2 for details), as well as the various dialects of Japanese that were brought to the island, the subsequently developed koiné variety of Japanese, and all English-related varieties, including not only the nineteenth-century Bonin Pidgin English but also Bonin Creoloid English and Bonin Standard English.

## 12.2. THE INFLUENCE OF ENGLISH
## ON OGASAWARA JAPANESE

12.2.1. VOWEL REASSIGNMENT OF ENGLISH-ORIGIN WORDS IN OGA-SAWARA JAPANESE. For the following discussion, it is important to remember that we must distinguish between Ogasawara Japanese and Bonin English. OML mixes words from both language systems, with both retaining their original phonology. Simply put, English words in OML are pronounced as they are in English, not in their katakana pronunciation. This is a crucial point.

It may sound contradictory, but some words from Bonin English have come to be widely used within Ogasawara Japanese. In these cases, the words are used even when the islanders are speaking only Japanese and are also used by ethnic-Japanese islanders. These cases are different from the structural mixing of OML, and they are simple cases of lexical borrowing, with the words altered to fit Japanese phonology. Let us examine a few examples.

In some English-origin words used in Ogasawara Japanese, [e] is used in place of the English sound [ɪ], as seen in *wentoru* (from English *winter turtle*) or *dampuren* (< Eng. *dumpling* [dʌmplɪn]). Of course, Japanese has no /ɪ/ phoneme, but normally English [ɪ] becomes /i/ in Japanese, not /e/.

The key to this mystery is in the difference in vowel reassignment between standard Japanese and Ogasawara Japanese. In standard Japanese, this reassignment is accomplished as shown in figure 12.1. However, in Ogasawara Japanese the reassignment is accomplished as shown in figure 12.2. This accounts for Ogasawara Japanese pronunciations like [wentoru] and [dampuren] in Ogasawara Japanese where we would expect [wintoru] and [dampurin] in standard Japanese.

Example (59) illustrates how words such as *shirt* ([ʃatsu] in standard Japanese) become [ʃetsu] in Ogasawara Japanese. The important thing to remember here is that the unique Ogasawara pronunciation of words like *shetsu, wentoru,* and *dampuren* shows that they entered Japanese independently of standard Japanese, as shown in the diagram below.

59.  a.  Mainstream English *shirt* → mainstream Japanese [ʃatsu]
     b.  New England Eng. *shirt* → Bonin Eng. [ʃɜːt] → OML [ʃɜːt]
         → Ogasawara Japanese [ʃetsu]

12.2.2. JAPANESE PRONUNCIATIONS WHICH REFLECT THE NEW EN-
GLAND ROOTS OF BONIN ENGLISH. There are still, however, some
sound changes in Ogasawara Japanese that figure 12.2 cannot explain. In Ogasawara Japanese, some English loanwords which originally had [i] unexpectedly change to [e]. This is seen in the word-
final vowels of commonly used words like *booby* [bube] 'a sea bird',
*nanny goat* [neːne goːto], and *billy goat* [bire goːto], and names like

FIGURE 12.1

Reassignment of English Vowels to Japanese Vowels in Standard Japanese

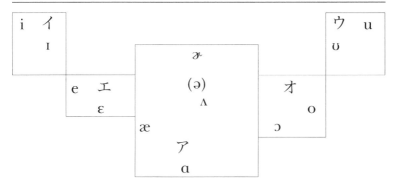

FIGURE 12.2

Reassignment of English Vowels to Japanese Vowels in Ogasawara Japanese

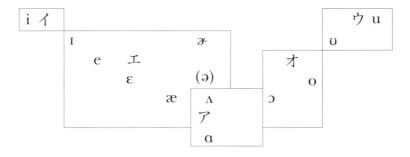

*Savory* [se:bore] and *Gilley* [gere:]. This pronunciation change cannot be explained by figure 12.2; common sense would indicate that English [i] would simply be pronounced in Japanese as [i] as well. The most likely explanation for this strange phenomenon has to do with the original variety of English spoken by early influential settlers. In New England, [i] has long been pronounced as a lower vowel, closer to [ɪ]. (Recall that Uncle Charlie had this pronunciation as well [section 5.3.1].) Thus, Nathaniel Savory and other New England settlers might well have pronounced *Savory, Gilley*, and *booby* as [sevorɪ], [gɪlɪ] and [bubɪ]. With this knowledge, we find that figure 12.2 does indeed explain the present-day pronunciation in Japanese of these words with an [e].

The pronunciation of *church* as [ʧɛ:ʧ] may be a reflection of [ʧɜ:ʧ], a pronunciation we would expect from speakers of New England English, rather than American English [ʧʌrʧ] (Wells 1982, 520–21). (Unlike the example of *shirt* mentioned above, *church* is used only in Bonin English and OML, not in Ogasawara Japanese.) Considering the vowels used, the absence of the *r*-sound in words like *shirt* and *church* (postvocalic rhoticism) seems also to be a reflection of the non-rhotic New England dialect of original settlers.


## 12.3. HISTORICAL SUMMARY

This book has shown that English has been a factor in the lives of the Westerners of the Bonin Islands for almost two centuries. This English has taken various forms, including mainstream native forms of English, nonnative pidginized varieties, a nativized creoloid variety and the English component of OML.

From the time of the first settlers in the 1830s, forms of English were used as the means of communication within the community and also to talk to outsiders. This was an Early Pidgin English variety that probably did not achieve a high degree of stability. This Bonin (Early) Pidgin English underwent "abrupt creolization," becoming a creoloid variety of English, but mainstream varieties of English have been used and understood by Bonin Islanders throughout the islands' history. This ability results from the strong influence of the small number of English natives, from contact with native English-speaking visitors, and from off-island experiences of island-born boys working on whaling and sealing vessels, or boys and (occasionally) girls attending English-medium schools in Honolulu, Tokyo, Yokohama, or Kobe.

With the arrival of the settlers from Hachijōjima came that dialect of Japanese, and others soon followed. These mixed into a koiné variety of Japanese that was acquired by the Westerners as they became increasingly bilingual. This bilingualism brought about code-switching, which increased in intensity and complexity, and before World War II, the two languages had become structurally intertwined. Westerners had used English as a marker of their separate identity; now even those Westerners who were Japanese-dominant could still use the intertwining of English and Japanese to express this identity.

Following World War II, the U.S. Navy provided an "other" at the opposite end of the linguistic spectrum. Now, the Bonin Islanders could distinguish themselves from the Navy personnel and their families by using the mixed English and Japanese variety of speaking they had developed. This increasingly important role for the mixed code caused it to coalesce into a single linguistic code, which became the first language of the children born and raised during the Navy period.

Following the reversion to Japan in 1968, this mixed code was the subject of criticism (as it had been to some extent by the Navy); increasingly many of its users opted for the prestige and linguistic security of Japanese (and/or English). Nonetheless, even today OML is still commonly heard when speakers of this generation get together. The offspring of this generation grow up with only a passive understanding of their parents' OML, acquiring mainstream Japanese as their first language. Even among this postreversion Japanese-dominant generation, though, there is a tendency to spend time in the United States, which they recognize as the country of their ancestors, but also where they have relatives, and these islanders have acquired a second-language proficiency in English. (I know of at least six such individuals, and I know of only one of their ethnic-Japanese classmates who has done the same.) This consciousness of a non-Japanese heritage and eagerness to acquire a practical command of spoken English sets these individuals apart from their ethnic-Japanese counterparts.

## 12.4. CURRENT STATE OF THE COMMUNITY

It has been 170 years since the original band of settlers began to carve out a home for themselves on Chichijima, 130 years since they and their offspring were naturalized as Japanese citizens, over a half century since their grandchildren returned to Western ways, and three decades since the latest transition back to Japanese ways. Have the Bonin Islanders endured? Has their community survived the reversion to Japanese authority and the incursion of massive numbers of ethnic-Japanese residents?

At present, the Bonin Islands are part of Tokyo Prefecture, and a sizable proportion of the population are temporary residents who stay on the island for a few years and then return to the mainland. Residents of the island are active, and they strike one as being do-ers rather than observers. This is seen in the fact that many are out playing tennis or gateball (croquet) several days a week, but also in the fact that any kind of lectures on the island are well attended and supported.

Recognition of the Westerners' place in Japanese society comes in other forms as well. Just as official representatives of the United States, such as Commodore Matthew Perry, met with Nathaniel Savory, the first Japanese governor of the island, Sakunosuke Obana, met with Benjamin Savory and Thomas Webb, and officials who visit the island continue to seek the opinions of their descendants. When Tokyo Prefecture Governor Shintarō Ishihara (a man whose electorate is larger than that of most European heads of state) visited Chichijima in 1999, he was shown on television speaking with Able Savory, one of the senior Westerners on the island.

The Westerners seem to be finding their balance—neither being swallowed up by the Japanese majority nor isolating themselves from the Japanese community surrounding them.

Linguistically the island is quickly becoming monolingual as the children—whether their parents are Westerners or Old Japanese residents or New Japanese residents—usually cannot speak English. This is ironic on an island that has a heritage of English usage, and indeed many islanders have expressed their regret at the disappearance of English. Ethnic-Japanese lament the loss of English because all over Japan people spend great amounts of time and energy and money to learn English, when on this island, it seems it should be possible to use English as a community language alongside Japanese. There are those working in the education of the island who have also expressed a serious desire to raise the status of English on the island to that of a language of daily communication, but at present none of us have been able to find the magic method for turning around the situation of English language decline.

The Westerners lament the loss of English for the same reasons; they know their children would be better off in a twenty-first-century world if they were able to speak English. But in addition to this pragmatic reason, they also lament the decline of English because they see it as the main pillar of their uniqueness. For them, losing English means losing their identity and becoming just like the rest of the people in Japan. It means losing their unique heritage and assimilating into the mainstream.

The attitude toward English and especially toward OML may be changing for the better. When I began conducting my field work just five years ago, I believe islanders were more reluctant to speak OML in front of me. They had been told for generations to speak "correct English" and "correct Japanese," which in their case usually meant not to mix the languages.

Since the reversion, countless numbers of Westerners have chosen to leave the island, either to live on mainland Japan or to migrate to Guam, Hawaii, or the mainland United States. Others have nonetheless remained on the island where they have rooted themselves. Today, members of the Savory, Webb, Washington, Gonzales, and Gilley families work in local government, run their own businesses, and are central members of the island community.

All Bonin Islanders today, Westerners certainly, but ethnic Japanese as well, seem to searching for a Bonin Islander identity—and most seem to be enjoying their lives in the process. Now, at the beginning of the twenty-first century, material signs of the Pacific heritage of the Bonin Islands are still found everywhere. Outrigger canoes used by the Westerners for fishing and collecting coral still line the beaches. Leis of hibiscus are placed around the necks (not of arriving tourists as in Hawaii but) of islanders leaving on the ship. Newly arrived Japanese residents to the island have continued the importation of Pacific Island culture, and practice kaka (hollow log) drumming, play ukuleles, and take hula lessons.

## 12.5. THE FUTURE OF THE BONIN ISLANDERS

What is the outlook for the future of this multiethnic band which coalesced into a group that refers to itself as the Bonin Islanders? Those who opted to remain on the islands as well as those who have chosen to make their lives elsewhere worry that the Bonin Islanders as a unique ethnic entity residing on Chichijima may be disappearing. I must admit that I myself find little reason for optimism when the issue is framed in this way. But perhaps our point of reference is skewed. Let us examine the issue from a different perspective.

Some aspects of the island's history seem to be cyclical. The language of community affairs was a variety of English in the earliest times, shifted to Japanese, then back to English, and then back again to Japanese. Many islanders profited directly or indirectly from whaling in the nineteenth century and today once again, many enjoy the benefits provided by a booming whale-watching industry. Perhaps the urge to leave home to wander and explore new lands is also a recurring "gene" that pops up every few generations. Almost two centuries ago, women and men grew restless in their homelands all over the globe and surrendered to their yearnings to travel, ending up in the Bonin Islands. The same insatiable curiosity and craving for adventure that originally lured people to these out-of-the-way islands from places as disparate as Agrihan, Bermuda, Bougainville, Bremen, Brittany, Brazil, Cape Verde, Denmark, Genoa, Guam, Honolulu, Lisbon, Madagascar, Massachusetts, Manila, Nonouti, Nuku Hiva, Ponape, Rotuman, Surrey, and

Tahiti, continues to this day, as islanders make their lives in points as far-flung as Alaska, Arizona, California, South Carolina, France, Guam, Hawaii, Pennsylvania, and Yokohama. Time marches on and the current diaspora of Bonin descendants may be seen simply as an extension of that process of exploration begun by these individuals' forebears.

Those of us who have lived through the end of the second millennium have grown weary of hearing clichés like "global village" and "world citizen," but such terms represent a fact about our changing world. When Nathaniel Savory left his home in Massachusetts, it meant never being able to return there again. The situation today is vastly different. Advancing technology (jet travel, cheaper international telephone rates, readily available Internet access) now enables individuals to retain their ties to their home community even as they expand their horizons. Bonin Islanders today are spread out all over the globe world—the Pacific, Asia, North America, and even Europe. But they still maintain contacts. Two global Savory family reunions (attended by Washingtons and Gilleys, as well) have been held. Relatives jet back and forth from the United States to Japan for visits, and many on the island are in telephone or e-mail contact with relatives in Japan or the United States several times a week.

Today we find that the Bonin Island Westerners are enjoying the freedom that successive generations of their ancestors struggled so hard to obtain. Like those who preceded them, they are independent individuals who have taken control of their own destinies, even as those destinies lead them away from the island. No longer are they "pawns of power" (Shepardson 1977), but self-empowered pioneers, forging their own futures, using their creativity and resources to forge a new community of Bonin Islanders, one which is anchored to—but not bound by—the shores of the Bonin Islands.

# NOTES

1. That people of African descent figure prominently in the makeup of this Pacific island community is not necessarily surprising. Walker (2002) writes, "By mid-[nineteenth] century, about 20 percent of the entire whaling force was African-American."

2. Official Japanese documents confirm that three "naturalized" islanders were chosen to teach at the elementary school, but names are not given. Joseph Gonzales was born in 1871, so was still only a teenager at this time.

3. William Awdry (1842–1910) later became bishop of Osaka (1896–98) and finally bishop of South Tokyo (1898–1908).

4. The United Society for the Propagation of the Gospel established a school over 100 years ago, in Kitanomachi, Kobe.

5. I myself remember the early 1980s when the law in Japan changed so that foreigners no longer had to adopt Japanese family names upon naturalization. I had assumed that the situation had always been like that, but such is not the case.

6. The use of "classmate" here as "classmade" is probably simply a spelling error. Japanese also has a voiced/voiceless distinction, and so, in the absence of other examples of this type, we have no reason to think that this represents a lack of phonological distinction on the part of the speakers.

7. Those ethnic-Japanese who married into Westerner households did understand and use the Ogasawara Mixed Language to varying extents. Many such spouses came to identify themselves as Westerners and to be seen as such by others.

# REFERENCES

Abe, Shin. 2002. "小笠原諸島に方言はないのか?" [Is there no dialect on the Ogasawara Islands?]. In Long 2002b, 57–94.

Aono, Masao (青野正男). 1978. 『小笠原物語』[Ogasawara Story]. Irima, Saitama: 松本精喜堂 [Matsumoto Seikidō Printing].

Arima, Midori. 1990. "An Ethnographic and Historical Study of Ogasawara/the Bonin Islands, Japan." Ph.D. diss., Stanford Univ.

Arima, Toshiyuki (有馬敏行). 1985. "返還直後の小笠原住民(特に小・中学生及び青年)のことばの実態" [The State of the Language of Ogasawara Residents (Especially Elementary and Junior High School Students, and Young Adults) after the Reversion]. 『音声の研究』[The Study of Sounds] 21: 409–17.

Bakker, Peter, and Maarten Mous, eds. 1994. *Mixed Languages: Fifteen Case Studies in Language Intertwining*. Amsterdam: Instituut voor Functioneel Onderzoel van Taal en Taalgebruik (IFOTT) [Institute for Functional Research into Language and Language Use].

Beechey, Fredrick William. 1831. *Narrative of a Voyage to the Pacific and Beering's [sic] Strait*. 2 vols. London: Colburn and Bentley.

Bickerton, Derek. 1981. *Roots of Language.* Ann Arbor, Mich.: Karoma.

Bickerton, Derek, and Carol Odo. 1976. *Change and Variation in Hawaiian English.* Vol. 1, *General Phonology and Pidgin Syntax.* Final report on National Science Foundation grant no. GS-39748. Honolulu: Social Sciences and Linguistics Institute, Univ. of Hawai'i at Mānoa.

Blake, P. I. 1838. *Report from the Officer Commanding H.M.S. Larne, on the Occasion of Her Visit to the Bonin and Caroline Islands, in Regard to Acts of Violence Committed on the Natives by British Subjects and Particularly by the Master and Crew of the Cutter Lambton of Sydney.* Photocopy of MS in Hamilton Library, Univ. of Hawai'i at Mānoa.

Britain, David, and Andrea Sudbury. 2000. "There's Sheep and There's Penguins: 'Drift' and the Use of Singular Verb Forms of BE in Plural Existential Clauses in New Zealand and Falkland Island English." *Essex Research Reports in Linguistics* 28: 1–32.

Buffett, Alice Inez. 1999. *Speak Norfolk Today: An Encyclopaedia of the Norfolk Island Language.* Norfolk Island: Himii.

Burg, B. Richard. 1994. *An American Seafarer in the Age of Sail: The Erotic Diaries of Philip C. Van Buskirk 1851–1870.* New Haven, Conn.: Yale Univ. Press.

Carr, Elizabeth Ball. 1972. *Da Kine Talk: From Pidgin to Standard English in Hawaii.* Honolulu: Univ. of Hawai'i Press.

Cholmondeley, Lionel Berners. 1915. *The History of the Bonin Islands from the Year 1827 to the Year 1876, and of Nathaniel Savory, One of the Original Settlers.* London: Constable.

Clark, Ross. 1979. "In Search of Beach-la-mar: Towards a History of Pacific Pidgin English." *Te Reo* 22: 3–64.

Clement, E. W. 1905. "Mito Samurai and British Sailors in 1824; with Appendix: 'List of Shipping Which Entered and Sailed from Port William, St. George's, Bonin Islands from 1 Jan. 1833 to 1 July 1835.'" *Transactions of the Asiatic Society of Japan* 33.

Collinson, Richard C. 1852. "The Bonin Islands in 1851, Port Lloyd." *Nautical Magazine*, Mar., 135–38.

———. 1889. *Journal of H.M.S. Enterprise, on the Expedition in Search of Sir John Franklin's Ships by Behring [sic] Strait, 1850–55.* Ed. T. B. Collinson. London: Sampson Low, Marston, Searle, and Rivington.

*A Compendium of the Ogasawara Islands* (小笠原島總覽). 1929. Tokyo: 東京府 [Tokyo Prefectural Government].

Corne, Chris. 1982. "A Contrastive Analysis of Reunion and Isle de France Creole French: Two Typologically Diverse Languages." In *Isle de France Creole: Affinities and Origins*, ed. Philip Baker and Chris Corne, 8–129. Ann Arbor, Mich.: Karoma.

DeChicchis, Joseph. 1993. "Language Death in Japan." In *Proceedings of the XVth International Congress of Linguists*, ed. André Crochetière, Jean-Claude Boulanger, and Conrad Ouellon, 133–36. Sainte-Foy, Quebec: Presses de l'Université Laval.

Dillard, J. L. 1976. *American Talk: Where Our Words Came From.* New York: Random House.

Ehrhart-Kneher, Sabine. 1996. "Palmerston English." In Wurm, Mühlhäusler, and Tryon, 523–31.

Eira, Christina, Melina Magdalena, and Peter Mühlhäusler. 2002. "Dictionary of the Norfolk Language." Unpublished MS.

Elbert, Samuel H., and Mary Kawena Pukui. 1979. *Hawaiian Grammar.* Honolulu: Univ. Press of Hawai'i.

Findley, Gordon. 1958. *A History of the Bonin-Volcano Islands.* Book 2, 1951–1958. Declassified government report in the U.S. Navy Archives, Washington, D.C.

Forgue, Guy Jean. 1977. "American English at the Time of the Revolution." *Revue des Langues Vivantes* 43: 253–69. Repr. in *Dialect and Language Variation*, ed. Harold B. Allen and Michael D. Linn, 511–23. Orlando, Fla.: Academic Press, 1986.

Forster, Honore, ed. 1991. *The Cruise of the Gipsy: The Journal of John Wilson, Surgeon on a Whaling Voyage to the Pacific Ocean, 1839–1843.* Fairfield, Wash.: Ye Galleon Press.

Fuller, Janet M. 1996. "When Cultural Maintenance Means Linguistic Convergence: Pennsylvania German Evidence for the Matrix Language Turnover Hypothesis." *Language in Society* 25: 493–514.

Gast, Ross H. 1944. *Bonin Islands' Story.* Monrovia, Calif.: Monrovia News-Post.

Goldschmidt, Richard. 1927. "Die Nachkommen der alten Siedler auf den Bonininseln" [Descendants of the Original Settlers of the Bonins]. *Die Naturwissenschaften* 15: 449–53.

Grimes, Barbara F., ed. 1996. *Ethnologue: Languages of the World.* 13th ed. Dallas, Texas: Summer Institute of Linguistics. Available at http://www.sil.org/ethnologue.

Hawks, Francis L., comp. 1856. *Narrative of the Expedition of an American Squadron to the China Seas and Japan, Performed in the Years 1852, 1853, and 1854, under the Command of Commodore M. C. Perry, United States Navy.* 3 vols. Ed. Sidney Wallach. Washington, D.C.: Nicholson. Repr. New York: AMS Press, 1967.

Hayward, Philip. 2006. *Bounty Chords: Music, Dance, and Cultural Heritage on Norfolk and Pitcairn Islands.* London: Libbey.

Head, Timothy E., and Gavan Daws. 1968. "The Bonins, Isles of Contention." *American Heritage* 19.2: 58–64, 69–74.

Hezel, Francis X., dir. 2006. "Micronesian Seminar." http://www.micsem.org/home.htm.

Hibiya, Junko (日比谷潤子). 1995. "ヴァンクーヴァーの日系人の言語変容" [Language Adaptation among Japanese-Canadians in Vancouver]. In『アメリカの日系人 都市、社会、生活』[Japanese-Americans: Cities, Society, and Life], ed. Toshio Yanagida (柳田利夫), 153–71, Tokyo: 同文舘 [Dōbunsha].

Hirayama, Teruo (平山輝男). 1941. "豆南諸島のアクセントとその境界線" [The Accents of the Southern Izu Islands and Their Boundaries]. 『音声学協会会報』[The Bulletin of the Phonetic Society of Japan] 67–68: 1–5.

Holm, John. 1988. *Pidgins and Creoles.* Vol. 1, *Theory and Structure.* Cambridge: Cambridge Univ. Press.

———. 2000. *An Introduction to Pidgin and Creoles.* Cambridge: Cambridge Univ. Press.

———. 2004. *Languages in Contact: The Partial Restructuring of Vernaculars.* Cambridge: Cambridge University Press.

Hymes, Dell, ed. 1971. *Pidginization and Creolization of Languages: Proceedings of a Conference Held at the University of the West Indies, Mona, Jamaica, April, 1968.* Cambridge: Cambridge Univ. Press.

Inoue, Fumio (井上史雄). 2000.『日本語の値段』[The Value of Japanese]. Tokyo: 大修館書店 [Taishūkan].

Ishihara, Shun (石原俊). "移動民と文明国のはざまから＿ジョン万次郎と船乗りの島々＿" [The "Civilized Powers" and the "Moving People" on the Ocean: Focusing on John Manjiro's Contacts with the Ogasawara/Bonin Islands].『思想』*Shisō* [Thought] 990: 94–115.

Jourdan, Christine, and Ellen Maebiru. 2002. *Pijin: A Trilingual Cultural Dictionary.* Canberra: Pacific Linguistics, Research School of Pacific and Asian Studies, Australian National Univ.

Källgård, Anders. 1993. "Present-day Pitcairnese." *English World-Wide* 14: 71–114.

Kamo, Motoyoshi (加茂元善). 1889. "小笠原島風俗記 附 帰化人種の区別" [Customs of the Ogasawara Islands, with a Classification of the Naturalized People].『東京人類学会雑誌』[Tokyo Anthropology Association Journal] 38: 322–27.

Kawasumi, Tetsuo (川澄哲夫). 2003. "Introducing John Manjiro." Manjiro Society for International Exchange. http://www.manjiro.org/manjiro.html.

Kenyon, John S. 1958. *American Pronunciation.* 10th ed. Ann Arbor, Mich.: Wahr.

King, Armine Francis. 1898. "Hypa, the Centenarian Nurse." *Mission Field: A Monthly Record of the Proceedings of the Society for the Propagation of the Gospel in Foreign Parts* (London), Nov., 415–21.

Kino, Yasushi (木野康). 2000. "小笠原CATVの盛衰とその存在意義" [The Rise and Decline of Ogasawara CATV and Its raison d'être]. In『離島とメディアの研究、小笠原編』[Research on Isolated Islands and Media, Ogasawara Edition], ed. Maenō Hiromu (前納弘武), 103–25. Tokyo: 学文社 [Gakubunsha].

Konishi, Junko. 2001. "Developing Tradition: The Origin and History of Music in the Ogasawara Islands." *Perfect Beat: The Pacific Journal of Research into Contemporary Music and Popular Culture* 5.2: 30–48.

Kurata, Yōji (倉田洋二).『写真帳小笠原 発見から戦前まで』[Photograph Album of Ogasawara: From Its Discovery to the Pre-war Era]. Kamakura: アボック社 (Abokku)

Labov, William. 1972. *Sociolinguistic Patterns.* Philadelphia: Univ. of Pennsylvania Press.

Lal, Brij V., and Kate Fortune. 2000. *The Pacific Islands: An Encyclopedia.* Honolulu: Univ. of Hawai'i Press.

Laycock, Donald C. 1989. "The Status of Pitcairn-Norfolk: Creole, Dialect or Cant?" In *Status and Function of Languages and Language Varieties,* ed. Ulrich Ammon, 608–29. Berlin: Mouton de Gruyter.

London, Jack. 1895. "Bonin Islands: An Incident of the Sealing Fleet of '93." *The High School Aegis.* Part 1, Jan. 18, 1895. Part 2, Feb. 1895. Oakland, Calif.: Oakland High School. Included as chapter 16 of *John Barleycorn,* New York: Century, 1913. Avaialble at http://www.fullbooks.com/John-Barleycorn-by-Jack-London2.html.

Long, Daniel (ダニエル・ロング). 1998a. "A Bibliography of Humanities and Social Sciences Works on the Ogasawara (Bonin) Islands." In Long 1998c, 175–90.

———. 1998b. "小笠原諸島における言語接触の歴史" [The History of Language Contact in the Ogasawara Islands]. In Long 1998c, 87–128.

———, ed. 1998c. 『小笠原諸島の言語文化』 [The Linguistic Culture of the Ogasawara Islands]. 日本語研究センター報告 6 [Japanese Language Research Center Reports 6]. Osaka: 大阪樟蔭女子大学 [Osaka Shōin Women's College].

———. 1999. "Evidence of an English Contact Language in the 19th century Bonin (Ogasawara) Islands." *English World-Wide* 20: 251–86.

———. 2000. "Examining the Bonin (Ogasawara) Islands within the Contexts of Pacific Language Contact." In *Leo Pasifika: Proceedings of the Fourth International Conference on Oceanic Linguistics,* ed. Steven Roger Fischer and Wolfgang B. Sperlich, 200–217. Auckland, New Zealand: Institute of Polynesian Languages and Literatures.

———. 2001a. "Insights into the Vanishing Language and Culture of the Bonin (Ogasawara) Islands: Mr. Charles Washington's 1971 Interviews." In 『日本語の消滅に瀕した方言に関する調査研究』 [Endangered Dialects of Japan], ed. Shinji Sanada (真田信治編), 46–85. Osaka: 環太平洋の「絶滅に瀕した言語」にかんする緊急調査研究 [Endangered Languages of the Pacific Rim Project] (A4-001).

———. 2001b. "Towards a Framework for Comparing Sociolinguistic Aspects of Isolated Language Variety Communities." *University of Pennsylvania Working Papers in Linguistics* 7.3: 159–74.

———, ed. 2002a. 『日本のもう一つの先住民の危機言語 —小笠原諸島における欧米系島民の消滅の危機に瀕した英語とその文化—』 [The Disappearing English Language and Culture of the "Westerners" of the Bonin (Ogasawara) Islands]. Osaka: 環太平洋の「絶滅に瀕した言語」

にかんする緊急調査研究 [Endangered Languages of the Pacific Rim Project] (A4-015).

———, ed. 2002b. 『小笠原学ことはじめ』[An Introduction to Ogasawara Studies]. Kagoshima: 南方新社 [Nanpō Shinsha].

———, ed. 2003. 『日本のもう一つの先住民の危機言語 —小笠原諸島にお ける 欧米系島民の消滅の危機に瀕した日本語—』[The Disappearing Japanese Language Variety of the "Westerners" of the Bonin (Ogasawara) Islands]. Osaka: 環太平洋の「絶滅に瀕した言語」にかんする緊急 調査研究 [Endangered Languages of the Pacific Rim Project] (A4-023).

———. 2004. "The Bonin (Ogasawara) Islands: A Multilingual, Multiethnic, and Multicultural Community in Japan." *Transactions of the Asiatic Society of Japan*, 4th series, 18: 41–55.

Long, Daniel (ダニエル・ロング), and Naoyuki Hashimoto (橋本直幸). 2005. 『小笠原ことばしゃべる辞典』[Talking Dictionary of the Bonin Islands Language, with CD-ROM]. Kagoshima: 南方新社 [Nanpōshinsha].

Long, Daniel, and Peter Trudgill. 2004. "The Last Yankee in the Pacific: Eastern New England Phonology in the Bonin Islands." *American Speech* 79: 356–67.

Lütke, Frédéric (Fedor Petrovich Litke). 1835–36. *Voyage autour du monde, fait par ordre de sa Majesté l'Empereur Nicolas Ier, sur la Corvette le Séniavine, dans les années 1826, 1827, 1828 et 1829, sous le Commandement de Frédéric Lutké*. Trans. F. Boyé. Paris: Lithographie de Englemann et Compagnie. Translation of *Puteshestvie vokrug svieta*, 1833. Repr. as *Voyage autour du monde, 1826–1829*. Amsterdam: Da Capo, 1971.

Lynch, John. 1998. *Pacific Languages: An Introduction*. Honolulu: Univ. of Hawai'i Press.

Maher, John. 1997. "Linguistic Minorities and Education in Japan." *Educational Review* 49: 115–27.

Maude, H. E. 1964. "The History of Pitcairn Island." In *The Pitcairnese Language*, ed. Alan S. C. Ross and A. W. Moverley, 45–101. London: Deutsch.

McArthur, Ian Douglas. 2002. "Mediating Modernity—Henry Black and Narrated Hybridity in Meiji Japan." Ph.D. diss., Univ. of Sydney.

Middlebrooke, Helen Widger. 2001. "Living on Guam, Staying on Guam." http://www.guam.net/home/inmiddle/guam.html.

Mishoe, Margaret, and Michael Montgomery. 1994. "The Pragmatics of Multiple Modal Variation in North and South Carolina." *American Speech* 69: 3–29.

Mizuno, Chikugo no Kami Tadanori (水野筑後守忠徳). 1861. "小笠原住民対話書" [A Dialogue with Ogasawara Residents]. Manuscript in the Obana Sakunosuke collection of the Ogasawara Village Office of Education.

Montgomery, Michael B., and Stephen J. Nagle. 1993. "Double modals in Scotland and the Southern United States: Trans-Atlantic Inheritance or Independent Development?" *Folia Linguistica Historica* 14: 91–107.

Mufwene, Salikoko S. 1996. "The Founder Principle in Creole Genesis." *Diachronica* 13: 83–134.

Mühlhäusler, Peter. 1986. *Pidgin and Creole Linguistics.* Oxford: Blackwell.

———. 1998. "Some Pacific Island Utopias and Their Languages." *Plurilinguismes* 15: 27–47.

———. 2002. "A Language Plan for Norfolk Island." In *Language Endangerment and Language Maintenance,* ed. David Bradley and Maya Bradley, 167–82. London: Routledge Curzon.

Mühlhäusler, Peter, and Philip Baker. 1996. "English-Derived Contact Languages in the Pacific in the 20th Century (Excluding Australia)." In Wurm, Mühlhäusler, and Tryon, 497–522.

Mühlhäusler, Peter, and Rachel Trew. 1996. "Japanese Language in the Pacific." In Wurm, Mühlhäusler, and Tryon, 373–99.

Myers-Scotton, Carol. 1993. *Duelling Languages: Grammatical Structures in Codeswitching.* Oxford: Clarendon.

———. 2002. *Contact Linguistics: Bilingual Encounters and Grammatical Outcomes.* Oxford: Oxford Univ. Press.

NHK放送局 [Japan Broadcasting Corporation]. 1987. "太平洋ブラザーズ〜東京都小笠原村〜" [Pacific Ocean Brothers, Ogasawara Village, Tokyo Prefecture].『ぐるっと海道3万キロ』[All Around the Sea Route 30,000 kilometers]. Show number 70, broadcast Apr. 13.

NHK放送局 [Japan Broadcasting Corporation]. 1990.『日本とアメリカの間で小笠原セーボレー一族の160年』[Between Japan and America, 160 years of the Ogasawara Savory Family]. NHKセミナー 現代ジャーナル [NHK Seminar, Modern Journal]. Broadcast Apr. 30.

Neustupný, Jiri (ネウストプニー, J. V.). 1997. "言語管理とコミュニティ 言語の諸問題" [Language Management and Community Language Problems]. In『多言語・多文化コミュニティのための言語管理:差異を生きる個人とコミュニティ』[Language Management for Multicultural Communities: Individuals and Communities Living the Differences], ed. 国立国語研究所 [National Language Research Institute], 21–37. Tokyo: 凡人社 [Bonjinsha].

Nishimura, Miwa. 1997. *Japanese/English Code-Switching: Syntax and Pragmatics*. New York: Lang.

Nobushima, Fuyuo (延島冬生). 1997. "小笠原諸島先住民の言葉" [Words of the Original Inhabitants of the Ogasawara Islands].『太平洋学会誌』(Journal of the Pacific Society) 72–73: 77–80.

———. 1998. "小笠原諸島に伝わる非日本語系の言葉" [Words of Non-Japanese Derivation Handed Down in the Ogasawara Islands]. In Long 1998c, 129–48.

Ogasawara Elementary School (小笠原村立小中学校). 1979.『十周年記念誌』[Commemorative Publication for the 10th Anniversary of the Establishment of Ogasawara Elementary and Junior High School]. Ogasawara: Ogasawara Elementary and Junior High School.

Ōkuma, Ryōichi (大熊良一). 1966.『歴史の語る小笠原』[Ogasawara as History Tells It]. Tokyo: 小笠原協会 [Ogasawara Kyōkai].

"An Outline of the Ogasawara Outlines" (小笠原島概況). 1888.『官報』[Daily Gazette] 1433: 120–21. Tokyo: 大蔵省印刷局 [Japanese Ministry of Finance Printing Office].

Palmer, Beryl Nobbs. 1992. *A Dictionary of Norfolk Words and Usages plus English-Norfolk Appendix*. 2nd ed. Norfolk Island: Palmer

Peard, George. 1973. *To the Pacific and Arctic with Beechey: The Journal of Lieutenant George Peard of H.M.S. Blossom, 1825–1828*. Ed. Barry M. Gough. London: Cambridge Univ. Press.

Peattie, Mark. 1984. "The Nan'yo: Japan in the South Pacific, 1885–1945." In *The Japanese Colonial Empire, 1845–1945*, ed. Ramon H. Myers and Mark R. Peattie, 172–210. Princeton, N.J.: Princeton Univ. Press.

———. 1988. *Nan'yo: The Rise and Fall of the Japanese in Micronesia 1885–1945*. Honolulu: Univ. of Hawai'i Press.

Pesce, Dorothy Richard. 1958. *A History of the Bonin-Volcano Islands*. Book 1, *1830–1951*. N.p.: Commander-in-Chief Pacific.

Platt, John. 1975. "The Singapore English Speech Continuum and its Basilect 'Singlish' as a 'Creoloid.'" *Anthropological Linguisitcs* 17: 363–74.

Quin, Michael. 1837. *Remarks on Peel Island, Bonin Groupe*. MS housed in the National Library, London, reference no. FO17/21.

———. 1856. "Notes on the Bonin Islands." *Journal of the Royal Geographical Society* 26: 232–35.

Reinecke, John E. 1969. *Language and Dialect in Hawaii: A Sociolinguistic History to 1935*. Ed. Stanley M. Tsuzaki. Honolulu: Univ. of Hawai'i Press.

Roberts, Julie. 1997. "Hitting a Moving Target: Acquisition of Sound Changes in Progress by Philadelphia Children." *Language Variation and Change* 9: 249–66.

Robertson, Russell. 1876. "The Bonin Islands." *Transactions of the Asiatic Society of Japan* 4: 111–43.

Ross, Alan S. C., and A. W. Moverley. 1964. *The Pitcairnese Language.* London: Deutsch.

Ruschenberger, William Samuel Waithman. 1838. *Narrative of a Voyage around the World, during the Years 1835, 36, and 37; Including a Narrative of an Embassy to the Sultan of Muscat and the King of Siam.* 2 vols. London: Bentley.

Sakanishi, Shio, ed. 1940. *A Private Journal of John Glendy Sproston, U.S.N.* Tokyo: Sophia Univ. Repr. Tokyo: Tuttle, 1968.

Sampson, Paul. 1968. "The Bonins and Iwo Jima Go Back to Japan." *National Geographic*, July, 128–44.

Sankoff, Gillian. 1993. "Focus in Tok Pisin." In *Focus and Grammatical Relations in Creole Languages*, ed. Francis Byrne and Donald Winford, 117–40. Amsterdam: Benjamins.

Schreier, Daniel. 2003. *Isolation and Language Change: Contemporary and Sociohistorical Evidence from Tristan da Cunha English.* New York: Palgrave Macmillan.

Sebba, Mark. 1997. *Contact Languages: Pidgins and Creoles.* New York: St. Martin's.

Segawa, Kiyoko (瀬川清子). 1931.『村の女たち』[Village Women]. Tokyo: 未来社 [Miraisha].

Sekiguchi, Yayoi (関口やよい). 1988. "小笠原諸島住民の言語使用に関する パイロット・スタディー" [Language Use of Bonin Islanders, Pilot Study]. *Sophia Linguistica* 26: 151–62.

Sewall, John S. 1905. *The Logbook of the Captain's Clerk: Adventures in the China Seas.* Bangor, Maine: Chas. H. Glass.

Shepardson, Mary. 1977. "Pawns of Power: the Bonin Islanders." In *The Anthropology of Power: Ethnographic Studies from Asia, Oceania, and the New World*, ed. Raymond D. Fogelson and Richard N. Adams, 99–114. New York: Academic Press.

———. 1998. "The Bonin Islands: Pawns of Power." Unpublished MS.

Shimizu, Rieko (清水理恵子). 1994. "小笠原欧米系島民言語生活研 究" [Research into the "Language Life" of the Westerners of Ogasawara]. Unpublished undergraduate thesis, 共立女子大学日本文学部 [Kyōritsu Joshi Daigaku Nihonbungaku].

Sibata, Takesi (柴田武). 1999. *Sociolinguistics in Japanese Contexts*. Berlin: Mouton de Gruyter.

Someya, Tsuneo (染谷恒夫), and Arima Toshiyuki (有馬敏行). 1972.『小笠原村初代村長と校長の記録』[A Record of the First Village President and School Principal of Ogasawara]. Tokyo: Fukumura Shuppan.

Sudbury, Andrea. 2001. "Falkland Islands English: A Southern Hemisphere Variety?" *English World-Wide* 22: 55–80.

Tamura, Norio (田村紀雄). 1968. "小笠原の文化とことば" [The Language and Culture of Ogasawara].『言語生活』[Language Life] 207: 70–74.

Tanaka, Hiroyuki (田中弘之). 1998. "How the Japanese of the Edo period perceived the Ogasawara Islands." Trans. and annotated by Stephen Wright Horn. In Long 1998c, 31–58.

Taylor, Bayard. 1855. *A Visit to India, China, and Japan, in the Year 1853*. London: Sampson Low.

Thomason, Sarah G. 2001. *Language Contact: An Introduction*. Washington, D.C.: Georgetown Univ. Press.

Thomason, Sarah Grey, and Terrence Kaufman. 1988. *Language Contact, Creolization, and Genetic Linguistics*. Berkeley: Univ. of California Press.

Trudgill, Peter. 1983. "Language Contact and Language Change: On the Rise of the Creoloid." In *On Dialect: Social and Geographical Perspectives*, 102–7. Oxford: Blackwell.

———. 1996. "Dual-Source Pidgins and Reverse Creoloids: Northern Perspectives on Language Contact." In *Language Contact in the Arctic: Northern Pidgins and Contact Languages*, ed. Ernst Håkon Jahr and Ingvild Broch, 5–14. Berlin: Mouton de Gruyter. Repr. Trudgill 2002, 68–75.

———. 1997. "Dialect Typology: Isolation, Social Network and Phonological Structure." In *Towards a Social Science of Language: Papers in Honor of William Labov*, vol. 1, *Variation and Change in Language and Society*, ed. Gregory R. Guy, Crawford Feagin, Deborah Schiffrin, and John Baugh, 3–22. Oxford: Blackwell.

———. 2002. *Sociolinguistic Variation and Change*. Washington, D.C.: Georgetown Univ. Press.

Trudgill, Peter, Daniel Schreier, Daniel Long, and Jeffrey P. Williams. 2003. "On the Reversibility of Mergers: /w/, /v/, and Evidence from Lesser-Known Englishes." *Folia Linguistica Historica* 24: 23–46.

Tryon, Darrell. 2000. "Ngatikese Pidgin." In *Leo Pasifika: Proceedings of the Fourth International Conference on Oceanic Linguistics*, ed. Steven Roger Fischer and Wolfgang B. Sperlich, 394–79. Auckland, New Zealand: Institute of Polynesian Languages and Literatures.

Tsuda, Aoi (津田葵). 1988. "小笠原における言語変化と文化変容" [Language Change and Acculturation on the Ogasawara Islands]. *Sophia Linguistica* 23–24: 277–85.

Tsuji, Tomoe (辻友衛). 1995. 『小笠原諸島歴史日記』 [A Historical Log of the Ogasawara Islands]. Tokyo: 近代文藝社 [Kindai Bungeisha].

Van Buskirk, Philip. 1880–81, 1898. "The Private Diary of P. C. Van Buskirk." Unpublished MS in the Univ. of Washington Library Manuscripts Collection.

Wagenseil, Ferdinand. 1962. *Rassengemischte Bevölkerung der japanischen Bonin-Inseln; ihre Anthropologie und Genetik* [The Mixed-race Population of the Japanese Bonin Islands: Their Anthropology and Genetics]. Stuttgart: Schweizerbart.

Walker, Bryce. 2002. "The Lives of the Whale Hunters." *American Legacy: The Magazine of African-American History and Culture*, Winter, 38–48.

Wells, J. C. 1982. *Accents of English.* 3 vols. Cambridge: Cambridge Univ. Press.

Williams, Samuel Wells. 1910. *A Journal of the Perry Expedition to Japan.* Special issue of *Transactions of the Asiatic Society of Japan* 37.2. Repr. Wilmington, Del.: Scholarly Resources, 1973.

Winford, Donald. 2003. *An Introduction to Contact Linguistics.* Malden, Mass.: Blackwell.

Wolfram, Walt, and Natalie Schilling-Estes. 1997. *Hoi Toide on the Outer Banks: The Story of the Ocracoke Brogue.* Chapel Hill: Univ. of North Carolina Press.

Wolfram, Walt, Kirk Hazen, and Natalie Schilling-Estes. 1999. *Dialect Change and Maintenance on the Outer Banks.* Publication of the American Dialect Society 81. Tuscaloosa: Univ. of Alabama Press.

Wolfram, Walt, Natalie Schilling-Estes, and Kirk Hazen. 1998. *Dialects and the Ocracoke Brogue.* Ocracoke, N.C.: Ocracoke School.

Wurm, Stephen A., Peter Mühlhäusler, and Darrell T. Tryon. 1996. *Atlas of Languages of Intercultural Communication in the Pacific, Asia, and the Americas.* Berlin: Mouton de Gruyter.